P9-CRB-939

closet

bathroom

fridge

the hall of awesome

kitchen

A

airbrush station
home of turkey jones

fondant station

recycling

E
E

L
S

K
B

M

G
S

tool area

A
K

contract wall

MA

photography

fortress of administration

J

D

A

done rack

main entrance

north

scale
0   5ft.   10ft.

WILLIAM MORROW

An Imprint of HarperCollins*Publishers*

DUFF GOLDMAN & WILLIE GOLDMAN

INSIDE THE WORLD *of* CHARM CITY CAKES

ACE OF CAKES. Copyright © 2009 by Duff Goldman. All rights reserved. Printed in the United States of America. No part of this book may be used or reproduced in any manner whatsoever without written permission except in the case of brief quotations embodied in critical articles and reviews. For information address HarperCollins Publishers, 10 East 53rd Street, New York, NY 10022.

HarperCollins books may be purchased for educational, business, or sales promotional use. For information please write: Special Markets Department, HarperCollins Publishers, 10 East 53rd Street, New York, NY 10022.

FIRST EDITION

Designed by Susan Walsh

Library of Congress Cataloging-in-Publication Data

Goldman, Duff.
    Ace of Cakes : inside the World of Charm City Cakes / Duff Goldman and Willie Goldman. — 1st ed.
       p. cm.
    Includes bibliographical references and index.
    ISBN 978-0-06-170301-0
    1. Cake decorating.   2. Sculpture.   3. Sugar art.   4. Ace of Cakes (Television program).
    I. Goldman, Willie.   II. Title.
    TX771.2.G65 2009
    641.8'653—dc22   2009020368

09 10 11 12 13   DIX/QWT   10 9 8 7 6 5 4 3 2 1

FOR THE STAFF OF CHARM CITY CAKES
THE CREW OF *ACE OF CAKES*
OUR MOM AND DAD
AND LUKE

CONTENTS

The Staff of CHARM CITY CAKES

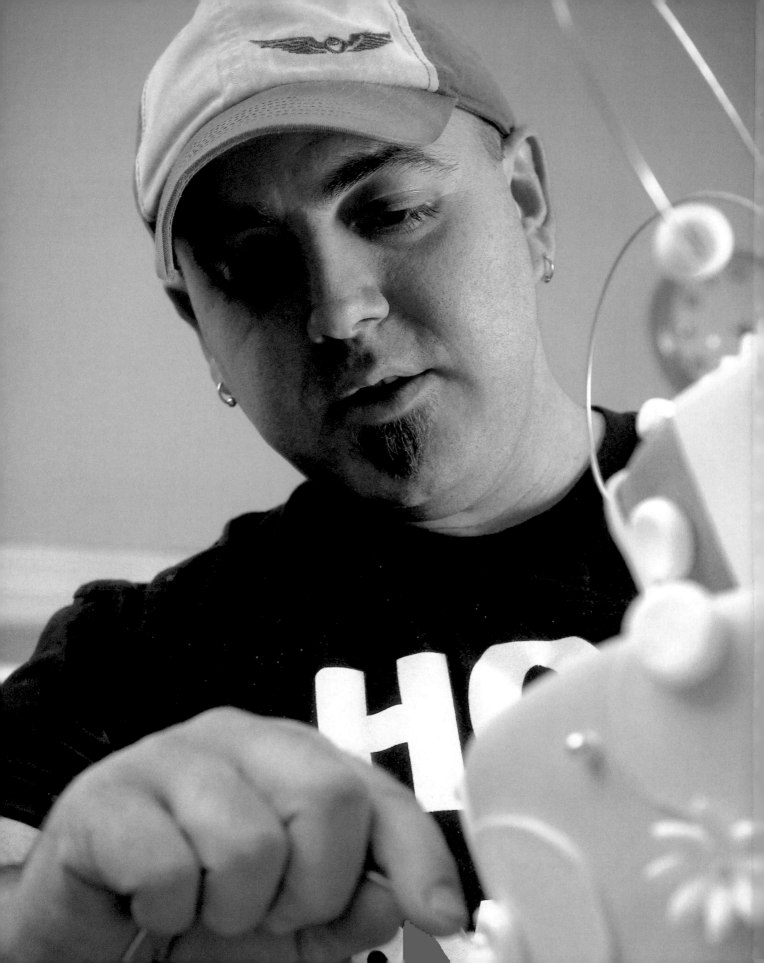

INTRODUCTION

"It's not the wand, it's the wizard."
—DUFF

Before we get started, we'd like to define what this book is not: it's not a cookbook or a how-to manual. With so many excellent cake-baking and -decorating books by some incredibly talented people out there already, we knew this book had to be different. One of the greatest joys for us is hearing our clients' reactions when they first see their cake, or a viewer's response to our show. If we were even to attempt a book, it was critical that we approach it the same way we do a cake, always mindful of the goal: to make the customer happy. Provide you with plenty of eye candy and feed the creative spirit in both kids and the kids inside us all. We wanted to create an artful celebration: a fun, visual, colorful scrapbook that reflects the spirit of both our show and our bakery.

But of course, Charm City Cakes has become much more than a bakery—it's more like a gigantic art collective where a group of artists, musicians, painters, sculptors, and chefs have been thrown into a mixing bowl with TV producers, directors, cameramen, sound techs, and more to execute their craft and create something, well, awesome. Though the majority of this book is about who we are and what we've done here at Charm City Cakes, we don't want to ignore the other artistic endeavor taking place inside the bakery: *Ace of Cakes*. *Ace of Cakes* isn't just a TV show, it's the wonderful result of the collaborative effort between the bakery and all of our writers, directors, producers, editors, and support staff at Authentic Entertainment in L.A., and of course, our friends and family at Food Network.

Before we go any further, we want to mention that we're going to be throwing the word "art" around a lot in the following pages. But just what is "art"? Is it something you see? Sense? Feel? Taste? Can it be all, one, or none of the above? Of course—art is how you define it. There's a scene in the movie *American Beauty* in which one of the characters finds wonderment in a small plastic bag that's being blown around in the wind. Some of the movie's viewers got it, some didn't, and others simply dismissed it as pretentious. It's that very division in viewers' opinions that allows us to create our own definition of the word. Art is the beauty, the near-unquantifiable force that moves

you when your senses interpret an experience—especially the first time your taste buds meet our award-winning Bananas Foster cake flavor.

Though some people may view art as something that hangs on a museum wall, we prefer a much looser definition. Picasso defined art as "the elimination of unnecessary"—and though we admit we don't fully understand exactly what he was saying, we *think* we get it. To us, "art"—the concept and even the definition of the word—is completely subjective. Yes, art can be something that hangs on a wall, but it can also be the shape of a building, the sleek lines of a race car, or lighted images projected on a screen. And, yes, art can be something you eat.

Food as art is as a temporary medium, but, like all lasting art, where it matters most is not on the plate but in your memories. Whether it's a painting, a TV show, or a four-tiered pumpkin chocolate chip–flavored cake in the shape of your grandmother's hatbox, art that is memorable stays with you forever. Bake, mold, shape, carve, sculpt, ice, fondant, paint, and decorate that taste into a physical object equally as extraordinary, and the food—the art—now has the power to become eternal.

Escoffier said, "We eat with the eyes first." It is important to us that this book be as visually interesting as the text it contains, if not more so. Cake, by definition, isn't a permanent art. Sure, it should be pleasing to the eyes, but it must also be pleasing to the palate. To us this is much more than a book, it's a visual record of some of the fun we've had and a glimpse at what we have planned for the future.

And for that we've turned to an incredibly talented group of artists, illustrators, and photographers, and the staff of Charm City Cakes. This book is as much a project of their imaginations as it is ours, and for that they will hold our everlasting awe.

We hope you enjoy the book as much as we did creating it.

DUFF GOLDMAN
Owner, Charm City Cakes
Baltimore, Maryland

WILLIE GOLDMAN
Co-creator and Co–Executive Producer, *Ace of Cakes*
Los Angeles, California

ME? A CAKE DECORATOR?

"I'm not going to change the way I look or the way I feel to conform to anything. I've always been a freak. . . . I'm one of those people."
—JOHN LENNON

One look at me, and it's easy to see why no one would mistake me for a cake decorator. Mechanic, maybe. Plumber, more often than not. Graffiti artist, possibly.

A bass player in a rock band—hope so. But how about someone whose job includes everything from painting several different shades of crimson on edible decorative flowers to maintaining the plumbing of a 5,200-square-foot bakery? A sales rep championing a product designed to be eaten? A deliveryman who drives from one coast to the other with an edible castle the size of Buckingham Palace in the back of his van? How about a mad scientist who knows how to adjust the ingredients of a cake just so in the sweltering miasma of Baltimore heat in August or a holiday confection in the dry and cold of a Mid-Atlantic winter? (I most definitely qualify as a weatherman, being intimately familiar with the humidity at any time of year and how it affects baked goods.)

That's okay; looks can be deceiving, and I've long grown to accept that I don't fit the mold. Screw molds. To hell with boundaries. Blast the limits. Forget established convention. And laws—well, okay, not all laws (we actually have a few in the bakery that are pretty useful at times).

For the most part, the human mind has this thing—this need—to put things in drawers and jars and plastic containers and give them labels. If you've seen *Ace of Cakes*, you know I'm not about the conventional rules, but I'm also not about breaking them just for the sake of it—and certainly not for an "image." I may have a reputation as a rule breaker, but you'll actually find no bigger proponent of a proper culinary education, such as the one I was fortunate enough to receive from

With Mamo in Wichita

the Culinary Institute of America, and of course all the on-the-job experience and advice I've picked up over the years from such mentors as Cindy Wolf, Todd English, Colette Peters, Thomas Keller, and others. This is not to say you need to have a Culinary Institute–level education or to apprentice under world-class chefs—not at all—but it *is* important to understand certain culinary fundamentals and the rules of food before you can set about breaking them and experimenting on your own.

So how exactly did I get here? I think serendipity did the job in the end, but the beginning of my culinary career simply involved my working my ass off in a variety of jobs (one of my very first jobs was at the McDonald's in Hyannis, Massachusetts) until I started doing something that worked for me. Before the bakery, I'd never had a job for more than a year or two, but now I'm closing in on my first decade (yikes, has it been that long?) as owner of Charm City Cakes, and it doesn't look as though I'll be switching careers anytime soon. Countless times I've been asked, "How did you know this is what you wanted to do?" I consistently give the only answer I know: "It just feels *right* . . ."

And it still feels right. Even through the soul-crushing stress of a cake falling apart or the emergencies that arise when the pipes burst, the walk-in goes kaput, the roof leaks, or the van gets a flat, it still feels right. Even through managing a team of highly creative, smart individuals, who can be just as tempestuous as I am, to taking care of the Dumpster bills and vehicle maintenance, it still feels right. My mom always lectured my brother and me to trust our instincts—to listen to those "voices," no matter how out there they might seem. I never really took that to heart until later in life, but it's advice I rely on every day.

BEFORE THERE WAS ME

Way before you and I were born, my great-grandmother, Esther "Mamo" Steinberg, left Ukraine at sixteen, passed through Ellis Island, and kept on passing across the United States until she settled herself in Wichita, Kansas. Let me type that again in case you missed it: Wichita, Kansas. That's right, a Russian Jew smack dab in America's heartland. They grow wheat there. Lots of it. Flour comes from wheat. I think you know where I'm going with this . . .

Mamo (my mom nicknamed her that when she was little) was an amazing woman, way ahead of her time—a freethinker and one of the most loving women on the planet. Though I have only brief memory flashes of her, there's one thing I recall very clearly: Mamo was a creator—of everything from food to all kinds of stitchery and knitting (my brother and I still have some amazing wool blankets she made for us before we were born). She was even a bit of an entrepreneur, buying and selling little properties all over town. She had her own millinery shop in downtown Wichita called the Hollywood Hat Shop (she thought the name sounded glamorous).

But it was in the kitchen where her cooking and baking skills merged with artistry to create dishes that are, quite honestly, legendary. One of the running jokes in my mom's family is that we may not have a lot of money, but one day we'll publish a book of Mamo's recipes and become millionaires. Family legend held that Mamo was known to keep her most special recipes in a safety deposit box along with her other cherished valuables. She also had a fairly serious ongoing competition with her cousin Sissy. Their culinary rivalry was as fierce as it was epic, and as a result we ate very well in our family.

One of her particular cooking habits was to put a bit of sugar in just about everything she made; it was one of her secret ingredients. Among her vast collection of savory dishes, a select few will stay with me forever.

Let's forget cakes for a second—I need to tell you about Mamo's strudel. I kid you not, this woman's strudel tasted as though God had made it. The surprising thing about the strudel was the genius in the way she made the apple filling. Unlike most strudel, in which the apples are uncooked, the day before she made her strudel Mamo would make an apple marmalade to which she had added another one of her secret ingredients. As if that weren't enough, Mamo's phyllo dough was inspired. She would make the dough from scratch, using clarified butter and seasoning it just right (using yet another secret ingredient), and bake it to a flawless buttery brown. Even the occasional misstep resulted in something equally delicious; when she had a bit of dough and filling left over, she would use them to make little individual strudels. She called them "bestards" in her Russian accent. My brother and I devoured them.

To a little kid of three or four, it was just this side of heaven. It was rich, it was sweet, it was messy and buttery and crunchy. All that was bliss to my little palate, which salivated at even the mention of things like mac and cheese, Dairy Queen, and gummy bears (still love the gummies, by the way).

THE NANA

Mamo's daughter, my grandmother Elinor Helitzer, inherited her mother's eye for style. Nana devoted herself to refining her study of many different art media, and though she was known mostly for her enameling and silversmithing, she also gained a reputation as a damned good lithographer and, later in life, a photographer. She even got my dentist grandfather, Bernie, into the act by having him make her charms out of dental gold for her bracelet. I was especially fond of one of a little toilet with the lid on a hinge. If you happen to come across a book on fine art enameling and silversmithing in the 1950s and '60s, you might even find her work in there. She was instrumental in opening my eyes to the world of art and nature, introducing me, as a kid, to a lot of the art and artists whose work I respect today.

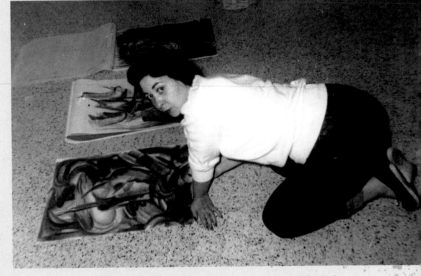

Nana

Nana was known mostly for her impressionistic images taken in the desert Southwest. She loved architecture and would examine it with her pictures. Light, shadow, and shapes fascinated her endlessly. She found them everywhere, from buildings and alleyways to mountains and boulders—there was always something that caught her eye. Other than a posed snapshot of her parents back in the 1940s, to my knowledge, she never took a photo that contained a human being.

One year when I was twelve or thirteen,

Nana's husband, my maternal grandfather, and Baltimore student Bernie Helitzer sporting his Maryland pride

Nana took me on a road trip from Kansas all the way to New Mexico (*long* before there was a Starbucks in the Santa Fe Square). We canvassed the region, driving out into the desert, taking pictures, checking stuff out, and eating some of the best cheese enchiladas I've ever had. One day we were driving by a pueblo, and as Nana had all her photo gear in the backseat and packed up tight in the trunk, she stopped the car, reached over, and grabbed my crappy little plastic 35 mm throwaway camera. She rolled down the window, leaned out, and took a picture. I got back home, and my mom had the film developed. When we got the pictures back, we sat down to look at them, and suddenly my mom gasped, holding up a picture and yelling, "Duffy! This is amazing! What made you take this picture?" Of course it was Nana's picture. The colors danced, the light hit the pueblo just right, the shadows made by the exposed logs were long and regular and at the right angle to offset the rest of the boxy building, and the background was of mountains and sky. The picture was so alive that you could almost hear and smell every detail. I often wonder what that picture would have been like had she used her own fancy camera with all the settings. I can't imagine it could have been any better.

Nana had an eye, no doubt. She bought a Roy Lichtenstein original long before he became popular. She had an autographed Annie Leibovitz poster of Keith Haring, she owned Georgia O'Keeffe prints, and everywhere she lived she made into a work of art. If she couldn't have the art, she'd buy books on the art she loved. She was a natural master of feng shui, and I bet she never heard the phrase. She just had the eye of an artist.

THE ARTIST AND THE BUSINESSMAN: MOM AND DAD

In the late 1940s, Nana gave birth to my mom, who is just the cutest little thing to ever come out of Wichita, Kansas. And surprise, surprise—behind that sweet little face lurked artistic brilliance. Speaking of which, there are two photos of the two of us at the same age where some people think we look alike, but I'll let you be the judge of that:

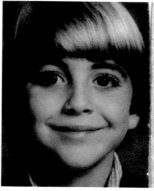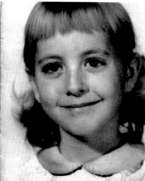

Mom and I at the same age

Me and mom

Dad and I at the bakery

I look at what I do, and if I ever need to put myself in my place, I look at my mom's art, and I am humble. From her landscaping to her paint color choices, she turns her dwellings into a place of refuge from a world that loves concrete. One day she decided to paint a room in the house plaid, and it was amazing.

My mom used to own a pottery studio, but now her art is glass; she makes windows to make Tiffany proud. She creates mosaics, many without grout—as if she "paints" with little tiny pieces of glass. Sometimes she makes things one wouldn't expect *could* or *should* be made of glass—much as we at Charm City Cakes make things that one might not expect *could* or *should* be made of cake. Once she made a table-size greenhouse in miniature, complete with hinged copper doors (with stained-glass windows) and working skylights. She broke up parquet flooring and made a wooden-slatted floor with tiny pebbles in between the slats. The little plants inside were real and needed careful tending.

Mom now lives in Palm Springs with my step-dad, Ronnie. On a recent visit to their house, I was delighted, but not surprised, to find a gazillion butterflies decoupaged on one of the dining room walls over a field of sky blue paint. In their office is a ceiling painted as a Scrabble board, complete with 3-D letters attached with Velcro. Yup, even though I was in the middle of the desert, I felt right at home out there in Palm Springs.

Maybe I am a mama's boy after all. Well, I'm proud of it.

As for my dad, luckily both my brother and I inherited a piece of his keen analytical mind. He's a business wizard with a PhD in economics. I would not be in business today if I didn't have my own entrepreneurial hot line: my dad's phone number. His guidance has kept me on the path for quite a while, and he's never at a loss for solving a problem. He calls himself my UFA: unpaid financial adviser. So, between his business savvy and Mom's artistry, my brother

At the Washington Monument in D.C.

9

and I were able to approach life with something of a fearless sense of adventure.

My brother and I were lucky enough to grow up in the Washington, D.C., area, and our parents were always taking us to the Smithsonian. From the local firehouse to aquariums, not to mention all the local art galleries, monuments, and museums, we were always taking field trips, discovering what the world had to offer. There was so much to see and do there, countless inspirational places that excited and delighted us. After our trips we would write about and create cartoons of everything we saw (my brother became a master of multidirectional and -dimensional drawings). Even if our masterpieces looked like scribbles and scrawls, our folks would ooh and ah—praising our every effort as *petit Picasso* and *very Van Gogh*. It wasn't long before our art (as well as life) styles developed into more of Lichtenstein for Willie and Fab Five Freddy for me.

Though my dad, like my brother, loved to *eat* food, it was really Mom who was responsible for my love of food and cooking and eating. When we were babies, she processed our food for us in the blender. She even made (and still does) the dog's biscuits and cookies from scratch. Now, if Mamo's strudel had a main-course equivalent, it would be Mom's brisket—so tender and full of flavor. Now, every Jewish kid is going to argue that his or her mom makes the best brisket (watch as Adam and I throw down over the very subject in *Ace of Cakes* episode 202), but let me say this: my mom's is so good, one bite and you'll see the face of God. She even puts matzoh balls around the sides instead of dumplings or potatoes, and they absorb the gravy and throw a little party in your mouth. The only thing better were the French dips she made out of leftovers the next day. Now, though Mom says she has a secret ingredient for that incredible brisket, I think secret ingredients just come with all Jewish mothers. It's in the genes. It's also a celebrated rite of passage when they reveal what it is. Like a mini Bar Mitzvah: "Today I am a *man*! I know what Mom puts in the chicken soup!" or "Finally, a chopped liver that doesn't taste all livery." Usually it's something artery-clogging or equally heart-stopping, but the flavor is always worth it.

Mom tells us that she learned to cook from Mamo by climbing on top of the refrigerator in Mamo's tiny kitchen and perching up there to get a bird's-eye view of the master at work. Mamo would even show her which hand to hold the crepe pan in when making cheese blintzes. With a family like this, who needs culinary school?

I don't consider myself particularly gifted. I just had the chutzpah to get off my tuchas. I'm just a cake decorator from Baltimore.

—DUFF

A TALE OF TWO BROTHERS

Life began in the suburbs of Detroit for us Goldman boys. My brother, Willie, arrived in early 1973 with the usual fanfare and hoopla most firstborns receive. Named for our great-grandfather, Willie got some pretty intense attention, as his every moment was cherished, recorded, and attended to. Twenty-two months later to the day, I came along. It was a dark and snowy December night, but there I was, and rue the day! Though there was plenty more fanfare and attention, even then, I was pretty much known as "Willie's little brother." Though I was born Jeffrey Adam Goldman, it was Willie who was responsible for naming me "Duffy." As hard as he tried to pronounce "Jeffrey," whenever he did, it kept coming out wrong.

Baby Willie

During grade school, the spotlight shone pretty brightly on Willie, not that I minded; I hardly noticed stuff like that. Although he was always the first to get to do stuff, there's no doubt I grew up a little faster by just being around him, our older cousins, and all his friends. Ahead of myself, sure—sometimes my downfall . . .

Willie took his big brother role quite seriously, a trait he has never abandoned, which is pretty much why we are where we are today. Ultimately, putting me and the high jinks at Charm City Cakes on television would be his idea.

Willie's early penchant for precision and order made him the perfect potential candidate for architecture school (or so our folks were convinced), while my all-over-the-place, hard-to-categorize style made my future seem most uncertain and sketchy (pardon the pun). After outgrowing his Tinkertoys, Willie was on to Lego cities and precision 3-D drawings, obviously honing his skills for that future in architecture. That is, until he saw *Star Wars* and got bit by the Hollywood bug at the ripe old age of four.

Baby me

Willie really enjoyed school and was completely delighted by every new experience and thing he encountered. I, by contrast, projected a more introverted front when I was young—a trait I'm pretty sure I more than made up for in the coming years. My lifelong love of music began early in life, although my instrument of choice morphed from harmonica to piano to bass over the years.

I did enjoy performing in some school plays, and I certainly loved art class and the creative activities, but I wouldn't say I was particularly *passionate* about them. I just went with the flow, soaked it all up, and had fun along the way. I was a huge fan of Shel Silverstein's

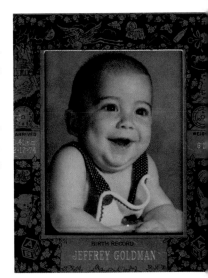

Willie + me + bowl of dirt = trouble

In Colorado

As "Dirty Dan" in the school play

books and poems. In fact, a school portrayal of one of his signature characters, Dirty Dan, was my very first experience in the performing arts—a role I took quite seriously.

As for sports, we loved all the winter ones: skiing, snowboarding, ice skating, hockey . . . we both played lacrosse at school and went on to play for our colleges' club teams. I played ice hockey, as well. But home life was still usually centered around the kitchen. Much time and care was taken up with buying, cooking, and of course devouring and savoring food—discussing it all the while. In our family we would sit around the table to a sensational meal, only to find ourselves reminiscing about other sensational meals in the past or longing for what we were to eat in the future.

With my grandfather, Bernie Helitzer in Wichita

Though Willie seemed content just to sample and graze through our childhood, loyal to an obsession with a few favorites (including Kansas' Lazy-R, Taco Via', Gates Bar B.Q., and Albert's Chinese), I, the relatively quiet and ever observant, started early in my fascination with the process of how all things culinary were created. Put simply: I cooked; he ate.

FOOD, ART, AND PAINTING WALLS

Mom and I spent a lot of time in the kitchen together, and I loved every minute. Most of the time we'd just talk, but I was always watching. When I was four years old, my mom caught me in the kitchen watching Chef Tell, swinging a meat cleaver, and chopping the hell out of all the vegetables in the fridge.

A pivotal moment in third grade heralded my future in the kitchen. While I was carving a pumpkin for Halloween, I decided that the stupid, dull *safety* knife Mom got us was not up to the job of creating the masterpiece I was planning. So I snuck back into our kitchen and emerged with the sharpest, evilest, most badass serrated steak knife I could find. Willie called it "the Knife of Hate." Boy, was he right. With one plunge into the pumpkin with Satan's Razor, I was *this close* to severing my pinky from my left hand. As I was rushed to the hospital with my digit dangling from nothing but a few tendons and a bit of skin, I learned what it meant to suffer for my art—even if it was just a Halloween pumpkin.

Despite the Great Pumpkin Incident of 1982, my interest in the kitchen grew. Along with Chef Tell, I kept a sharp eye on the Galloping Gourmet and my (still) favorite, Julia Child. I'd study Mom as she confidently put our meals together, always wondering how she knew all that stuff.

Sure, I'd see her with a cookbook occasionally, but mostly she just *knew* what to do. How much of this or that to put in, how long to cook it, when to stir, what level to adjust the flame to. I kept wondering why she didn't just put it on full blast so it would cook faster. I had *so* much to learn . . .

Along with the food, there was art. Mom sometimes took us to Meredith Stained Glass, where she worked as a studio artist and instructor. I was pretty fascinated by that place, especially all the dangerous glass and equipment around. They had one class for parents and kids together: sandblasting. *Sandblasting.* I didn't know what it was, but it sure sounded cool. Mom enrolled Willie and me, and it sure enough, it *was* cool. First we made a design on a clear plastic drawer liner, then we transferred the design onto glass and used an X-ACTO knife (yes, Mom helped me) to cut out the negative space, which would be etched by blasting sand at it. Then we put the glass in the enclosed chamber of the blasting machine, aimed the sand gun at it, and pulled the trigger.

The sand was powered by compressed air and made a ton of noise. The powerful sand etched away the part that I had cut, leaving the part covered by the plastic sheet still shiny. When I was finished blasting, I peeled off the plastic and my design was there. It was amazing—and the process taught me a lot about the use of negative space in art. I knew then I needed to be doing stuff like this, and I started getting more and more focused on rather out-of-the-ordinary ways to create. And of course I loved equipment and tools. I even had an inkle loom and learned to weave. Yeah, I said inkle loom—you got a problem with that?

I had a natural ability to have fun, but sometimes I would get ahead of myself. I had to learn the rule of cause and effect early on. One day I strung the electric cord of our best lamp across the steps and yelled for Willie, knowing he'd trip

With Willie in high school

and fall over it. It never occurred to me that the lamp would fall instead and break into a thousand pieces. Or that I would get into a ton of trouble. Nope, never gave it a thought.

In the mid-1980s, our mom and dad got divorced and confusion ruled the day. Realizing that things weren't going to be so easy from now on and discovering a need for a car and money to buy said vehicle, Willie went off to scoop ice cream at Tysons Corner Center. And with him gone most afternoons, it was then that I discovered a new art medium. I had always liked to doodle and draw and even illustrate a little, so what high and noble cause did I strive for? What beauty did I seek to arouse from a blank space? What discipline did I hone my young skills on? Drum roll, please . . .

> *I'm pretty confident in my ability to make cool cakes, things people haven't seen before.*
>
> —DUFF

13

GRAFFITI

Graffiti. n. pl. graf·fi·ti (-te) a drawing or inscription made on a wall or other surface, usually so as to be seen by the public.

Defiant by nature, I walked a fine line between the law and the needs of my creatively fertile mind. Never settling for the mundane or mainstream, I had to find my way in a world that I found slightly askew. School wasn't challenging or exciting enough. Boredom set in, and, like most undirected and/or misdirected young boys, I found that the "creativity" that had been so celebrated in my younger years was suddenly a bit of burden. My graffiti may have had some

At McLean High School

artistic value, but the police had other ideas—such as enforcing the law, of all things. But oh, man, I found heaven in a spray can.

I remember one day very clearly. I was walking in the woods near a road and came to a bridge that was parallel to the road. It was a beautiful day, and the bridge spanned a wide creek and a willow-bordered gully. I stopped at this cool un-discovered (by me) place and took it all in, just digging on it. Then I turned and looked at the other side, where the road was. Ugh. The creek flowed under me and then under the road, but the underpass of the bridge was vandalized with swear words and stupid drawings. It looked like a bathroom stall at a truck stop.

So I went home and starting doing some drawings for what I thought should be there instead. Once I was satisfied with them, I con-nived some money from my soft-touch mom for "art supplies" (how could she say no, right?). I then went to the hardware store, bought a bunch of spray paint, and went back to the overpass. I climbed down into the gully with two *borrowed* milk crates full of paint, my drawings, and some lunch, and I got to work. I won't dis-grace the name of graffiti by calling it that, but at least it was colorful and covered up the nasty stuff. And the place was great—you could work all day and nobody ever saw you down there. I took some pic-tures of what I did, took them home, and started drawing some more; then I went back and covered my earlier stuff with new stuff. It still sucked, but I was getting there. I don't know how many layers I went through before I

asked my mom to go on a drive with me so I could show her my art. I didn't tell her what it was—I just let her see it for herself. It was kind of funny for me to see her struggling with conflicting emotions—should she be mad because I was defacing public property? Or should she be bursting because I had come out of my shell as an artist? She was a little unnerved, but she was happy in the end; in the corner of the mural I had written, "To Mom and Ronnie." I think that's what did the trick.

So I kept going back. Mom and Ronnie got me some books on graffiti, and I was hooked. I started getting bolder, and I found a few other places around town that other writers were painting and started painting there, too. When we went to London to visit Ronnie's family, I managed to find the most amazing work in Europe. I was totally inspired—not just by the art and the scene but by the ever-lurking danger of creating it, which hooked the rebel in me.

Of course my new means of self-expression meant that trouble followed me around. I was becoming a pain. Schoolwork came too easily, and a minimum of time spent studying translated to maximum time "creating" with a can of spray paint. My mom was worried about me (she still is!) and knew she had to find something constructive to occupy my time.

A month after my Bar Mitzvah, Mom sent me to Israel on a trip with a group of older kids from Washington Hebrew Congregation, and it turned out to be the experience of a lifetime. Not particularly excited about going, I came back vowing to return one day, claiming it had been a pivotal point in my life—one that had given me some needed perspective on what I wanted and where I was going. I was inspired to achieve. Israel is full of superachievers, and the experience was very eye-opening.

With my mom's fairly fierce cam-

paign to keep me focused and out of trouble, at fourteen I found myself enrolled at the Corcoran School of Art, Washington's most prestigious art school. I surprised myself by really liking it there and rose to the occasion by becoming an exemplary art student. My instructors were impressed with the wit behind my work and even used my drawings for publicity for the school's graphic arts section. Mom's efforts at keeping me off the streets and out of trouble were the beginning of a deepening passion: serious art. I loved it, and it challenged me—unlike school, which generally bored me, unless I was reading books—something I love to do to this day.

Of course, I still needed money for my "art supplies" (spray paint). Like Willie, I found myself drawn to food establishments for employment, and my first real job was at the newly opened Skolnick's Bagel Bakery in the mall where Willie worked. At first I was relegated to the broom and mop, but the day I was finally allowed to handle the food was a memorable one. True to my family's passion for eating until your sides ached, I decided that the allotment

15

of filling for Skolnick's wide selection of bagel sandwiches wasn't nearly sufficient, so I secretly began stuffing my lucky customers' bagel sandwiches with enough deli meat to feed a family of five. By channeling Mamo's generous spirit I probably cost Skolnick's as much as my salary, but I loved the happy customers, and they loved me. Of course my managers got wise as soon as customers started coming in and asking for me specifically.

In high school I led a little bit of a double life. I played football and lacrosse by day, and at night I would go out and paint walls. One day in my sophomore-year photography class I was drawing in the notebook I usually drew graffiti in, and this older kid walked by. He came around to the other side of my table and furtively asked if I was the one responsible for a few of his favorite murals. I said I was, and he pulled out his notebook and showed me his sketches. It turns out we'd been sharing a few of the same walls together. Suddenly I found a new partner in art; Jason was light-years ahead of me in tagging, but he was very giving with his art and taught me things about color and wall surface and different brands of paint. The craft of the job and

the art as well. He helped create a new tag, and we would work on murals together whenever we came up with something worth doing. It was great fun.

Well, one night I was out by myself writing behind a strip mall, and right behind me a door burst open. I didn't even flinch—I dropped my can, grabbed my bag, and took off. I was in good shape and I could run, but the cops were a little faster. I got caught. It happens. My mom wasn't thrilled, to say the least, and made me promise that I would stick to my private little overpass and concentrate more on *in-studio* art.

My art teacher at McLean High School was a really cool guy named Jeffrey Meizlik. He tried his best to get me to focus on clay and line drawing and rendering and brush painting, but I just wasn't into it. It turned out that he was a metal sculptor, and his work was amazing— now, *that* I liked! If I couldn't get chased by the cops, at least I could burn myself! What's the fun if there isn't a little risk, right? So I started some attempts at working metal, but I quickly realized I'd need a teacher if wanted to learn how to manipulate metal, and teachers are not easy to come by. So I started using found objects and metal screws and my mom's soldering iron, and then I plucked up some nerve and enrolled in some college art classes in the summer at the Corcoran School of Art in Georgetown. They didn't offer metal sculpture to high school kids, but I really tried at doing some more studio art. It was a fiasco—I was fifteen and taking classes with art-school college kids. It was hard, but I stuck it out. At the end of my first summer, my portfolio development teacher told me I would do well to try a career path that didn't involve art.

Ouch.

So I said, screw that guy, I'll make my own art. I'm not too dumb, so I reasoned I could figure it out as I went along.

CCC: CAPE COD CALLING

At the end of my sophomore year of high school, my mom and Ronnie decided to move up to Cape Cod to a town called, of all things, Sandwich. Off I went, kicking and screaming. Actually it was pretty cool, although I hated to admit it. The very first week we went clamming with a crusty old Italian named Bob Gianferante. He was a fisherman/restaurateur/builder/real estate agent /cranberry bog man (everyone on Cape Cod has at least three vocations, one of which is always a fisherman and the second is either a framer or a roofer) who really knew the Cape. Digging in the sand and filling up my bucket was a blast. He actually initiated me to Cape Cod clamming by making me eat a fresh live clam right from the sand. I think it's because of him that now when it comes to food, I'll try anything (catch Ben and me eating a box of Milk-Bone dog biscuits in Ace of Cakes episode 507).

That night, Bob taught me how to make a serious, homemade New England clam bake, complete with the works—fresh-caught lobster, right off the boat down at the docks, and our own quahogs and steamer piss clams. Piss clams (aka "littlenecks" or "Ipswich clams") got their name because they squirt seawater when you step on them or take them out of the sand. They also toss local corn, red potatoes, and linguiça (Portuguese sausage, a specialty up there) right into the pot with everything else. There at the picnic table in their front yard, I had one of the greatest meals of my life.

I had many memorable experiences at my second high school, Sandwich High—some that perhaps I shouldn't be bragging about—as not only did I love to fish (legal), but I had a whole new town on which to hone my graffiti skills (not legal). I was definitely what one might call "a haver of shenanigans," as I constantly stayed up until midnight to sneak out and meet my friends to tag down by the tracks or go fishing. Both on a good night. Though "netting" at the herring run wasn't allowed, it sure was fun. Seemed as if all the stuff that wasn't allowed was the most fun.

After a few more "incidents," I had some, shall we say, "meet and greets" with various members of local law enforcement. I personally like to remember those times as a mutually beneficial relationship with the fine men and women of the Sandwich PD. I got to do my art on the largest canvases I could find, and they got lots of exercise chasing me. We laughed. We cried. We learned about each other. One evening my folks and I were sitting around the dinner table when the rather strong knock on the door interrupted (another) perfectly good meal. Guess who? It was the cops, who were looking for me because I'd paid a "special visit" to a guy who had gotten physical with his girlfriend.

When the school authorities heard through the campus grapevine that I had my eye on the handball courts for an upcoming (I rush to say—highly uncondoned) graffiti fest, they countered my plans with an offer I couldn't (and shouldn't if I knew what was good for me) refuse: instead of a study period, I could paint the wall across the hall from the office. Extortion? Could be. Fun? Absolutely.

Aside from some (relatively) harmless pranks and other rather goofy and unexplainable teenage behavior, I found some other outlets for my energy. I took over my parents' huge two-car garage, making one car run out of two that didn't. Funny how I always had pieces left over after I had reassembled every part. It became a joke, actually. After that, I traded in the entire mess for a VW Bug with no floor, just like the car from The Flintstones. You've heard of sunroofs? This car had a sun floor. This poor beast of burden came to an untimely end when I made an unfortunate left turn at one of Sandwich's two stoplights.

Sandwich High School, Sandwich, Massachusetts

I still made art in Sandwich, but metalwork isn't cheap, so I worked after school. I tried a few things—a shoe store, landscaping, that kind of thing—but the only thing I really excelled at was cooking, so I graduated from fast food and got a job as a breakfast cook for a summer at a real old-fashioned diner: The 6-A Café, one of the more popular eateries for the locals on the legendary road that runs the entire length of the Cape, route 6A. It was always crowded, and I really got a workout keeping those customers happy in the mornings. After that I went to work at one of the coolest places in town, Sandwich Pizza. Man, if you got a job at Sandwich Pizza, you were *in*, you know? It was at Sandwich Pizza that I decided what I wanted to do in life. Really, no joke. I was standing at the griddle making a steak-and-cheese grinder (a sub or hoagie), and I had just been accepted to college to study who-knows-what, and my mind wandered as I was chopping steak, toasting bread, frying onions, and melting cheese. I looked down on the griddle and I saw that I'd made a resplendent steak and cheese without even consciously thinking. *That* was it. I wanted to be a chef.

THE CALL OF CHARM CITY

I finally graduated from Sandwich High School in spring 1993. (My God, were they happy to have me out of there—the vice principal just beamed the whole day. I think they named the gym or something after me just to entice me to go.) My high school grades weren't so fabulous, but I totally aced the ACTs, which got me into the Baltimore campus of my grandfather Bernie Helitzer's alma mater, the University of Maryland. When I told my parents I wanted to go to culinary school instead, they weren't totally thrilled. But they did say that if I finished college in four years and got good grades, they'd help me out if I still wanted to go to culinary school—and that I should get a job in a nice restaurant that would teach me a few things before I went. Maybe they thought a good dose of new influences would change my mind. So I packed my stuff, gave my mom and stepdad a hug, and headed south to college. My dad was living in Annapolis at the time, so in Baltimore I would be closer to him.

I majored in history and philosophy in college. To supplement my tuition, I was the superintendent of our dorm, which is a fancy way of saying I was the handyman/plumber. I even had one of those handyman's belts. Now I know why their pants are always falling down. Anyway, one day a girl in the building called me frantically, saying she'd dropped her grandmother's strand of pearls down the sink. The girl's name: Mary Alice Fallon (more on her in a bit).

INTO THE KITCHEN

College was fun. I played lacrosse and hockey, created art (although I didn't take any art classes), and started playing bass in a band. I still had a yearning to go to culinary school, but it was on the back burner for the moment. My junior year, however, I was fortunate to meet someone in archaeology class who was a server at Savannah, one of the best restaurants in Baltimore. I had an interview with the chef, Cindy Wolf, and told her I wanted to be a chef. She looked at my résumé, with all my fast-food, pizza joint, and greasy spoon experience, and said, "So basically you don't know anything, huh?" But she found it in her heart to give me a job . . .

. . . baking.

Cornbread and biscuits. That's it. Cornbread and biscuits. "Baking?" I thought; it wasn't what I'd had in mind. "Who wants to *bake*?" It turned out *I* did. I loved it. Cindy was very serious about everything that came out of her kitchen, her food was sublime, and her team was a bunch of the best cooks in the city. Working at Savannah

(Above) With my mom and stepdad Ronnie at high school graduation

Sandwich high school graduation

19

My dad checking on his investment at the Culinary Institute of America

puccino, and then I'd sit down, make a list of mise en place for myself, talk to the cute servers, and bake my cornbread and biscuits. And then one day I looked over on the line, and it was total flipping chaos. Organized chaos, but man, those guys were sweating like crazy, burning themselves, cutting themselves, moving so fast, and tickets would just keep pouring out of the squirrel. Total chaos and urgency.

I liked my job a lot better—it was much more methodical. I was learning kitchen chemistry and math and working with tricky products like chocolate and dough that don't always behave the way you want them to. It was then that I realized I wanted to be a pastry chef. Though there was an excellent culinary school in Baltimore, I decided it was time for a change of scenery. While at a party at the sous chef's house, I saw a catalog for a culinary school, and not just any culinary school but the Culinary Institute of America. The catalog was for a brand-new school that had just opened in California (check!). In Napa Valley (check!). In an old monastery/vineyard (double check!).

I knew that I *should* go to school. Now, you don't have to, and 90 percent of what you learn you learn on the job, but I figured that as awesome at teaching as Cindy was and as giving with knowledge that the pastry chef was, pastry is a science you really need to study. There are percentages, chemical reactions, protein contents—things that people in a very busy restaurant just don't have time to teach you. So I graduated from college, hung out in Baltimore for the summer, and then headed out west for a whole new adventure.

Eagerly, I packed my car with all my earthly possessions and drove all the way across country. Words don't do justice to the gastronomic shrine of the Napa Valley. The setting, the vineyards; it was peaceful, it was beautiful. A whole new feeling was emerging inside me, and when I got to school, oh man—it was straight out of

was one of my best restaurant experiences. The place was a well-oiled machine. There wasn't any griping or whining, nobody begrudged anyone else being promoted, sauté didn't grumble at grill, expediter didn't grumble at garde manger—I loved every single minute. And anyone who has worked in fine dining knows that there aren't many places like that.

Cindy had real a knack for bringing out the best in people, and I think that if I had been working anywhere else, I might not have followed my career in food for as long as I have. I was lucky to be learning all kinds of stuff—knife skills, how to make stock, and *pastry*! We had this real French pastry chef who taught me everything. Ice cream, sorbet, meringue, pâte à choux, pâte sablée, pâte sucrée, cakes, piping, crème anglaise, pastry cream, roux, fresh fruit tarts—you name it. He found me a very eager student, although I hadn't even known what a pastry chef *was*. I was able to hold my own, and it felt right. That and one more thing—see, I would come into work and make myself a cap-

that scene when Harry Potter arrived for his first day at Hogwarts. The building itself was simply stunning, and it contained the most unbelievable kitchens I've seen in my life.

I found an attic to rent from a guy in a house on top of a mountain. (The valley had the some of the most difficult mountain bike terrain I've ever ridden; I used to come to school wearing bandages more often than not. I loved riding mountain bikes; I just wasn't very good at it.) I miraculously found a job with the right hours as the night baker at an artisan bread bakery, and once I was settled in, I bought myself a pony bottle of Veuve Clicquot, a baguette, and my first raw cheese (Le Rustique) and ate a celebratory lunch in the parking lot of school, drinking out of the bottle and using a pocket knife to cut the bread and cheese. Life was good.

We started school, and the classes were small—perfect for studying the subtle art of pastry. About a month in, I was driving around the valley with Orion, a friend from class, looking for places for him to skate, and we drove through a little town called Yountville. And then Orion said, "Whoa, there's the French Laundry!" I had never heard of the place, but it was apparently one of the most renowned restaurants in the world. We were sitting there and looking at the gorgeous little place when Orion said, "You should work there!" I said I already had a job, and he told me told me to go in and ask to apprentice. Well, I figured they probably had people coming in all the time, but from sneaking into train yards at night I had developed a sense of which way the wind blows, so I found the back door to the kitchen, walked in, and asked the pastry chef (an amazing human being by the name of Stephen Durfee) if he needed any free help.

Well, it just so happened that he did. He needed someone with strong arms to roll out cookie dough. They couldn't pay me, which was fine. They had the best cooks in the world

Celebrating at Mary Alice's brother Neil Fallon's wedding with my very first Charm City Cake

in there, but I wasn't *too* scared. Contrary to what people like to speculate about top chefs, Thomas Keller was an incredibly cool, giving, understanding, funny guy without ego or attitude, only a love of the pursuit of excellence. So I showed up the next day and rolled out cookie dough. And the day after that, I got to roll out more cookie dough, and by the end of the week, I got to keep on rolling cookie dough! Well, they didn't kick me out, so that was really something, and little by little I learned. I called my former chef, Cindy Wolf, and told her about my amazing experience there. In true Cindy fashion, she said, "Good for you—now, keep your eyes open, your mouth shut, and your hands moving, and don't embarrass me by being a jackass!"

Well, sorry, Cindy, but I was a jackass. One day I was plating cheese courses, ran out of mise en place, and got behind in my tickets, and Steven yelled at me. It wasn't just the yelling— I knew I was just plain out of my league. So I

The very first "Charm City Cake"

some lemon juice and a little salt. He looked surprised, but he gave me a little cup of the purée to experiment with. I flavored it, he tasted it, and then he let me fix the sorbet. He was so cool about it. Look at it from my perspective: he had been voted pastry chef of the year, I was still in school, and he was asking my opinion on how to fix the sorbet. He was so short on ego and so confident in his abilities that he wasn't afraid to take advice from a peon like me.

I've really taken his attitude to every aspect of my life, and I'm never afraid to learn from anybody, no matter who they are. Someone always knows something you don't, and if you have too much ego or are too self-conscious, you'll stop learning (and you'll be a jerk).

After close to a year in culinary school I decided to head back to Vail. My head was in a pretty messed-up place, and I didn't even know if I wanted to cook anymore. I figured a little R and R in the mountains, riding bikes and snowboards, was a good place to figure out what the hell I was going to do with my life. So I hung out with my snowboarding friends Greg, V-Boy, Whitey, and Tom, and they convinced me to stay in the mountains for a bit, get a job, and regroup.

So I got a job baking bread at the Vail Cascade Resort. The executive chef, Jesse Llapitan, was an incredibly cool guy with a passion for food and life that I'll always treasure as a source of inspiration. He pushed me to my limits and beyond and really taught me not only how to cook but to love the food, love the life, and care, care, *care*. I was also fortunate to work with a sous chef there, Jason Rogers, for whom perfection in cooking seemed to be second nature. He was my go-to guy when I was freaking out about the broken-down walk-in freezer holding my 1,200 sorbet napoleons. Jason, along with Clay and Steve from Olives in Washington, D.C., was probably the best line cook I've ever seen. He was a restaurant athlete who was always laughing, no matter how far in the weeds he was.

waited until lunch was over, grabbed my knives, went home, packed my car, and drove to Vail, Colorado, that very day to see some friends who were pro-am snowboarders.

I had committed the cardinal sin of a kitchen—I'd bailed. To this day I'll never forgive myself for letting down some very caring, wonderful people, but I use that now as a source of strength. To this day, I try to uphold standards that won't let Stephen and Thomas down. I don't expect forgiveness or sympathy; I was just a kid with his head up his ass. I betrayed their trust once, and I won't ever do it again. Sorry, guys. Having said that, let me digress and give you an anecdote that illustrates one of the most important lessons I learned from Steven.

At school we were learning the scale of flavors and the balance between salty, sweet, and acidic. At the same time, I was helping Stephen make some honeydew sorbet, and it didn't taste right. It tasted like honeydew, but puréed; it didn't have that honeydew punch. It was just kind of bland. Well, Stephen and I were wondering what to do, and he asked me for an opinion. Me! Some dumb intern! So I suggested adding

THE CALL TO CAKE

One day I got a call from Mary Alice back in Maryland, and she asked if I would make a wedding cake for her older brother, who was living in Denver at the time. Now, not only was Neil Fallon Mary Alice's brother, but he happens to be the lead singer of my favorite band of all time, Clutch. So I instantly agreed to make his wedding cake. It was a glorious six-tier cake with thousands of hand-painted marzipan flowers all over it. I took the cake to a venue near Red Rocks and set it up. Little did I know that I was about to receive a major impetus to my career. The owner of the wedding venue freaked out when he saw the cake, saying he'd never seen one like it before. He asked me for my card, and I told him I didn't have one—I was a pastry chef at a hotel in Vail. He then said that I should quit my job and open up my own cake shop! Well, I was still getting my sea legs and had no intention of starting my own business, let alone being a cake decorator. But even then a little light went on in my head. Hmm, I thought, maybe I could open up a cake shop and have enough time to be in a band, go on tours, and make a living! Maybe. So I headed back to the hotel and checked out how much money the hotel was getting for the cakes I was making for them—and I thought, Geez! I could live off of a few cakes a year at that rate!

Once again, serendipity stepped in. My parents called from Cape Cod; they had eaten the night before at a restaurant in Boston called Olives. Knowing it had to be *the* Olives owned by the celebrated, award-winning chef Todd English, I told Mom the guy was a legend and that I'd kill to work for him. She said the private dinner had been given by our cousin and that he was friends with Todd, and the cousin arranged to have an audition for me at the Olives in the Bellagio hotel in Las Vegas.

The audition consisted pretty much of tossing me into the pastry kitchen at the Bellagio and having me bake bread and pastries for Steve Mannino, the executive chef at Olives in Washington, D.C. He must have liked what I made, because I got the job—just a few miles from where I'd grown up and gone to college.

I told my chef at the Cascade, and he was really happy for me and told me to go for it—and not to screw up this time (see a recurring theme in the advice?). So I packed up all my stuff again and headed back to the East Coast. Well, I made some amazing friends there, and it was at Todd's that I *really* learned how to cook. A lot. Too much, in fact. I spent about a year there and felt myself getting burned out fast. So this time I stuck to my guns and quit like a real man. I realized I wanted to own my own shop, be in a band, and get some control over my life. So I moved back to Baltimore, got a job as a personal chef, and made enough money to start a website, buy some business cards, and make cakes on the side.

On March 3, 2002, I left my job and started decorating cakes full-time. In my apartment in downtown Baltimore. Health Department? Permit? Tax ID? Nope. I figured I would cross those bridges when I came to them (or, more appropriately, they came to me). There is nothing, I repeat, *nothing* that can get you motivated to run a business like when I woke up on March 4 and realized I didn't have a paycheck anymore. Want to learn how to jump? Paint yourself into a corner. I won't say roll the dice, because I knew I had no choice but to succeed. Well, so far trusting my instincts had never felt so good.

> *Cake is a physical manifestation of joy.*
> —DUFF

23

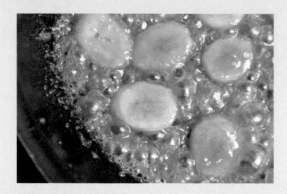

Q: Why isn't this a cookbook? Where are the recipes?

A: This is a book about us doing things in a way that we have found works. You can just use your favorite cake recipe or even a cake mix and experiment with it. There are plenty of books out there that can tell you how to bake a cake; we're not reinventing the wheel, we're just playing with our food.

Q: How much do your cakes cost?

A: How much you got? You can't put a price on happiness.

Q: Your cakes look good, but I bet they don't taste good.

A: In all honesty, we get this one a lot, especially on the Internet—where people just love to throw up all kinds of snarky comments. First off, forget the TV show—do you really think Charm City Cakes would be in the bakery business longer than a week if our cakes didn't actually taste good? By the time you read this, one in every twelve homes in America will have tasted a Charm City Cake—with numbers like those, it's hard to imagine they wouldn't taste good.

Okay, so we're exaggerating on the stats, but truth be told, cake itself is kind of hard to screw up—it's just flour, sugar, butter, and eggs. Of course, we do make forty-nine different flavors, which we're adding to all the time—take a look at the list on page 79. Our cakes have a layer of buttercream, on top of which is placed a decorative layer of fondant—which can be eaten or not. Though it's hard to convey flavor without handing you a piece of cake, let's take our Bananas Foster cake as an example. Imagine a smoother, silkier version of Nutella, with bits of fresh sautéed bananas mixed in—that's what a Charm City Cakes cake tastes like. One bite, and you'll see the face of God.

Q: What *is* the deal with fondant?

A: Though fondant is edible, the point isn't to put it in your mouth. Our cakes are designed so that the fondant seals in the freshness and preserves the cake and icing underneath. Think of fondant as a thick, dense coating that's meant to be peeled off like a banana skin; you want what's underneath. That's not to say you can't eat it—it's just that it's pure sugar.

Q: Why are your cakes mostly Styrofoam?

A: This is another misconception, thanks to the magic of TV and the Internet. Like most bakeries, we have a display rack that highlights cakes for prospective clients. We also create display cakes when a client says he or she would like to be able to show a cake for a longer period of time, something that wouldn't work with edible material that would spoil. On average, Charm City Cakes creates more than sixty cakes a month—all edible—and maybe one or two display cakes for (usually) a corporate client. So, no, even though you may have seen one or two on TV, our cakes are definitely not "mostly Styrofoam."

Q: What are rice cereal treats used for?

A: The treats are a very stable, sculptable edible material that are great for making parts of cakes that might not be as structurally sound otherwise. They're an easy way to add mass and volume without the support needed for the heavier weight of cake.

Q: How come we never see you guys wash your hands on the show?

A: The sink broke a few years ago, and we just haven't had time to fix it.

Q: No, really, how come we never see you guys wash your hands on the show?

A: You're not going to let up, are you? It's a simple matter of editorial direction. The *Ace of Cakes* production team films more than 120 hours of footage for a single twenty-two-minute episode—so the boring stuff, like us washing our hands, is left on the cutting room floor. But for the record: yes, we wash our hands . . .

. . . sometimes even once a week!

Q: Can I work there?

A: As much as I wish you could, if we hired all the incredibly talented people who've asked, we'd need a much, much bigger building!

Q: Do you have an open internship program?

A: Not really. Though we've had a few interns in the past, we currently don't have an open internship program.

Q: Can I have an autograph?

A: Sure, send us an email.

Q: Is working there really your job?

A: Yes, it is.

Sofia ices a cake with buttercream before the fondant is applied

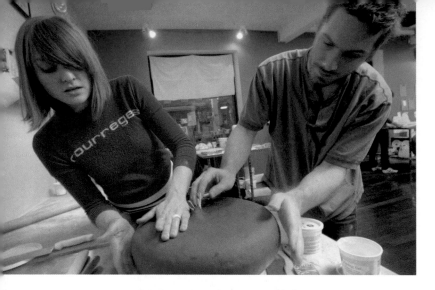

cake we make is handcrafted to order, and though that makes for some really spectacular cakes, it doesn't leave us with a lot of time for visitors and jibber-jabber. So we can't have people stopping in to watch. We do realize that you're special, but we simply do not have the time or resources for visitors.

Also, our evil lawyers have told us it's a no-no to have folks traipsing through here. Would *you* want a parade of visitors walking through a place you were ordering food from?

If you ask to visit, we'll be forced to say no (see above re: evil lawyers) and then we'll feel like meanie heads. If you show up anyway, we won't be able to let you come inside, and then we'll feel like megajerk meanie heads. We don't want to let you down, and we don't want to feel like megajerk meanie heads. We're very sorry to be so stern and such, but there are no exceptions to this policy.

Q: Do you ship your cakes?

A: We tried. Once. Epic fail. Never again.

Q: Can I visit the bakery?

A: Though we love to have visitors, between decorating the cakes and producing the show, it's a little too crowded inside to entertain company. We are a very small, very busy shop. Every

Q: I want to learn how to do what you guys do. Any advice?

A: Good artists borrow. Great artists steal. For example, get your craft down pat so you can make a perfectly iced square fondant cake. Now pick up a book of Picasso prints, choose a favorite, and replicate it on top of that cake. Or—have you ever wanted a cake in the shape of something that wasn't a cake? Easy. Stack up three or four sheet cakes with butter cream

between the layers, get out your handy-dandy serrated knife, and carve away until you get exactly what you want. So much of what we do is sculpting, painting, coloring, shading, piping, and defying gravity. We're not the best decorators out there—and we don't claim to be—but we're definitely having some of the most fun doing what we do. So if you want to do what we do, do what we did: just figure it out. Bake, ice, carve, experiment. And have fun. I started in a one-bedroom apartment in Baltimore decorating cakes on my coffee table—and the rest is history.

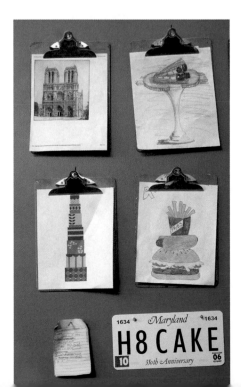

If you're looking for cake technique info, check out the books *Cakewalk* by Margaret Braun, *Cakes to Dream On* by Colette Peters, and *Larry Powell's Big Book of Cake Decorating*. The Web forums at sugarbuzz.us and cake-central.com are also wonderful resources. We also suggest taking a Wilton class at Michael's or Jo-Anne's, which can help get you started on the path to becoming a decorator.

Be creative. Be artistic. Be imaginative. And be yourself.

Q: Are there any schools you recommend?

A: Though it would be really hard for us to play favorites, there are several culinary and art schools that can serve as great launching pads for careers in the culinary arts as well as art in general. Some of the schools we've attended include the University of Maryland, Culinary Institute of America, Maryland Institute College of Art (MICA), the Corcoran College of Art + Design, and many, many, others. The simple truth is that there's no one path—culinary schools and colleges aren't the only way into a career. With no connections in the industry, my brother thought the only way he could get a job in Hollywood was through film school. He got an internship instead and has been a producer ever since. My advice: work in a kitchen and learn all the proper jobs, all the terminology. Try working under several chefs before attending culinary school. Though schools are fantastic, there's no substitute for real-world, on-the-job training.

CHARM CITY CAKES ELEMENTARY
BALTIMORE, MARYLAND

Elena Fox

Katherine Hill

Mary Alice Fallon Yeskey

Adam Goldstein

Sofia Rodriguez

Duff Goldman

Sherri Chambers

Jessica Curry

Adrienne Ruhf

Benjamin Turner

Mary Smith

Erica Harrison

Anna Ellison

Katie Rose

Lauren Friedman

Mark Muller

(No Image
Available)

Geof Manthorne

GEOF MANTHORNE Sous Chef

Hometown: Pottstown, Pennsylvania
Favorite movies: Anything by Wes Anderson or Akira Kurosawa
Favorite hobbies: Playing instruments—trumpet and guitar
Favorite music: The Beatles, Bob Dylan, Neil Young
Favorite nondessert dish to create or eat: Guacamole, pot pie
Fun fact: I appeared as an extra in the 1997 film *The Curve*.

In his own words . . .

I see cake everywhere.

I look at a car and wonder how to construct it with cake. I see the strata of strawberry buttercream in a skyscraper. I am icing a stranger's head and covering a mailbox with fondant. A traffic light: circle cutters, red fondant, green fondant, yellow fondant. How would I build the bench I'm sitting on? What materials should I use? How can I glue them together? Why?

These questions never used to trouble me. Sure, I had seen a few cakes before: wedding cakes, ice cream cakes with funny names, homemade cakes from heart-shaped pans. But I knew nothing of fondant or marzipan or pastillage. You may wonder, as do I, how it all came to this point. Well, I guess it all started with a meeting . . .

Meeting Duff

If I remember correctly, Duff's reputation preceded our first meeting; he was a friend of many of my friends, who all spoke of his jocular and boisterous nature. After he moved back to Baltimore, he began dropping by the warehouse space where I lived along with some of his college friends. A group of friends had the idea to create a live cooking variety show theater piece starring Duff called *F—— You Let's Bake*. Over a couple of years we put on several perfor-

mances that included local musicians and quirky performers, obstacle courses, egg targets, burlesque superheroes, and ninjas.

Organizing and performing the show along with running a bakery became too much for Duff to handle alone, so our mutual friend Kevin suggested that he hire me—even though I had no background in cake or pastries and only a few months' experience working in a kitchen as a prep cook, preparing salads and sandwiches and working the fryer and grill at a local restaurant. At the time, I was working as needed at an architectural firm building models, so I started off as a two-day-a-week employee for Duff while I kept the architectural job. As the bakery grabbed the attention of the local, then national, press, business picked up and my job at the bakery went from two days a week to six.

Our First Cake Disaster

We were producing more and more cakes and needed a larger, legitimate bakery. Because of the increase in the number of cakes, I began making deliveries. One of the first weekends I went out alone, I took two cakes. I don't remember the name of the first cake delivered, but the second I'll never forget: it was called "Oops." As I made the turn into the parking lot of the first reception site, I heard an awful, sucking sound—something I had never heard before. When I turned around, I realized that was the sound of the top two tiers of a cake falling off.

I hadn't expected that.

So I called Duff. No answer. Well, I have to finish this first drop-off, I thought. No problem. I called Duff. No answer. I had to start driving. I called Duff. No answer. I was at the fork in the highway where I had to decide to go on or go back. I called Duff.

"Where are you?"

"At the drive-through."

"I have a problem. Cake fell over. I'd go back to the bakery to attempt a repair, but I don't have keys yet!"

"I'll meet you there—want a burger or something?"

We met up at the bakery, fixed the cake, delivered it on time, and named the cake "Oops."

I learned a couple of lessons that day. I now understand the importance of smooth driving and the proper speed at which to make a turn. We also made some changes to the way we built our tiered cakes. And decided I should have keys to the bakery. And that cheeseburgers are more important to Duff than answering my calls.

Jeep Cake

Most savvy television viewers are keenly aware that "reality" shows are often molded by editors and writers to create a narrative and build excitement. People often ask me when referring to the show, "Did that really happen?" Most of the time, they're wondering about the Jeep cake from the very first episode of *Ace of Cakes*. In case you haven't seen this episode, after working on this cake for a week, I look on as a groom heartily devours the cake replica of his Jeep while the rehearsal dinner guests are still eating dinner. Most reality show viewers are used to contrivances and situations being staged for the camera, but I can assure you that this really happened.

Ace of Cakes

It wasn't that long ago that Charm City Cakes consisted of "three friends who listen to a lot of music and eat a lot of sushi." We eat much less sushi and listen to music less frequently (since it's prohibited while filming) and are now fifteen or so staff members. And now strangers talk to me—and not because they just got out of jail and need money to take the light rail back to Owings Mills. Occasionally one will misspeak and refer to me as a character: "I really enjoy your character on the cake show!" I don't mind, I just smile and say thanks. And though it often feels as if I'm playing a role, it's a fun one, as one of the reasons I enjoy making the show is the freedom we have to play around, move from our day-to-day cake decorating to a silly skit or mock game or cooking show. It's sort of as if we all have two jobs now: one is making cakes, the other is making TV. Though there's some over-lap, I do have to reflect and explain a lot. Before TV, we finished cakes and went home. Now we answer questions about the cakes before they're made, while we're making them, and after they're done. For about two hours every week the production staff interviews the others and me for what the editors whittle down to sound bites and seconds of screen time. I also

have to schedule our deliveries for the week to meet production's needs.

Though we all enjoy it, the show does add a great deal of pressure. There are many amaz-ingly talented decorators out there who aren't given this platform, and though our angle is cer-tainly not that we're the best cake makers in the world, we're still under the microscope. I think in a way this pushes us—we're constantly trying to innovate and improve. But in the same way, participating in the show adds to our workload, and we often don't have as much time as we'd like to experiment.

Regardless, though we all enjoy being a part of *Ace of Cakes*, personally I'm surprised at how successful our show has been. I didn't imagine that anyone would want to produce a

> **TIP** *Look around you for inspiration and tools. Items in your kitchen can be used as molds to create interesting shapes.*
>
> —GEOF

show about a bunch of cake decorators from Baltimore. And I certainly didn't expect so many viewers and enthusiastic fans. Though most of the attention and praise falls on us, the "cast," it's really the production company that's responsible for making us, and the show, look good. We're not really that interesting. Some days there are boring, silent epochs of time. Another reason for the show's success is the association with Food Network and its devoted fans, an association that I think grounds the show. Though it's a "food program," it's not always necessarily about food. It's comforting to know that the focus of the show will always be the cakes and not any of the negative drama you see on other reality shows.

Why the Bakery Works

Prior to Duff and Charm City Cakes there was an unfilled niche in Baltimore. Many of our early clients were peers of ours looking for a different kind of wedding cake or personalized cake for special events, and with his charm and custom design ideas, Duff was able to show people that there is a nontraditional way to view cakes. Charm City Cakes clients want elements of their cakes/celebrations to reflect themselves or their loved ones—something close to impossible with store-bought items. That customization

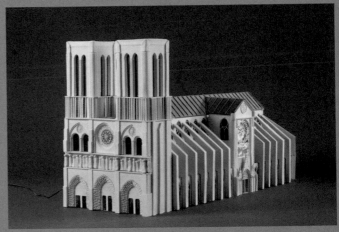

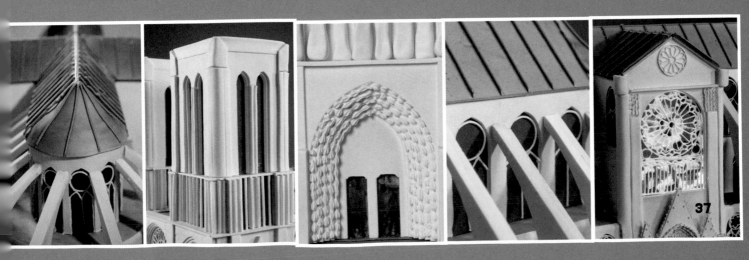

pulls from many disciplines, from art technique to social and political studies. Personally I've never really felt completely comfortable creating something called "art," as I consider myself more of a craftsman than an artist. A client orders a replica of a car or building, and I craft it out of cake. That's it.

Now, of course, I have to figure out how I'm going to build it. I decide what are the important aspects, the details that make that building or vehicle unique, as often it's the smallest details that draw people in. One of the many things I learned when making architectural models was the importance of detail. No matter how late or how long we'd been working, we'd always take the time to add the smallest things: miniature people and cars, awnings, streetlights, shrubbery, flowers. These little touches really make a project come alive, whether it's an architectural model or a cake. I often recall those rushed hours when we're finishing a big order, and though the cake itself is done, we're all huddled around it, decorating the base with sidewalks or waves or trees. When you hear things like "Oh, look, there's the fountain that's in the courtyard!," you know you've done your best to make a client happy.

Building models is a time-consuming job that requires accuracy and meticulousness, which naturally can lend itself to some long days. Luckily my model-building background prepared me for life in the bakery, as it's a time-consuming job that requires accuracy and meticulousness.

Once I made the transition from models to cake and learned the new materials, I was able to use those prior skills for the new job of cake decorating. Thinking back, I'm amazed at some of the weeks we survived with such a small crew—there was a time when just four of us completed more than fifty cakes in one week—but back then we certainly had many fewer distractions . . .

is appealing to both individuals and companies that want to incorporate their buildings or brands into their events.

I came to the bakery with a very different set of skills from the other decorators'. I didn't attend art school; in fact I think the last hands-on art class I took was in the ninth grade. But I've always been interested in art history, as it

The Future

The opportunities presented to us have been satisfying and unexpected, and the kinds of affairs and cakes we've worked on have been more and more gratifying. We've been invited to participate in some fantastic events that do not fall into line with a cake decorator's job description. We've voiced characters on *King of the Hill*, visited Jay Leno at *The Tonight Show*, gone places most civilians don't get to go, and met some of our favorite sports stars, actors, and musicians.

This chapter of my life has to end sometime. What happens after *Ace of Cakes*? *Ace of Cakes: The Musical*? *Ace of Cakes: The Animated Series*? *Ace of Cakes on Ice*? The *Ace of Cakes* Reunion Tour? That's where it all ends.

> **TIP**
>
> *If you have the time, think through the process of decorating the cake. Your cake will be cleaner and fresher if well planned.*
>
> —GEOF

DANA TERRY

Dana is what we call a "superclient," as she has come back for more than half a dozen cakes over the years. Not only has Dana ordered an air hockey table cake for her parents' fortieth anniversary and an off-roading landscape cake for her daughter Rosalie's eighth-grade graduation, but she's also ordered several of our favorite pop culture-themed cakes.

Her first cake was for a birthday party for Rosalie, who was really into Phantom of the Opera. Charm City Cakes recreated the famous gondola from the show and even included the phantom's mask and single red rose. Dana was so thrilled with the cake that she promised to come back within a few months to get another one. And she did—but this time she placed an order for a *Star Wars*–themed cake. Ahh, *Star Wars*—two simple words that instantly make a client a staff favorite. Nothing puts us into a more playful and excited mood than the prospect of a cake from a galaxy far, far away. . . . Dana attends several sci-fi conventions, and she loves to order a cake to wow all her friends at the show every year.

The Star Destroyer Cake

Speaking of that epic space fantasy from a long time ago, we have happily created several *Star Wars* cakes for various clients and charities, including the Death Star I, an Imperial Star Destroyer, the Millennium Falcon, an X-wing fighter with light-up engines, and even a Slave I . . .

. . . for a wedding! Best. Wedding cake. Ever.

One of the tough things about having repeat clients is the need to top yourself with each successive cake. It's easy to impress someone once, but five times in a row? With each of Dana's successive orders, we challenge ourselves to outdo what we've done in the past so that Dana will be just as thrilled as she was with the first cake she ordered. So what's next for this Charm City Cakes superclient? Word has it she's planning an Invader Zim–themed cake for Rosalie's Sweet 16 . . . and for her own birthday, Han Solo frozen in carbonite, err, we mean, cake!

A collection of Star Wars–themed cakes created by Charm City Cakes over the years

STAR WARS™

Death Star
Space Station

Imperial
Star Destroyer

Imperial Shuttle

Millennium Falcon

X-Wing Fighter

FREE BOBA FETT
Fondant figure included with Slave I cake.

Pit Droid

Slave I

Baker

PROOF OF FRESHNESS SEAL

Ace of Cakes
FUN GROUP

STAR WARS®
CAKES

© 2009 Lucasfilm Ltd. & ™. All rights reserved. Used under authorization.

BEGINNING A BAKERY

"You can't wait for inspiration. You have to go after it with a club."
—JACK LONDON

So I called my dad, business guru extraordinaire, and asked, "Hey, Dad, how do I start a cake business?" And he says, "Get some business cards, get a website, and sell some cakes!" Astounding, basic advice, but I followed it. At the time I was living in the top floor of an apartment building right in downtown Baltimore, so I got a nice little website, bought some cake supplies, designed some business cards, and sold a cake! I made that cake in my rickety joke of a home oven, decorated it on my coffee table (oddly enough, the same table I'm typing on right now), and delivered it in my little hatchback VW to my new clients down in Washington, D.C.

I still remember the cake: it had this really cool peach-and-ivory color scheme, with a very 1950s mod piping, and was inspired by some of Shag's art. Who knew I was doing something different? Certainly not me. When I met the potential clients before they placed the order, they told me what they wanted, I drew them a picture on the spot, and they liked my idea. Simple, right? That's exactly how we do things today. We don't have a big book of designs for people to choose from; every cake we make is custom-designed for the client. I had no idea that this is very different from the way most cake shops operate.

Soon enough, I was selling cakes to catering companies and hotels and individuals, so I quickly built up a big stack of cake pans, other cake supplies, and even a snazzy little five-quart mixer! I outgrew my apartment in no time and bought a row house with the intention of turning the master bedroom into the decorating studio, the kitchen into a cake production shop, and the dining room into a reception area where I could meet with potential clients and hold tastings and design consultations.

While all this was going on, I was playing music and even doing a bit of satirical theater. Me! Onstage! I was that guy who gave the thespians in high school a hard time—I never thought I would be treading the boards!

Geof

I had a funny little spoof of a cooking show that was called *F—— You Let's Bake!*—a title that had been conceived years earlier at my going-away party as I was headed to culinary school. Some of my theater world friends thought it was ludicrous that this dumb rock-and-roll jock was going to school to become a pastry chef. Well, when I got back to Baltimore, my friend Mike Smith called me one day and asked if I thought the idea of a cooking show was still worthwhile. I said sure, but only if he wrote, directed, and produced it, because if anyone was going to get me to act, it had to be someone whom I trusted and knew could get the best shtick out of me.

The show was, how do I say this—well, it wasn't exactly a *family* show. Let's just say we didn't advertise it, for fear of being raided. Surprisingly, our little stage show was a success, and we did many more of them. Soon we were playing to standing-room-only crowds, so we called our friend Kevin Weston, who was living in an old warehouse, and asked if we could have the show there. He eagerly agreed. Among those living with Kevin were some friends from college, namely Matt Dickenson—my right-hand man onstage—and another guy whom I knew from the music scene but never got close with, Geof Manthorne. So, here I was, running a business, playing bass in the emo band Two Day Romance, acting in Mike's show, and also acting in a synchronized swimming outfit called Fluid Movement.

NOW HIRING

With the popularity of the stage show and all the incoming orders, I was beginning to think that I had bitten off more than I could chew. More than anything, I didn't want it to show up in my work, so one day Kevin called and said that since I was just way too busy and Geof was ready to leave his job building architectural models, he was hiring Geof to work with me on my behalf (you just have to know Kevin to understand why that works).

And that's how I got my sous chef, Geof Manthorne. Yin to my yang, Frick to my Frack, Spock to my Kirk—er, well maybe Chewie to my Han (or the other way around). I'm the crazy, overoptimistic one, and over the years Geof has become one of my best friends and my logic personified. Geof keeps me sane. If I'm about to do something dumb or am too eager to go over the top, he's always there to talk sense into me, reason things out, and, in the worst-case scenario, pick up the pieces when things fall apart, literally and figuratively.

Establishing Charm City Cakes was my idea for how to create a fun, creative, challenging job that would allow me the time off I needed, but I would probably still be dodging the health department and making adequate cakes if it weren't for Geof. He's also a musician, a much better one than I am, and the job worked out perfectly for him as well. He's an amazing singer, composer, and guitar player and plays trumpet with his older brother in a Fela Kuti tribute band called the Baltimore Afrobeat Society, which, incidentally, was home to another musician friend of mine, Chris Donohue. Chris is no doubt the funkiest white man on the planet; he's got the Long Island guitar skills and the soul of Motown. Chris was my second hire as a baker. So here we were, the three of us—making cakes, playing music, and working in my house. I was even fixing some pretty tasty three-hour hot lunches for all of us every day. If I had the time, I still would. Often we'd order in sushi and watch the History Channel and *Star Trek* until . . .

Anna.

One day I received an email from an art student here in Baltimore. Anna Ellison was attending MICA, the Maryland Institute College of Art, and was looking to fulfill an internship requirement. An intern? Here? What the hell would we teach an intern? So I ignored her first email, but Anna sent another one. Wow, this girl was persistent. So I replied with a vague "We'll see," and I thought that would be that.

A few days later I heard a knock on the door. I thought it would be some eager art student wanting to work for me for free, but instead it was an official from the city, complete with a big bad badge. He asked me if I was making cakes in my house without a permit, which of course was illegal. Someone had ratted me out! So I replied, "No, sir. Look at me—do I look like I make cakes?" He said no, I didn't look like a cake decorator, but if he came back with a warrant, he better not find any cake-decorating items in my house. Yikes! So, I started searching frantically for a place with the proper zoning for commercial baking. I got lucky and found an old catering kitchen a few blocks from my house and got a two-year lease, and under cover of darkness

we moved all our equipment out of my house and into this new place. Then I immediately got a real license and permit, posted them for the world to see, and boom—we were legit! Since we now had the physical capacity to handle the increasing workload, it was time to fill it with personnel; so I called back my persistent art student, Anna, and offered her an internship. That's one phone call I'll never regret. Once while we were working, the subject of Scrabble came up. I fancy myself a pretty verbose and loquacious individual, and Anna asked if I wanted to play. Well, I felt kind of bad, as she was still in school and I could usually beat the pants off my friends. I said sure, deciding that I'd take it easy

Anna

45

A promotional image from the first Ace of Cakes *website*

had to work hard to find a word that went across two letters—and somehow I did. This time Anna laid across mine on a double word score. Four words in, and I know I'm beaten. After we finished the game, Anna laughed and said she'd never won by so much, *even after she'd become a ranked Scrabble competitor!* It turned out she'd memorized every two-, three-, and four-letter word in the English language. I've never played her since, but I'm glad to have her on my team.

Through the synchronized swimming group Fluid Movement we met an amazing artist named Sherri Chambers who taught me that, although I thought I knew how to sculpt, I really didn't know squat. Sherri very quickly took us to the next level. I've said before—on the air and anyplace else I have a chance—that Sherri is an art machine. She works so fast and so well that the camera crew rarely has time to set up a time-lapse camera on her. By the time they do, she's already done with whatever she's working on.

Here's Sherri in a nutshell: it was her first week in the new place, and I showed her how to make a parchment piping bag and apply dragées to a traditional wedding cake. She was doing that while I was carving a pug dog for a client. I saw Sherri watching me, and she asked if she could do the dog. Well, it was her first week, so I figured we should work up to carving. Sherri says okay and keeps applying the dragées. After a few minutes she says, "Ya know, I think I can do that!" I see that look in her eye, so I figure when she screws up, I can always bake more cake. So I hand her the knife and I pick up where she left off, applying the dragées to the wedding cake.

Well, I saw that Sherri was moving pretty fast, and then she started icing the cake! Where the hell did she learn that? She'd never worked in a bakery as far as I knew, and I'd never shown her how. Then she started rolling out fondant as if

Sherri sculpting a gumpaste figure

on her. The next day Anna came to work and pulled out this awesome vintage board with a built-in lazy Susan. She set the game up and we drew for first word. I won, so I looked at my tiles and tried to come up with a really good opening word. I looked up and saw Anna just sitting there, staring at me with a poker face that would make Matt Damon nervous. She got me a little off balance, but whatever—she was just some punk-art school kid, right? So I laid down a really good word, and without missing a beat she laid down hers. Directly parallel to mine. She drew her new tiles and resumed the stare. So now I

she'd been doing it her whole life. She covered the pug; then she went to the airbrush area and started mixing colors to paint the dog. She got done in a few hours what would have taken me all night. It was perfect—better than anything I could have done. When she asked me if it was okay, I smiled to myself and said, "Not bad for your first time!"

customer service was better than mine. It's hard to be nice on the phone when you're covered in buttercream and trying to smooth out quickly drying fondant. One night as we were firing on all cylinders, I looked around at our little family and thought, "Wow, check us *out!*"

OUR GROWING FAMILY

Working with Sherri and Anna, not to mention Geof with his amazing architectural skills, made me realize that I didn't need cake decorators—I needed artists! I could show the artists how to work with my materials, but I couldn't make an artist out of a cake decorator. Where could I find some artists? Anna. So I asked her if she had friends who needed jobs. My hunch was a good one—eventually she led me to hire her college roommate, Katie Rose, who's one of the most deliberate, incredible brush painters I have ever seen. She also has an amazing sense of proportion and composition. I am constantly in awe of what she's able to pull off. She has the gift, and has created some of the most amazing hand-painted cakes Charm City Cakes has ever produced.

Now with all of us as decorators, we were rocking, so I started taking more orders and people slowly begin shifting around and doing what they're good at. Since we were so busy with decorating duties, I needed someone to help with all the administrative work, such as answering calls and emails. Chris's girlfriend, Beth, was looking for work, and she's very level-headed and organized. So she stepped in, and it was painfully obvious that her

Anna

Katie

IT ALL BEGAN WITH A
PHONE CALL . . .

Though I knew things were picking up, it wasn't until I received an unexpected phone call that I really started to believe we were onto something. My cell phone rang, and the caller ID displayed the name Colette Peters. I was a little nervous, not because Colette is probably the best cake decorator on the planet but because I'd copied every one of her published cakes and proudly displayed them on my website. I answered the phone and sure enough, there was Colette—asking if I'd like to compete in a cake competition in Beaver Creek, Colorado. I said, "Wow, I would love to! Thanks! And by the way, I'm a really big fan of yours!" With a laugh she said, "Yeah, I can tell from the pictures on your website! I'll email you the information." Click. Ouch, oh, the burn!

So off I went to Colorado. The theme of the competition was "nature." Now, if you ask a pastry chef to make something that represents nature, you'll no doubt get flowers or the seasons or something bland like that. So I took a chance and rolled a steel peach tree, complete with peaches hanging from the ends of the branches. It was then that I learned that I'm kind of a weirdo when it comes to cakes. I didn't really get that I was doing something different until I was onstage with some serious pastry chefs. They had sugar lamps and racks and molds and tools I'd never seen. All I had were some cakes, some metal, a *very* loud air compressor for my airbrush, an arc welder, a belt sander, a blowtorch, an electric Dremel tool, and some black gaff tape (just in case).

I made what I thought was the best piece by far and naturally came in dead last. I wasn't bothered by that, as I got a free trip back to the mountains to see my friends, and I also learned

a lot from Colette and two people who would go on to become my best cake buddies, Carol Murdock and her assistant, Cathy. The two of them were snickering with me as I broke pretty much every single rule in the competition. Don't get me wrong, I wasn't trying to be rebellious or anything—I've competed in ice carving, chocolate sculpture, sugar sculpture, and plated desserts and done quite well. It's just that the rules of this particular competition didn't really fit with what I wanted to make and how I wanted to make it. So after the competition, Colette, being the awesome sweetheart she is, pulled me aside and told me that I had taken a chance and made a nice cake, but I had broken *every* rule she herself had written. Seeing that I was less than half the age of any of the other competitors, we both just laughed about it. I was also the only one who hadn't brought an assistant, as Geof was back in Baltimore running the shop.

Little did I know that Colette had some friends back at Food Network and told them to keep an eye on me—not because I was the best decorator in the room but because I was an entertaining diversion. Right about then, my brother Willie's roommate, Dana Leiken Richards, was a producer for a talk show called *It's Christopher Lowell.* She somehow persuaded them to do a short segment about me, the "crazy cake guy from Baltimore," and put me on TV for the first time. I didn't realize how big a deal it was until some friends said that their moms had seen me on the show and gave me hell like all good friends should. Now, keep in mind that most of my friends consist of hockey players, lacrosse players, and metal musicians. So my appearance on the show was about as cool to them as, well, posh interior decorating. Hey, whatever, I thought it was cool, and if anything, the appearance would be good for all of us at the bakery.

BACK IN BALTIMORE . . .

Meanwhile, Charm City Cakes was growing. Mary Smith had just started working with us. I swear the girl must have been born with a piping bag in her hand, as she has a pretty firm grasp of the extrafine details that turn good cakes into amazing cakes. Her patience is astounding, and she's relentless in her pursuit of exactly what she wants out of her art. She was the one of the quickest hires I've made thus far—I think she was an intern for a week or so before I hired her. I made some smart-ass comment to her, and without missing a beat she turned and gave it right back. My kinda girl. I would have hired her on her talent alone, but her sassiness sealed the deal.

I'd known our baker, Adam Goldstein, from way back. When I was a personal chef, he used to sell me produce, and his dry wittiness and staggering intelligence used to crack me up when I was shopping for veggies. Well, one day, Adam came walking through the bakery door with his fiancée and ordered their wedding cake. I didn't know he was coming over, and he didn't know I was making wedding cakes, but fate brought him to Charm City Cakes at an opportune time for both of us. Chris needed help baking, and Adam needed a job. Kismet, I thought. So Chris started training Adam, and the two of them were great—both brilliant, and both men of few words. Adam caught on fast, and between the two of them, I had created an all-star cake-baking team.

As we were still using my crappy old website, I figured by this point I should hire a new design firm to build me one. There's a place here in Baltimore called Mission Media that has a full-on recording studio and gallery space for art shows, and they promote some of the best music venues in Baltimore, *and* they make websites—so I figured it was a perfect match. I

Mary Smith

Duff and Adam Goldstein

traded my website for a wedding cake for one of the co-owners. It's amazing what deals you can make when you throw in a cake.

> *They may say, "Wow! That sucks!!" But at least they'll say "Wow!"*
>
> —DUFF

THE GATEKEEPER

Enter Mary Alice. No, she didn't work at Mission Media, but she did work across the street from their offices. One day I was going to Mission to approve some new design, and afterward I went over to visit Mary Alice, whom I didn't see very often at that point. I walked into her office building and asked the receptionist if she was in. She came downstairs and said hello and asked if I wanted to go up to her office. I was perplexed, but I went. When we got into her office, she shut the door and proceeded to burst into tears. She was miserable—she hated her job and didn't know what to do. Well, I already knew Mary Alice was a whiz at organization, so I asked her if she wanted a job that paid about half what she was making and had no benefits and much longer hours. She gasped and asked, "You mean, work at Charm City Cakes? For you?" I said yes, and

she immediately put in her two weeks' notice and came to work with Beth on trying to get my place to run smoothly.

It seems that my inspired plot to turn all my friends into pastry chefs was working out.

FOOD NETWORK CALLING

Soon after, the phone rang and Beth handed it to me and said, "It's someone from Food Network." Uh oh! What had I done now? So I picked up the phone, and they asked if I'd like to compete in a Food Network Cake Challenge. I asked Geof, and typical of him, he said, "Sure, why not?"

Soon enough, Geof, Anna, and I were driving the van to Georgia to make a haunted house cake on TV! We came in third, which was actually pretty good considering that there were some incredibly talented decorators in that room. But it wasn't the placing that got people's attention—it was our method. We showed up with my array of power tools and crazy stuff, and that made people take notice. What really got the producers fired up was that before the com-

petition, instead of practicing our drill, Geof, Anna, Carol, and I went skeet shooting. During the competition, I was messing with the audience, goofing with cameras, goading my fellow competitors, and basically just having a good time and laughing. A lot.

They kept having Geof and me on, and we'd never win, but we always had fun. Soon we were doing other specials for shows like *Roker on the Road* and *Sugar Rush*, with my very good friend Warren Brown, who I simply cannot say enough complimentary things about—he is absolutely the real deal. We always had fun with Warren, especially when I made a cake for him in the shape of a cannon and blew off hundreds of rounds of mortar fireworks out of the cake in my dad's backyard. We had a huge party and got all our friends on TV drinking keg beer and blowing stuff up. It was all caught on camera. We freaked out Warren's producers a little bit with how illegal the whole thing was, but everyone had a good time. I was Warren's first guest on his premiere episode of *Sugar Rush*, and it was a rush, all right—yeah, I'll give you a "Bam!"

Soon after that Geof and I were invited to do another Food Network Challenge, held in Scottsdale, Arizona. This time the theme was a secret until we got to the event. It turned out to be sports, so we chose sport fishing and got to work in our hotel room making a fishing boat cake. I guess when you're pushing the limits of a given medium, you'll find out what those limits really are. It just stings a little when you find out on national television. Our boat completely fell apart with about thirty seconds left on the eight-hour clock.

But when it fell apart, you know what I did? I laughed and laughed and laughed. Who cares? Then I had to go out into the audience and console my mom, because she was crying that her son had just crashed and burned on national television. As a joke I said to her, "Don't worry, they'll give me my own show after this, watch!"

Careful what you wish for. The producers of the show had another reaction: they loved my appearance and said it brought a certain "something" they'd never quite seen before on their Challenge series. What that "something" was, they didn't say, but they invited me to do another.

And another, the Spooky Cake & Candy Cook-Off. Working my way up in the rankings, after doing pretty well in the Elvis Birthday Cakes competition, I finally won my last Food Network Challenge, the Cereal Skyline Crispy Treat Challenge. I created the skyline of my beloved Baltimore. Here I am a cake decorator, and I finally get a win—with no cake in sight.

In the spring of 2005, NBC got wind that our bakery was doing some pretty dramatic wedding cakes and invited me to be one of the bakers for the "*Today* Throws a Hometown Wedding" segment airing that September. I made a four-tiered pumpkin and chocolate chip cake that used Swarovski crystals on several layers of the cake in a nod to the bride's gown, as well as black magic roses to work in the bridesmaids' gowns. Our cake came in second, but the exposure really boosted sales, and it was a lot of fun to compete in something where an audience voted instead of the judges.

When I was competing on the Food Network Challenge, my reputation as an unpredictable cutup (and dare I say "klutz") was becoming a part of the Network's newest campaign to draw younger and "hipper" audiences to its new nighttime show lineup. It signed me up to do one of the biggest ad campaigns it has ever launched. TV, billboard, and print ads in the top magazines appeared in what seemed like overnight, and my bakery was enjoying the biggest jump in orders since it opened.

Excitement served nightly

Food Network Challenge & Iron Chef America
Sundays & Thursdays

food network

nighttime
WAY MORE THAN COOKING

51

GROWING PAINS

Cake orders were coming in faster than we could fill them, and that's when we made the decision to move yet again. It had become clear that we needed some serious kitchen and decorating areas. So in August 2005 I started looking around, and just around the corner I found an old church for sale. The now recognizable Charm City Cakes building was the perfect space, allowing for steady expansion for what was now fifteen people. The tall ceilings and gorgeous wooden flooring made a perfect start for the complete renovation. I suppose it was a gutsy move, but something told me to just believe in the vision. It was about five times the size of our current location, it had a lot of nice large windows, and the mortgage was less than our rent. It had two basements and a small apartment upstairs. To afford the place, I rented out my house to some college kids and moved upstairs over the bakery. I made one of the basements into a recording studio for my band, . . . *soihadto* . . . , and converted the other basement into a gym. I had all my groceries delivered; I rarely left the place! But I now had this awesome bakery just

Geof, Elena, Sofia, Katie, and I in Los Angeles at the Kung Fu Panda premiere

behind the Johns Hopkins campus in the Remington section of Baltimore.

Word was out by now that some pretty serious cakes were being crafted at the Charm City Cakes bakery, and without even one dime of money spent on advertising, we were getting orders that were taking us fifteen-hour days to fill. Things got so crazy that soon I was no longer working on my own specific cakes. Just like a pinball, I was bouncing from artist to artist, cake to cake. I was training my rather unconventional group of artists and musicians the arts of piping and rolling fondant, and even how to use the complicated machinery, from the airbrush to the power tools I kept over in the shop area of the bakery. Sometimes I wonder whether the bakery was leading me or I was leading it. But I do know that I trusted my instincts—something Mom has always lectured my brother and me to do. Sometimes it's not that easy, and there can be a lot of second-guessing, but as time goes by I'm still finding she's right about that, and it does get easier.

Chris had a really good job offer as a project manager at an architecture firm, so, a true stand-up guy, he found his own replacement, Elena Fox. Elena was hired to ice cakes with buttercream to go under the fondant, but it quickly became apparent that Elena wanted to decorate cakes. So she iced her cakes as fast as she could just to get a chance to show me what she do on the outside of cake—and wow, she got really good, pretty much immediately.

Shortly after Elena came, I hired Sofia, a born-and-bred French girl who comes from a family of fantastic cooks; her brother is a pastry chef back in France, her dad used to make huge paellas for parties, and her mom, who cooks traditional French cuisine every day, makes the best escargot ever. Sofia has a passion for good food that rivals mine, but even as we speak, she has been getting out from behind the cake icing wheel and is rapidly becoming one of my most

stalwart decorators. Sofia's unique sense of style is so freakin' cute. She'd been delivering cakes for a while before she came to work full-time at the bakery, but she'd always had regular jobs working at Johns Hopkins and selling apples at the farmer's market. So I stole her away, and she's become a rock in this place. On the rare occasions when we don't *always* get along as a group, Sofia has been our commonsense diplomat and can usually keep us from beating the crap out of each other.

As time went on, I found that in some areas my new decorators were even surpassing me in their skills and abilities. I decided to cross-train everyone, but it turned out that each of us has skills we excel at more than others, so we are truly a team in every sense of the word.

THE BEGINNINGS OF
ACE OF CAKES

All this time, with the sale of several screenplays, book adaptations, and TV series pilots, Willie was beginning to carve out a career as not just a writer but a producer as well. Along with his friends—mostly all in "the business"— he always had his eyes and ears open for ideas and opportunities wherever he could find them. In 2005 I went on vacation to L.A. to visit him, my mom, and my stepdad. I was staying with Willie

in the Valley, and on the way to visit Mom and Ronnie, we stopped at a production company in Silver Lake called Authentic Entertainment. Evidently, Willie and Dana had shown them some videos of me that featured me throwing food around and being loud and obnoxious. After Willie and Dana introduced me, we sat down in Authentic's conference room, and I met Lauren Lexton and Tom Rogan, Authentic's owners and founders. Scary, right? They started asking about me and what I do, so I told them funny kitchen stories and some of the high jinks we were all up to now that I had my own place.

It was cool; I had those guys laughing, which I guess was a good thing to do, in retrospect. Willie and I have always had this weird ESP thing that siblings have where we can talk without talking, and he was telling me to keep going and have fun with these guys. So I started getting a little more raunchy and telling the stories that shouldn't be told outside a kitchen, and we were all laughing really hard. We were in there for about an hour and half, and then all of a

Mary Alice, Dana Leiken Richards, and cameraman James Mann taking a break after filming.

Josh Spector

about the whole thing. But they kept saying to just go with it, be ourselves and do our thing. I was thinking about how all the work we do is very tedious and slow, and we're usually very silent when we work. So these two guys, Jeff Daniels and Josh Spector, went back to Hollywood to edit together what is called a "sizzle reel," which is a short proof-of-concept pilot to present to potential networks to gauge their interest in possibly picking up the show. Well, before Authentic sent out the sizzle reel, they sent it to us, and through the magic of editing, they'd somehow made it as hilarious as it was interesting. All of us were simply floored. They'd really *gotten* us. So they started doing their Hollywood thing, trying to sell the show, while we got back to business moving into our new space.

Soon enough we got the call, and after some interest from a couple of networks, Food Network wanted to place an order for a six-episode first season. Authentic Entertainment would become the production company, with Tom and Lauren as executive producers and Willie and Dana as co–executive producers along with a fantastic reality producer named Kelly McPherson. Although we'd just started filming our first season of what at the time was called *Bake It to the Limit*, and not a single episode had aired, in May 2006 my agent, Lisa Shotland, got a call from *The Tonight Show with Jay Leno* to make an appearance. The people there asked me to create a cake for Jay and present it to him on the show. It was pretty amazing, to say the least, but we flew to Los Angeles, and I built a car engine cake that could shoot real fireworks in my very-inadequate-for-cake-decorating hotel room. Authentic filmed the entire behind-the-scenes action for our show, so there were about twenty of us in a hotel room built for one—talk about stressful.

On *The Tonight Show*, Jay and I talked about my upcoming new show on Food Network, and

sudden they stood up and said, "Okay, we'll call you tomorrow." Strange.

So after the meeting, outside in Authentic's parking lot, Willie and Dana gave me this huge hug and said, "That was best pitch meeting I've ever seen!" I asked them, "What's a pitch meeting?" and they told me I had just sold a TV show! I asked, "About what?" and they said "About *you*, dumb ass!" Here I'd thought the whole time we were there for some business Willie and Dana had to take care of on the way to Long Beach. I don't remember ever being more stunned. Willie knew me well enough to know that if he had told me he was taking me to a pitch meeting, I probably would have run for the hills. Certainly he never would have gotten me to go to an actual audition, so he did what he had to to get the job done. That's Willie. Whatever it takes . . .

I was thinking that a reality show about my cake shop wouldn't be very entertaining, and after I got back to Baltimore and Authentic sent out a two-man film crew to follow us around to make a small demo reel, I was really pessimistic

I had to tell a joke. We had rehearsed earlier in the day, but it's all a big blur now. After the show, while everyone went out to celebrate, I found a stairwell in my hotel and fell asleep. Thankfully no one found me for hours.

Back in Baltimore we had a lot of space to fill and room to grow, so we did. Katherine Hill was a full-time dog walker who was interning with us a few days a week until one day she fell down and shattered her kneecap. Well, she couldn't walk dogs for a while, and she was getting *unbelievably amazing* at decorating cakes, so I quickly put her on the payroll before she had time to think about it. We had a handicap ramp and a nice, big, wide-open space so she could roll around in her wheelchair and decorate cakes. And man, did she take to the craft. She starting ruling the place from that chair, and then when she got done with her physical therapy and started walking around, she really started coming into her own.

Now Katherine, or "K-Money," as I like to call her, is my go-to for any project. She can pipe like Mary Smith, she can sculpt, she makes both crazy out-there stuff and realistic stuff, and she creates some of the most stunningly beautiful wedding cakes this place kicks out. However, beyond her mad skills as a cake decorator, it's her ridiculous sense of humor that has made her such an integral part of team at Charm City Cakes. She has a great work ethic and does what she needs to do, but the whole time she is a complete goof who loves playing practical jokes on all of us. Which in turn makes all of us play jokes on her and one another, and now, if you watch the show very, very, *very* closely, you'll see some of our little jokes. Most of them the editors don't catch, but every now and then, one slips through . . .

Things started really getting away from us, and Mary Alice was getting swamped, especially since we had started selling T-shirts and hats and all things Charm City Cakes on our website

With Anna, Katherine, and the crew

Jessica Curry

(to quote Mel Brooks from *Spaceballs*, "Merchandising! Merchandising! Merchandising!"). She needed help. So we hired Jess Curry, and at first I thought she was very shy and quiet. Well, I was half right, she is pretty quiet, but she is anything but shy. Recently Jess started answering all our emails, keeping the books, and tracking receipts, and generally became the gyroscope keeping us all steady as we go . . .

55

On August 17, 2006, *Ace of Cakes* made its Food Network debut. The name was changed shortly after the Leno appearance and the network began advertising it by showing me blowing up a cake and getting covered with frosting, an idea that originated from the cake I'd made for *Sugar Rush*. That must be when they gave me the "Bad Boy of Baking" moniker, which honestly I'm doing my best to shed. Well, maybe not that hard; I'm always up for some good hard rock.

BEHIND THE CAKE

See their story in
ACE OF CAKES episode 403,
"Mascots and Mice"

ROMMEL AND JESSICA LORIA

I first met Rommel in the autumn of 2006 during his design appointment, when he explained that he wanted a cake to propose to his girlfriend, Jessica. Wedding cakes: we do plenty of those. But a proposal cake? That was a new one. But I liked the idea—and besides, who am I to stand in the way of true love? Rommel described how he wanted the cake to be a "happily ever after" scene: a cute little house with a picket fence, the two of them sitting out front, all smiles, with their dog. He wanted to incorporate the engagement ring into the cake, so we came up with the idea for him to hang it from a lamppost on the sidewalk outside the house.

As this was Charm City Cakes' first proposal cake (since then a few more have followed), naturally the entire staff was very excited about the prospect of being a part of Rommel's proposal. To make it even more interesting, I decided to surprise Rommel and wire the lamppost so it would actually light up.

The day Rommel came to the bakery to pick up the cake, he was visibly nervous but was definitely pretty stoked that we had illuminated the light. After he took the cake home, we all waited anxiously to hear word of how the night went. The next morning, Mary Alice received an email from Rommel with the subject line "SHE SAID YES!" He included a great photo of a very teary-eyed Jessica holding up her ringed hand in front of the cake.

When time came for the couple to design their wedding cake, of course the bakery was thrilled to have them back (I had promised Rommel a discount if she accepted). As the couple wanted to include their alma mater, Georgetown University, in their cake design, they chose a four-tier asymmetrical cake with a second cake that looked like the Bulldog mascot biting into the first cake. Both cakes came out fantastically, and everyone was thrilled to see pictures from the wedding afterward. Now we're anxiously awaiting a call to help out with a baby shower . . .

CLUTCH

Chief Martin Brody Bird

I MADE THIS CAKE • Right!

OMG~ MARY'S RULE

daddy's little girl 1979

Message:
I just wanted to say that your show is awesome and it gave me a great tips on how to make my cakes. Also I believe that Alice really deserves a raise after everything that she goes through. Oh and Mary Alice, don't worry we will still love you, you kill your flowers in the front of the store.

The infamous BIKE CAM!

Malice's Morning Mix
1> Here Comes the Sun / Nina Simone : 3:49
2> Story of My Life / Social Distortion : 5:48
3> The Sick Bed of Cuchulainn / The Pogues : 2:59
4> Take It On The Chin / William Elliott Whitmore : 2:27
5> The Gambler / Kenny Rogers : 3:35
6> Put it Down : Mike Doughty : 3:54
7> Flathead / The Fratellis : 3:17
8> Generic in Love / J Roddy Walston and the Business :
9> Revolutionary Kind / Gomez : 4:33
10> Tusk / Fleetwood Mac : 3:30
11> Starfish and Coffee / Prince : 2:49
12> Hell Yes / Beck : 3:17
13> Party at Ground Zero / Fishbone : 6:29
14> Jerusalem / Dan Bern : 3:44
15> Lucretia MacEvil / Blood, Sweat, & Tears : 5:30
16> Carry On / Bran Van 3000 : 4:50
17> Immigrant Punk / Gogol Bordello : 3:45
18> Cypress Grove / Clutch : 2:45
19> Up / Palomar : 3:27
20> My United States of Whatever / Liam Lynch : 2:06

Duffs First Wedding Cake!
(for my brother Neil & his wife Angela)

Always, I hope to grow brighter, funnier. I hope to learn to be even more well-rounded. But right now, I cannot be any better than I am.
— maya angelou

TEAM YESKEY (my sweetheart)

SMILE! You're in Baltimore!

me & my bro

UMBC
UNIVERSITY OF MARYLAND
BALTIMORE COUNTY
SP95
MARY ALICE FALLON

CHARM CITY ROLLER GIRLS

Best presents from FANS: Alice in Wonderland Coffee Cup & Mousepad

MAKE·A·WISH

Happy Birthday, You Old Bird!
Love, The Bakery

i heart my coworkers

my wedding cake! (By Duff)

CHARM CITY CAKES

CHARM CITY CAKES

(this is what I do)

my view of the bakery

Old friends (circa 1998)

MARY ALICE FALLON YESKEY Manager

Hometown: Gaithersburg, Maryland

Favorite movies: *Bugsy Malone, Jaws, Amélie, Office Space*

Favorite hobbies: Cooking, the *New York Times* Sunday crossword, singing show tunes while cleaning, hanging with DY, Dexter, and Brody

Favorite music: William Elliott Whitmore, J. Roddy Walston and the Business, Clutch, Bruce Springsteen, Rilo Kiley

Favorite books: *The Little Prince* by Antoine de Saint-Exupéry, *The Princess Bride* by William Goldman, *Skinny Legs and All* by Tom Robbins, *Mary Alice, Operator Number 9* by Jeffrey Allen.

Favorite nondessert dish to create or eat: I am known for my deviled eggs. They are redick. I also make a mean roast chicken. My favorite thing to eat is extremely fresh sushi with a big glass of pinot grigio.

Fun fact: As a child, I wrote a series of stories about a character I created named Mimi Kinderlan: The Girl with the Steel Hand. She was awesome and could punch the living daylights out of anyone with her steel fist. Seriously.

In her own words . . .

Duff and I met while we were both attending the University of Maryland, Baltimore County, in 1994. I was a freshman and Duff was a sophomore and we lived in the same dorm (shout out to Chesapeake Third North!). He had taken a job as the dorm's maintenance assistant through the Resident Life office.

One morning when I was getting ready for class, I was leaning over the sink and putting on my pearl necklace. Well, not my pearl necklace. It was actually my mother's, and I had taken it to college without telling her. As I leaned over the sink, craning to reach the clasp behind my neck, the necklace slipped and fell into the sink, right down the drain. I stood there, dumbfounded, not really sure what to do. Panic struck. I bolted downstairs to the front desk and asked the guy on duty for a maintenance request form. I filled it out frantically, using phrases such as "extreme tragedy" and "urgent family emergency" and "save me!" I think I may have even drawn a small portrait of my anxiety-ridden face. I submitted the form, went back up to my room, and waited.

With my mom on Cape Cod, 1986

With my mom on Cape Cod, 1986

With Duff at UMBC

Not fifteen minutes later, there was a knock on the door. I opened it and was face-to-face with Duff for the first time. He was beyond scruffy, sporting ripped-up jeans, an absolutely threadbare tie-dyed T-shirt, and a tool belt. "I hear you need some help with your sink," he said.

"That was quick," I responded.

In walked Duff, and he took out a huge wrench and proceeded to pull out the U-pipe beneath my sink. He stood up, turned the pipe upside down, and out dropped my wet but otherwise unscathed pearls. I think I may actually have applauded, I can't remember. But I do know that I thanked him profusely and declared him my hero.

As freshman year went on, every time I saw Duff I addressed him as "my hero" or "my knight in shining tie-dye" or some other grateful moniker. We got to be pretty good friends as we lived in the same dorm, but it wasn't until the next school year that our friendship was really forged in blood. We have Kiefer Sutherland to thank for that.

My sophomore year, I also took a job with Resident Life, as front desk staff for our dorm—the easiest job on the planet. For a few shifts a week, I had to sit at the front desk and check people's student IDs as they passed by. I logged in visitors, answered the phone, and pretty much watched the front lounge TV and twiddled my thumbs. It was easy money. Duff was still the maintenance assistant, so we got to spend a lot more time together as we were both on Res Life staff. But the night that Duff and I truly bonded for life came when I was working the graveyard shift at the desk, I think it was 2 to 5 a.m. The TV in the lounge was airing (much to my joy) the 1987 classic vampire flick *The Lost Boys*. The movie had just started when Duff wandered in. We discovered a mutual adoration for the movie, and he sat down to watch it with me.

"You ever notice how many times they say the name 'Michael' in this movie?" he asked me.

"A lot," I responded. I suggested we keep a tally. So I started keeping count. There's this one scene when Kiefer Sutherland and his gang of vampire cronies are mocking Jason Patric's character, Michael, teasing him and egging him on to join them. They say "Michael" about ninety-seven times within ten minutes. It's hilarious. We were screaming with laughter as I ticked off every time they said it.

> **TIP** *Never get involved in a land war in Asia.*

Duff's impression of Kiefer's character, David, is spot on. "Maggots, Michael. You're eating maggots. How do they taste?" To this day Duff says that line whenever I'm eating Chinese food, and it absolutely kills me.

Despite our differences (Duff was a lacrosse jock and I was an English major do-gooder), we got along famously. Duff and I had many a ridiculous night behind that desk—one night before Thanksgiving break he convinced me to give him dreadlocks. He had maybe ear-length hair at the time, and I knew dreadlocks weren't really the most, um, fetching way for him to style his hair, but I did it anyway. I spent several hours teasing and spraying and waxing and gluing his hair to itself until he had about eight cute little white boy dreads. Apparently when he went home for break his mother was so disgusted that she made him shave his head. After that, he just kept shaving it. So I guess in a way, he has me to thank for his baldy style.

I ended up transferring to University of Maryland, College Park, halfway through sophomore year, but Duff and I stayed in touch through

email, sometimes several dozen times a day. He's an incredibly talented writer, and we both have a passion for taking the English language to its poetic extremes. We took great joy in penning ludicrously verbose and tangential emails to one another. We fit really well together—he was a tortured artist and I was an overly theatrical romantic. We still sort of are.

After college, both Duff and I ended up in Baltimore. We ran with the same friends (still do), and while I took an administrative job at a nonprofit, Duff was busting his ass as a personal chef to a family up county that could afford such a thing. We saw each other when we could, eating inordinate amounts of sushi and going to our friends' bands' shows at local clubs.

Fast-forward to 2004. I was working for another nonprofit in Baltimore and was pretty miserable at my job. I was overworked and stressed and at the end of my rope—ready to quit but terrified to do so. One morning in May, Duff unexpectedly stopped by my office. I had spent the better part of that particular morning crying

At my brother's wedding, 1999

61

Top: *With my brother, circa 1985.*

Middle: *circa 2002.*

Bottom: *With my brother, 1976.*

in the bathroom and trying not to throw up. I met Duff in the lobby, and he asked, "Are you okay?" I think the look I gave him said it all. I explained to him (in whispered tones) that I needed a new job but didn't have the courage to quit the one I was in. "That's weird," Duff said. "I was actually going to ask if there was any way you could come work for me, but I figured you wouldn't have time with your job here and all."

I know this may sound ridiculous, but there are moments in your life when everything lines up just right, you know you are exactly where you are supposed to be, and what is happening is absolute providence. This was one of those moments. I remember telling my mother later that at that moment, the skies parted, angels sang, and God came to me in the form of a big hairy baker to save me from my misery.

In July 2004 I went to work for Charm City Cakes. I inherited my job from Beth, who had been keeping Duff's books up until then. The day I came in for Beth to train me was actually the last day that the Authentic TV crew was at the bakery to shoot the "sizzle reel" to sell the then-nonexistent television show. The director interviewed me about who I was and why I was there. I remember being very uncomfortable and nervous. I didn't expect to be included in the finished pilot, and I certainly didn't expect the show to go anywhere.

Back then, our bakery was in a very small

space around the corner from where we are now. We were a staff of six, putting out about ten to fifteen cakes a week. My job consisted of setting up tasting appointments, making sure contracts were in order, and answering emails and the phone. It's a ginormous understatement to say my workload wasn't what it is today. To put it into perspective, back then, on Thursdays and Fridays I would typically finish my work at around two o'clock and then help the decorators with their cakes. It seems unreal to me now that there was a point when I could be "finished" with my job—all emails answered, all phone calls returned, and everything in order. These days I'm thrilled if my inbox contains less than one hundred emails.

Though the administrative part of my job came easily, I had no experience whatsoever with cake decorating. Duff taught me how to dragée, make piping bags, color fondant, and do lots of other cool stuff. Back then, Friday evenings were always the most fun. Those late nights I would hang out and help Sherri, Mary, Geof, and Anna and we would listen to music and drink beer, and the whole time it just blew my mind that this was my *job*.

I came to the bakery with seven years of nonprofit job experience. I was pretty regimented to nine-to-five office life. It was hard for me to lighten up and adjust to the anticorporate culture of Charm City Cakes. Case in point: my first week of work Duff hadn't had a key to the bakery made for me just yet. One morning I showed up so early that no one was there to let me in. I sat on the stoop for over an hour in the July heat until finally Duff showed up. "You don't have to get here so early," he told me. "This isn't like your other jobs." How right he was.

I was born in Boston, twelve days too late to be a proper bicentennial baby. My family moved to Washington State in the early eighties (one of my first clear memories is the aftermath of the Mount St. Helens eruption) and then to Mary-

land in 1982. We've been here ever since. I had a normal, if not idyllic, childhood. My brilliant and wonderful parents are still happily married, I have an older brother whom I idolize, and despite our general Irish kookiness and predilection for bad puns, we've always been incredibly happy and blessed. Growing up in suburban Maryland, I excelled in language arts and had an extraordinarily active imagination. As a young girl, my career goals were, at any given point, to be a truck driver, a ballerina, a Broadway star, an author, a stand-up comedian, a butcher, a professional roller skater, a singer, a veterinarian, a teacher, an Irish step dancer, or a comic strip writer.

The night *Ace of Cakes* premiered, the whole staff and a great number of our friends gathered at the bakery to watch. To be honest, I was terrified. I had no idea how the show was going to depict us, if it would be funny and favorable, filled with conflict and nonsense, or totally horrible and unflattering. Though we'd been given every assurance by Food Network and Authentic that they had our best interests in mind, having not seen a moment of the show before it aired, we were all really nervous. I can still remember the absolutely electrifying feeling when the opening credits started. We were all gathered around a TV, drinking beer and laughing, and then there was a huge round of *shhhhh*ing, and when we heard Duff's voice say, "After pastry school . . ." we all just erupted in clapping and screaming. It was truly unreal. As we sat and watched that first episode, surrounded by friends and giddy at our fifteen minutes of fame, I happened to notice something in the background: the phone was ringing.

Since *Ace of Cakes* began airing, everyone who works at the bakery has seen changes in their lives and their jobs. But I daresay that no one's job has changed more than mine. Since the night the show premiered, the number of people contacting us via email and phone has increased exponentially. I also end up doing quite a bit of administrative work for the show itself—helping the production company communicate with the clients they want to film and assisting with the scheduling for the shooting.

Jess Curry came to work full-time at the

My husband, David, and I on our wedding day

bakery in February 2007. I truly have no idea how I ever survived without her. She helps wade through the piles of email, voice mail, contracts, bills, payroll, scheduling, and merchandise sales. She's also completely in charge of the accounting and bookkeeping, which is a good thing, as math is not my forte. The merchandise for sale on our website used to be somewhat manageable, but as the show continued to air, the orders continued to pile in. Last Christmas season was pretty hellish. Jess and I spent hours every night processing, packing, and shipping out hundreds of T-shirts, hoodies, and aprons, and merchandise had pretty much become a full-time job. For that reason, Jess's friend Adrienne Ruhf came to work for us in March 2008. Adrienne is in charge of all the merch sales and helps answer emails and schedule appointments. The three of us form what I like to call the Administrative Triumvirate, and we sit behind the Fortress of Administration (a huge, U-shaped black desk from Ikea).

Of course, other things have changed since the show started airing. Our formerly quiet block in Remington has now become something of a tourist attraction. At least a few times a day and practically all weekend there are people milling about, usually in out-of-state cars, taking pictures of the building and the street corner. This never ceases to befuddle me. Even after nearly three years, it still sort of blows my mind that there are people who think enough of *Ace of Cakes* to travel out of their way to see the building. I certainly don't mind people taking photos, but it can get a little irritating when people feel the need to beg to get into the building. Jess and I have made every effort to make it very clear that we do not have a visitor policy, we do not offer tours, and we can't let anyone into the bakery just because you drove all the way from [insert faraway state here]. I've actually had people berate me over the phone because I wouldn't let them come inside. As if it's my fault that they were so impetuous with their reality show road trip that they failed to go to our website and read the paragraph that says in no uncertain terms that we do now allow visitors, for insurance reasons among others. Sorry, but after the millionth time explaining this, I can get a little curt and impatient.

Of course, most of the attention is flattering and sweet. I've tried to get accustomed to being recognized and even occasionally asked for an autograph, but in truth it's not something I've ever gotten completely used to. Because my hair has changed a lot over the last three years, I get a lot of "the look"—people see me and do a double take, and I can tell they have no idea why they think they know me. I get asked a lot what college I went to. Being stopped in the street or airport or grocery store is really totally flattering. And though there have been a few occasions when I was out with friends and I've been a little embarrassed when some stranger came up and asked to take a photo with me, it's nearly always great to hear from fans who like the show.

The opportunities the show has given

that when I actually met Steve Carell I wouldn't say anything stupid. I failed.

For some reason, one of the things a lot of fans do when they meet us is repeat things from the show. Like "Remember that time when you couldn't fit the flamingos in the van?" "Remember that one where you went to Asbury Park?" "Remember the episode when you said that funny thing?" I don't mean to sound like a jerk here, but there really isn't a good answer to these comments. It's, like, "Um, yes, I remember that, as I was there. Thanks for recalling that thing that happened two years ago. That was awesome." Those comments are always just sort of awkward and weird.

So, anyway, flash forward to the *Get Smart* premiere, and we're being introduced to the Carells. I'm totally freaking out on the inside, trying to play it cool and not say anything annoying or asinine. So I get introduced to Steve, I shake his hand, and then suddenly, I say, "I saw you on *The Daily Show* last night! It was hilarious!" To which he nods and smiles and says, "Yes, that was fun." And I immediately want to crawl into a hole and die. I'd just done to Steve Carell exactly what I told myself I wouldn't. I'd done that repeating-what-they-clearly-already-know thing that I know firsthand is totally annoying. Ugh!

Hands down, the best part of being a part of *Ace of Cakes* is being able to use our fame, however small it is, for the power of good, such as granting wishes for three Make-A-Wish kids (so far). Laura, Marianne, and Kelsey are pretty much the toughest, most amazing girls I've ever met, and it's an absolute honor to have been a part of their wishes. We've been able to donate gift certificates and merchandise to hundreds of local charities to raise money for everything from animal shelters to pediatric cancer research. We've provided t-shirts to soldiers stationed in the Middle East, toys for kids at the Ronald McDonald House, and cake for our

---

TIP *If you'd like to order a cake from us and decide to send us an email, don't regale us with your entire medical history, the details of your recent divorce, your child's struggles with algebra and fitting in, and your dog's last trip to the vet. This will not increase the likelihood that you'll get a cake from us. We fill orders on a first-come, first-serve basis, regardless of who you are or the circumstances of your life. The number of emails we receive with way, way too much personal information is kind of horrifying. My tip? Keep it short, sweet, and to the freakin' point.*

me to travel and meet people have been really quite thrilling. Meeting famous folks like John Waters, Jeremy Piven, and Steve Carell have been some of the most surreal moments of my life. Meeting Steve Carell was particularly amazing because I'm such a huge fan of his work. We met at a special fund-raiser screening of *Get Smart*, and he and his wife told Geof, Duff, and me that *they* were huge fans of *us* and of *Ace of Cakes*. What? Excuse me? Steve Carell watches *our* show? You just blew my mind, dude. Seriously. The worst part was that before it happened I had promised myself

neighborhood block party. I'm not listing these to be self-congratulatory. It's simply that being able to assist people and organizations in need has been such a blessing—truly the highlight of my job for me. On my worst days (and believe me, I have them) I look at the picture next to my desk of Laura on her visit here, and her smile makes me put everything into perspective. All my jobs before I came to work for Duff were for nonprofit organizations, so to be able to have a little bit of that giving-back-warm-fuzzy that I got from my other jobs here is really important to me.

The last three years have been a wild time. If you had told me ten years ago that I would be working for Duff, at a wildly successful cake shop, and that we were all going to be featured on a reality show on Food Network, I would have laughed really hard. Or punched you in the face. No one saw any of this coming. Despite the surreal nature of our situation, it's true that every day we simply try to do what we do best: make exceptional cakes and relish our friendships and creative workspace. And I think that's why *Ace of Cakes* is so popular. We're not contestants or models or jerks. We're just a bunch of weirdo kids from Baltimore with a passion for what we do. That speaks to people, and though sometimes I don't understand why, I'm glad it does.

TIP *Showing up to your wedding cake consultation driving a Hummer, wearing a fur coat, and sporting a golf ball–size diamond is not going to make your cake any cheaper. We notice these things. I'm just sayin'.*

WHY BALTIMORE?

So why Charm City Cakes? Why not in New York or Chicago or Philly or D.C.? Because Baltimore rules. Our slogan is "The Greatest City in America," and we're not kidding. Our town is the best. You know it, I know it, and the American people know it.

The thing about Baltimore is that it is unpretentious. It's not all frilly and supercool and subject to the whims of what is "in." Baltimore likes what it likes and really doesn't care what other people think. It's a little rough around the edges, sure, but the heart of Baltimore is strong, alive, and very unique. I like to think of Baltimore as the SoHo of the beats, not the new, superhip SoHo, but the SoHo where anything goes and everything is judged on merit, not by what everyone else thinks. This is a city of individuals, and you can see it in Baltimore's artists, actors, musicians, local heroes, and, yes, bakeries.

I didn't grow up here, but I did go to college here and made some really good friends in that four years. Well, I left, and then I came back. Some of my friends were still here, some had moved away, and some I had yet to meet. But slowly I built my home and my bakery in Baltimore. I think the reason we've done so well here is that Baltimore loves different stuff. Baltimoreans love variety, and we can certainly provide that. From really pretty, elegant wedding cakes to crazy cakes that defy gravity, insurance regulations, and sometimes the law. Baltimore is not xenophobic. A bakery like mine wouldn't last in Washington, D.C., where most people have a very clear idea of what a cake should look like. One trip to Baltimore neighborhoods such as Hamden, Mount Vernon, Waverly, the Harbor, Federal Hill, Canton, Charles Village, Remington, Roland Park, Guilford, and/or Govanstown, and you'll see that Baltimore loves the wacky and Baltimore loves its art.

✦ In one Saturday afternoon in Baltimore, you can . . .

✦ See the USS *Constellation* and the place where "The Star-Spangled Banner" was penned

✦ See sharks and the rain forest at the Baltimore Aquarium

✦ Buy some awesome indie rock at Sound Garden in Fells Point

- Visit Lexington Market for some of Faidley's world-famous crab cakes

- See art from all over the world and from many different eras at the Walters Art Museum

- Hear the amazing classical music students practicing at the Peabody Institute

- Have drinks at Club Charles, where both Lenny Bruce and Mary Alice met their spouses

- See the beautiful brownstones of Charles Village

- Stroll through the Johns Hopkins campus

- Pick up a DVD categorized by director at Video Americain

- Stop by the Baltimore Museum of Art and see one of the finest collections on the East Coast

- Head over to the wonderfully retro Baltimore Zoo and see baby elephants, pink flamingoes, and our thriving community of Panamanian golden frogs

- Hit up the Frisbee golf course in Druid Hill Park

- Pay my respects to Edgar Allen Poe at Westminster Hall

- See a game at the most beautiful stadium in the world, Camden Yards

- Check out the fierce derby ladies of the Charm City Roller Girls

- See where we kicked some British ass, again, at Fort McHenry

- Chow down on some incredible BBQ at Chaps, Big Bad Wolf, and Andy Nelson's

- See the Patterson Park Pagoda, designed by Charles Latrobe

- Buy some top-quality produce, seafood, and cheese and say hi to friends at one of Baltimore's outdoor farmer's markets.

- Catch a Broadway show at the beautifully restored Hippodrome theater

- See the latest offering out of Cannes at the Charles Theatre—and have tapas right next door

- Catch my band and many other awesome indie acts at the Ottobar, our rock-and-roll haven

- See the world's largest trash can on Russell Street

- Lose count of Michaels Phelps's gold medals

- Head up to Hamden and get some awesome vintage clothes, vintage food, and the ultrasupercool stuff at Atomic Books (where you can buy this book)

John Waters

Edgar Allan Poe

Cal Ripken, Jr.

- ✦ Go see Fluid Movement, a bunch of tattooed urban hipsters doing synchronized swimming

- ✦ Marvel at the Kinetic Sculpture Race and see some really awesome contemporary art at the American Visionary Art Museum

- ✦ Visit friends at the kitchens of Charleston, John Steven Ltd., Five Points Tavern, and Woodberry Kitchen

- ✦ See the National Great Blacks in Wax Museum on North Avenue

- ✦ After visiting the Babe Ruth Museum downtown, cross the street to visit Geppi's Entertainment museum

- ✦ Send my brother out for mind-blowing sandwiches at Isabella's in Little Italy

- ✦ Experience the best Indian food on the planet at the Ambassador Dining Room
- ✦ Take a picture outside Charm City Cakes!

I think John Waters (a proud citizen of Baltimore) put it best when he was describing the difference between Baltimore and New York: "In New York, the people are weird and they know it; in Baltimore people are weird and they don't."

When patterns are broken, new worlds emerge.
—TULI KUPFERBERG

If you want to teach your kids eye-hand coordination, get them a hammer, some nails, or maybe even the latest game console. There, that's done.

If you want your kids to develop an imagination and to embrace creativity, give them good blank paper, colors, and the best paint and brushes you can afford. In other words, no coloring books—ever! Coloring books have lines. Lines say "Do not cross," "Stay within," "Go no further," They also imply that if you do, it's a mistake. The F-word: Failure. Start over on the next page, and be more careful next time.

Every kid has imagination; he or she just needs space (and permission) to unleash it, nurture it, and let it fly. If there are no lines, there are no limits. How simple is that? Sure, some ideas may bounce off a wall or two, but that's okay. Rebound is learning. Experience is learning. Success is learning, and even failure is learning. Of course there are some laws of physics we have to contend with, and even (as much as I hate this word) obey (e.g., gravity), but otherwise, our possibilities are as vast as our minds can imagine.

I believe imagination must be continually fed by inspiration. Speaking of "feeding," here are some rather prophetic photos of what was to come; my love of food and my love of art.

What better expression of my future than a huge Big Mac complete with a sesame-seeded bun made of clay? True to Bauhaus teachings, form follows function; I made the top bun a re-movable lid to reveal a container for my mom's quilting pins. It's interesting that I included a single white sesame seed among the brown

7

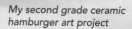
My second grade ceramic hamburger art project

AN ART EDUCATION

When my mom sent me to the Corcoran Art School in Washington, D.C., at fourteen to occupy my time while she was at work, she hoped that it would keep me out of trouble. I guess I picked up a thing or two about art there. A couple of years later, I had an art teacher who on the first day of drawing class instructed us to begin our masterpieces in the center of the paper. Well, I decided to start mine in the corner. The art teacher got mad. And I walked out of class . . . and kept on walking . . . and walking . . . three miles to home, where I graffitied our *entire* basement. It was epic.

Despite the fact that I got suspended for walking out of school, my renown for becoming a quasitalented, loosely defined "muralist" of culverts (as my mom likes to refer to it) had by then reached the ear of the vice principal (there's a reason they call him "vice" principal). After some give-and-take negotiations, mostly give on my part, I eventually was actually "given" an entire wall right across from the principal's office (so the staff could keep their collective eye on me) to tag. With their blessing, I painted the most glorious fiftysome feet of "mural art" they've ever seen at Sandwich High School.

It took me several weeks; I worked slowly to keep it going, but it did keep me out of (more) trouble *and,* thankfully, out of art class.

toasted ones. It doesn't take a high-paid shrink to tell us what that meant. As I said, ever the defiant one. Even then, I knew I wasn't ever going to go with the flow, and I was always finding ways to express that, especially through art.

So what *is* my inspiration? Where do I find it, and how do I feed it? There's inspiration for creativity *everywhere*—from writing and speech to art and architecture to food and yes, even to business. I'm here to say, I'm living proof of everything I'm saying here.

A TURNING POINT

It finally dawned on me that I was receiving more positive responses from my graffiti—oops, sorry, Mom, "mural art"—than not, even from the adults, although some were slower to admit it than others. I liked that people liked my stuff. It sure felt better than being in trouble all the time. Being my clever self, I always made sure I dedicated every work to my mom and Ronnie. That way they couldn't get *too* mad.

As you've probably heard me say on *Ace of Cakes*—that "After pastry school, I decided to make cakes *my* way"—the ever-defiant kid in me still lurks inside the older, wiser, certainly more educated person I am becoming. I still say, "There are no rules when it comes to cake." No one can say "You can't do that" to me without getting my full attention very quickly. I will fight people and I will even fight cake, but I will make it happen with my imagination being the only limitation. Oh, that *and* the pesky law of physics I mentioned before: gravity.

NO LIMITS

My training was in everything culinary, and I loved it all, but when I first started baking, I had so much fun letting my mind go, imagining a cake with no restraints, no compromises, and no traditional physical limitations. My art training, which was just naturally a part of me by then, seemed to blend perfectly with the materials of pastry, but especially cake decorating. As I became more proficient at the science of baking, I continually pushed the limits of my decorating materials, as I had done with clay, glass sandblasting, woodshop, inkle-loom weaving, fiber, sculpture, wire/metal/paper sculpture, paint, and all my other art and creative experiences. It's impossible to ignore the ubiquitous smiles,

laughter, and celebration that surround a cake, and so cake itself, to me, is synonymous with joy.

At the same time, I was struck by the downright stunning cakes that the pros such as Colette Peters do, and I realized there were not nearly enough Colettes out there for brides to have dream wedding cakes they could see only in magazines or in their own imaginations. That's when I decided to fill a need and being something new to the game, I just let the customers tell *me* what was special to *them*. It all came so naturally for me to put my own twist

when I was a kid, *there are no limits* as far as I'm concerned with our cakes today. When I started, the clients of Charm City Cakes helped me by giving me their ideas to interpret within my medium. Over time I developed a particular style, and people could easily distinguish my cakes from those of other decorators. There was no question when a cake I made was what my little brother Luke calls "a Duff cake." And though some people have labeled my style "cartoony," I was breaking molds and stereotypes with each new creation. My cakes could be Martha Stewart elegant, crazy punk, adorable, indie, shocking, or even—yes—traditional, but they still had a style that was unique to me. I think people may have been surprised by how much they related to this rather daring style, and the appreciation just served to light my fire—to make me want to do more and more and more.

It wasn't long before I needed help. Serious help! Geof was a model builder and had a saint's patience with the materials and the precision it took to turn out the masterpieces you see on the show. Subtle, quiet, and very funny, Geof has managed to fill the gaps of patient, practical, and analytical thinking I've lacked—and so, together, we've worked as a true team to engineer some pretty amazing feats of cake. Our collaborations have been more than a meeting of the minds—we've locked souls working on some of our more spectacular creations. The shared inspiration has propelled us to reach further than I think either of us would have dared to alone.

As the Charm City Cakes staff grew, so increased our skills, our cakes, and overall artistry.

Of course, that is the product of zillions of hours of practice, which is something we do put in here—hours and hours and more hours. The clock on the wall sometimes looks like a spinning wheel when we're up against a deadline, which, come to think of it, is pretty much *always*.

and style onto their personal desires and ideas, and I was continually motivated by the expressions of joy, delight, and surprise on their faces when they finally saw their own special cake for the first time. Cake after cake after cake, it kept happening; this wonderful, awesome reaction to my work. The cakes were perhaps not so traditional, but they were very uniquely theirs—and for me, that's what keeps the creative juices flowing as strongly as ever.

Just like the lineless notebook pages I filled

Truth be told, I believe our best work comes under time pressure, although some of us would always wish for just one more hour.

I think that's another quality that makes us the artists we are. We don't punch time clocks, and our creations are always more important than the time we spend on them. It's not at all uncommon to see lights blazing in the bakery on any given night until the wee hours of the morning, as that's when many of us do our best work.

WHERE WE ARE TODAY

Whatever cake I design and make, I embrace it fully, and by putting myself in the customer's shoes, I create the most awesome cake I can imagine. I put powerful colors together without agonizing—if they look good together to *me*, they look good. If they don't, I start over. Color is a very important aspect of all our cakes, and I never shy away from using color with depth. I multilayer colors—it's more time-consuming but so worth it in the end.

I've become increasingly fearless—some might even say daring—in combining color, design, sizes, and even shapes in my cakes. Once one barrier comes down, on I go on to the next challenge. If people can imagine it, we can make it. Even if they can't imagine it, we'll imagine it and make it for them. We personalize these edible creations into art forms; always pushing, always daring to top the last in form, size, and any way we can, really. When the cake is delivered to its destination, it's our reputation, it has to make you stop, even for just a moment, and say, "Wow!"

CREATIVITY BEGETS CREATIVITY

I bought this great old building with lots and lots of character in the old Remington section of Baltimore and let the contractors have at it. It used to be a church, so the bones were there. Knowing we wanted (and needed) a happy, cheerful environment, we painted the walls some great shades of happy, cheerful, yet soothing colors. We saved the character of the original building as much as possible, down to the rich deep honey wood flooring. The bakery is much more of an art studio than it is a traditional bakery, and that's where and why the magic happens. We've got all kinds of music going on and lots of bright, natural light. Again, I believe that keeping the senses stimulated in a positive manner is the best incubator for creative activity. We play off one another, too. There's no room for competition at Charm City Cakes. We're very much unique individuals on a very special team.

Never one to want to be bored with the safe, tried, and true, I always look for new fresh approaches to cake decorating. I've blown 'em up, hung 'em up, lit 'em up, motorized 'em, and electrified 'em. There's close to nothing we can't do with cake, and there's certainly nothing we won't try. I'm always learning, always teaching, always reaching, and always expanding—by observing and keeping an open mind, I'm always ready to accept a challenge and interpret anything I see into cake design. We must and do keep our work fresh, fun, and exciting.

What also keeps me creative and motivated, besides the limitless creative ideas and the challenge to make cakes with the "wow factor," is the pure and simple fun and inner satisfaction it gives me to bring joy to so many people. My customers must *never* be disappointed. It's up to me to see to that. There's nothing like watching the face of a cake recipient when he or she first sees the cake. I can tell immediately if they love it, and *I* love it when they do. I couldn't do this for long if I didn't get that payoff. No amount of money can buy that kind of satisfaction. It's what makes me excited by the creative process—thinking as I go while working on a planned design; getting even more excited in the middle of a project because I just thought of something new for the cake that I can integrate into the original idea. I don't worry about sticking to my plan so strictly, because I know that if I get an inspired idea while working on it, I can make an immediate adjustment. I just add it, subtract it, change it. Remember, there are no lines stopping me.

I get stoked and will spend inordinate amounts of time and energy on the smallest detail, just to get it right. Sure, they're the client's cakes, but we like to think of them as "our" cakes. They may not have asked for lights to flash or for things to move or spin around, but if we think it will make a better cake design, we'll do it. Though we're delighted by the fact that most of our clients give us free rein, it's never a requirement. There's a difference between doing something for its own sake and doing it because it's right.

MAKING THINGS HAPPEN

When I first take on a new cake challenge, I begin by learning about my customer—what inspires, defines, or speaks to him or her. Of course, the cake is most likely being made to commemorate a special occasion, so the subject matter is often predetermined to a large degree. That's where I pick up the puck and skate. Although I look back to the customer for the initial inspiration, I look forward and all around me—for depth, dimension, color, and even strength.

To help envision the idea, we draw a sketch of the main elements the cake should have. We add details and go through the entire process of making the cake in our heads before we begin to work, much as a dancer or skater visualizes a choreography before taking the first step. We see the end result in our minds and work back, imagining each step in getting there—all the steps in order, all the plans. Then we get to work by gathering all our materials and tools.

Charm City Cakes is filled with all the expected tools of cake decorating, such as tubs of fondant. That's the dryish, matte-finished, rolled-out marshmallowy cover we put over the buttercream cakes. The fondant basically serves as a "canvas" for our special designs, while also serving as a freshness sealer. Form follows function, here as in other pursuits! We have an airbrush station where we spray edible color onto the fondant and many specialized tools to work our materials, such as coloring methods (you can knead the color in, you can airbrush it, you can hand paint it, you can pipe it, or you can do a colored appliqué) and special paper for making piping bags. Many of our tools are just everyday,

The 49 Flavors of Charm City Cakes

almond	chocolate chip muffin	peanut butter cup
almond amaretto cream	chocolate espresso	pear compote and ginger
apples and cinnamon	chocolate mint	pear spice
banana caramel	chocolate orange	pecan pie
bananas foster	chocolate raspberry	pineapple coconut
beurre noisette	dulce de leche	pumpkin and cinnamon
black forest	egg nog	pumpkin chocolate chip
blackberry sour cream	ginger and green tea	red velvet
blueberry muffin	Italian orange and vanilla	s'mores
brownie	lemon	strawberry shortcake
butterscotch walnut	lemon curd and berries	tiramisu
cardamom and pistachio	lemon poppyseed	white
Caribbean black cake	marble	white chocolate
carrot	mudslide	raspberry
cherry and almond	orange and ginger	yellow
chocolate	peaches and cream	yellow with chocolate
chocolate cherry	peanut butter and jelly	buttercream

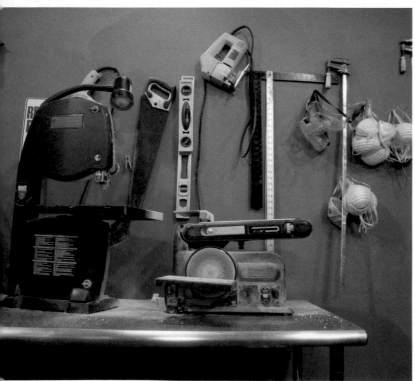

ordinary household kitchen items, and many more are art studio staples. We have countless small hand tools for clay, sculpture, and model building; dental tools; paintbrushes; faux painting tools, you name it—the list is almost endless and always changing as we come up with new techniques. If you were able to rummage through our stuff, you'd no doubt be very surprised by what you'd find. I know I am half the time.

Of course, the cake within the fondant must taste amazing as well. When you see an incredibly intricate cake, it's easy to assume that it can't possibly taste any good, but (1) though it is edible, fondant is meant to be peeled away to reveal the icing and fresh cake underneath, and (2) out of the thirty-plus cakes we make a week, the few that are featured on TV tend to be the "wildest"-looking. But trust us, if they didn't taste good, you wouldn't be reading this book. Our kitchen is well stocked with all the expected baking equipment: pans, mixers, and giant stainless-steel bowls, of course. We also have dozens of types of chocolate, fruits, nuts, and so on to create every cake flavor, from Bananas Foster to Pumpkin Chocolate Chip.

Another thing that sets Charm City Cakes

apart is that our tools include a band saw, a drill press, soldering and welding equipment, a belt sander, a hammer, an assortment of screwdrivers, pliers, wrenches, and just about everything else I can remember from my days in my high-school shop class. Yup, I took shop. I also took home ec. A great class to meet girls in. In fact I was the only guy. What am I, stupid? Besides, I learned how to sew and make 3-D trapunto quilts. Comes in handy in cake decorating. Sometimes. Well, maybe one day.

I can envision some pretty amazing creations, but it would be physically impossible for me to fabricate most of them without some heavy-duty equipment. We use them to build sturdy bases to support the cake—we're not actually taking a chain saw to something you would eat. Though you may not usually associate such power tools with delicately artistic cakes, when you think about it, some of the worlds' greatest art treasures could not have been created without them. So why *not* cake? *Art* cake. If I had a coloring book mentality, I wouldn't have con-

Elena

sidered using my power tools for cake construction. That's why I'm reminding you about those pesky imagination-stifling, possibility-limiting lines again.

CLIENT INPUT

Once we've taken on new clients, we like to meet them in person. Sure, we know the basic idea they're looking for, but we want to get a feel for who they really are and what they like, as conveyed by nonverbal communication.

The next step is the visual concept. Okay, so we have a design—a sketch—that we've created from a mix of our experience and talking to a client and figuring out how to realistically make his or her cake desire a reality. Now we need to transform the design into a finished cake. Generally, we have five days to create the cake from start to finish. That may sound like a long time for one cake, but it really isn't. There are many, many steps involved in creating just one cake, and some weeks we can have close to forty cake orders—and some cakes can require from three hundred to up to five hundred man-hours to create.

With the cake concept determined, we have to figure out how to get there. First of all, support—will it need special interior infrastructure to keep it secure? Cake is very heavy. We don't want to take any chances with gravity. Do we have all the supplies we need? If not, can we get them in time?

The next step is to explore the shape and design. Do we have all the tools we need to create the shape? Is a trip to the hardware store necessary, or the electrical store or even the plumbing store? Will we need to carve, to build up, to rethink our original idea or even create a negative space? Will the cake have moving parts or parts that make other parts move? How will they be hidden and/or made part of the overall design? What will the base be like? Will there be special added elements, such as a melted sugar-water feature? Molten lava? How will the colors be created? Modeling chocolate, fondant, royal icing? Will we need hours and hours of intricate piping on this cake? Will there be wiring or PVC plumbing or a dramatic use of dry ice?

These questions and many more need to be addressed before even a bit of cake is baked. But the big questions are always, Can we take a chance with this one? How far can we push the limits of the materials we have to work with? And how far can we push ourselves?

AGAINST THE NORM
IN ALL WAYS—ALWAYS

Charm City Cakes is an artistic democracy. Impossible, you say? Not only is the business humming right along—some would say booming—but we're going against most conventional small-business models. I don't just want to make cakes creatively—I'm always trying to think of creative ways to keep everybody happy and in the creative mood, which means keeping it fun. So I don't mind donning a kilt and having a bagpiper come in to play for us when we're making a Scottish yak cake.

Or taking a little field trip when asked to make an elephant cake for the Baltimore Zoo (hey, it's important to see that elephant skin up close to be able to recreate it in fondant, right?).

We even went to the local army base and actually drove a tank just to get into the mood to make a birthday cake for the U.S. Army. It was supposed to be a reconnaissance mission, Charm City Cakes style, to get up close and personal with an Abrams. Yeah, sure. I just wanted to get a chance to drive a tank!

That's for inspiration, joy, and just plain fun. What else do you think our cakes are? In my opinion, that's just about as perfect as you can get.

As Picasso once said: "Every child is an artist. The problem is how to remain an artist once he grows up."

> *I can understand why fame is so fickle and fleeting. . . . What I need to do is figure out what I want—and use my temporary pass into this kind of accessibility to get what I want. Hopefully, I can use this as a springboard to make better and better and better cakes.*
>
> —DUFF

Photographer Vincent Lupo captures Katie at the airbrush station.

BEHIND THE CAKE

See their story in
ACE OF CAKES episode 511,
"Tanks, Trucks, and Vikings"

AMANDA AND STEPHEN WARD

Although they were officially married in April 2007, prior to his deployment to Afghanistan, Army Captain Stephen P. Ward and Amanda Sessoms Ward decided to renew their vows upon his return and receive a blessing of their marriage in June 2008 at St. Paul's Episcopal Church in Wilmington, North Carolina. Captain Ward had sustained dual injuries during his deployment with the 97th Civil Affairs Battalion, U.S. Army Special Operations Command: one in combat and the other in an accident.

With the hope of both honoring the couple and turning the military experience into a positive healing process for them all, the groom's mother, Pam Ward, contacted the bakery and requested a special cake for the occasion, in the shape of (of all things) an M1A1 tank. Sharing her plan with her new daughter-in-law, Amanda, gave them focus, unity, and joy as they planned the surprise presentation.

According to Pam and Amanda, the most indelible memory of the event is the look on Stephen's face when they rolled in the tank: "Just priceless," they said. The *Ace of Cakes* production team insisted on including the story and the cake in an episode, and a story about the couple and the cake appeared in the Annapolis Capital newspaper.

I'm proud to say the staff at Charm City Cakes rose to the occasion by embracing the meaningful gesture, creating a "happy tank" with love for Stephen and the 165 guests. I dubbed the vehicle "Tankish," which pretty much said it all.

The Events of CHARM CITY CAKES

AN **INTER VIEW** WITH

ANNA ELLISON
Artistic Director

Position: Artistic Director

Hometown: Richmond, Virginia

Education: James River High School in Midlothian, Virginia, 2001; Maryland Institute
College of Art with a major in graphic design, 2005

Interests: Scrabble, soccer, swimming, iced coffee, and sunny days

Fun fact: When Katie Rose and I lived together, she would do my packing whenever I went
on trips. Even though I moved out, I still try to get her over before traveling.

Favorite books: *Franny and Zooey* by J. D. Salinger, *Middlesex* by Jeffrey Eugenides,
100 Years of Solitude by Gabriel García Márquez, *Lolita* by Vladimir Nabokov

Favorite music: Fleetwood Mac, The Kinks, Os Mutantes

Favorite movies: *Rushmore, Clueless, The Unbelievable Truth, Badlands,
Masculin Féminin*

How did you start working at Charm City Cakes?

During a summer home from college (I think in 2003) I was in a Michael's craft store and on a
whim signed up for a Wilton cake-decorating class. Not long after that, a friend told me that if I was
into cake decorating I should check out Charm City Cakes—he had just been to a wedding where
they had made the most amazing cake he had ever seen. When I looked up the CCC website and
gallery, something just clicked with me, and I knew that I had to be a part of whatever craziness
they had going on. The company was just Duff
and Geof at the time, and they were working
out of Duff's house. I got in touch with them,
and Duff invited me to come over so I could
see them at work. I was immediately hooked
on the world of professional cake decorating!
Before leaving I asked Duff if I could intern at
CCC for free in exchange for school credit.
Even though I was turned down that first day,
I persisted. Two months later I emailed Duff,
"Can I intern for free? I'm a super hard worker
and into fun." He wrote back, "Anna—I'm into
fun too. Let's work something out." To this day
I'm convinced that the "I'm into fun" was what
sealed the deal.

What was it like when you started?

I remember walking in and just being totally amazed, not only that such a great job existed but that you could make a living doing it too! I remember on my first day being given the most basic task of glueing tiny flowers onto a wedding cake. I was incredibly nervous that this amazing cake maker was putting so much trust in me, and I was terrified that I was going to ruin the cake (I didn't). The whole first-day experience is really indicative of my career and relationship with Duff. He trusts us completely to dive headfirst into projects, and he also creates this environment that allow us to explore and experiment as artists and therefore thrive on our own.

Everyone on the show seems like such good friends. Is this true?

Some of my best friends were hired over the years, and I've become great fiends with a bunch of other people that I didn't know before they came to CCC. We're all close, and sometimes even after insanely long days at work, we'll still want to go out and get drinks together. If we didn't get along, the business wouldn't be so successful. Our work depends on integrating all of our various talents. No one could do every cake we get by themselves.

As the artistic director at Charm City Cakes, what does your job consist of?

Anything that needs to be done! Usually I do a lot of the painting, figure making, color coordinating, and designing. I also do some of the design consultations, helping our clients develop their ideas into a more finished cake concept.

What do you like so much about working with cakes?

I've always loved the idea of cakes—they're almost always associated with joyous and cel-

ebratory events where people come together and are happy. Even before I made cakes, my artwork and design projects were colorful and happy.

What is the most challenging part of your job?

Every day is different from the last. As our company grows in experience and size, so do our projects. Even when we redo an old cake design, we're always trying to figure out ways to make it better and more impressive than before.

What's the best part of your job?

Everything, really. The environment is incredible. I work with a bunch of really talented artists who function like a second family to me, and Duff is the best boss ever. He really cares about the people that work for him, and he gives us all a tremendous amount of freedom to execute our projects however we see fit.

The most rewarding?

Seeing the reaction of a client who really loved their cake. A few times clients have cried because they were so moved, which definitely made me tear up.

What's a typical day like?

Each day of the week is a little different. Most cakes are due on a Saturday. Mondays we have a big meeting and assign each contract to a person. The first part of the week is spent in preparation—dyeing colors, making flowers,

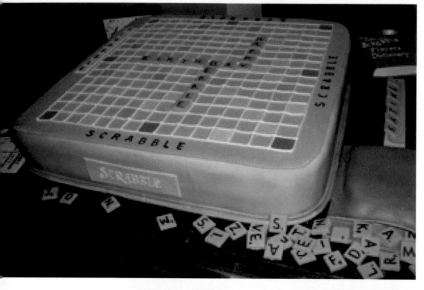

carving the cakes, and so on. On Thursdays and Fridays we ice the cakes, cover them in fondant, and finish decorating them.

What's the most memorable moment you've had so far?

When Warner Bros. asked us to make a cake for the Harry Potter movie premiere! What an amazing opportunity—we flew out to L.A. to make a giant Hogwarts castle. We got to walk the red carpet, see the premiere, and hang out with the actors at the after party (where our cake was on display)!

What's the craziest cake your team has ever made?

We made a giant Super Bowl cake in Miami, and the humidity there nearly ruined it and cost us our sanity.

What was your personal favorite?

I'm a huge Scrabble nerd, so making a Scrabble cake for a fellow aficionado was really fantastic.

What was your reaction to *Ace of Cakes* before it started?

I wasn't into it. I've always been really shy and not totally comfortable in front of cameras.

When the show first started?

My first impression of the show was actually pretty negative at first. Before the show aired, a few people came down to film a pilot. During that period I think the crew were more aggressive in their style of interviewing and trying to create conflict and dramatic situations. It seemed as if they were overcompensating in order to make sure someone would want to pick the show up. The whole week they were there, I was completely stressed out and hated the invasiveness of it all. I remember thinking that if the show got picked up I would quit. A couple of months later

Mary Smith and Anna

it did get picked up, and I decided to give it a chance. I spent time getting to know the crew and had a change of heart. It also definitely helped that the crew were more natural and relaxed in their style of interviewing and being in the bakery. It's completely surprising to me that the show is successful with little to no conflict and no interpersonal drama, but for my own sanity it's the reason I'm still at Charm City Cakes and on TV.

How do you feel about being on TV now?

It's mostly positive. I don't mind things as much. I'm completely used to all the crew and cameras. Having cameras around all the time only gets hard when I have no idea what I'm doing (which happens often) and I have to pretend otherwise. Also, the crew are all really wonderful people who we've all become close to and even hang out with outside of work.

Do you get recognized? Has it changed your life at all?

My fear of losing anonymity has become more of an indifference. I get recognized sometimes, but it's mostly just in Baltimore. At first I didn't like that aspect, but I'm into being more positive about it all, and I'm learning to love it. The best was actually getting to be on a CCC float at a local parade. I never imagined that would be something I'd enjoy. But in fact having hundreds of people waving and cheering felt really amazing and completely validating for me. In general, though, nothing is that different— my peers and people I'm friends with outside of work don't really have cable or watch the show. If anything, they usually say, "Oh, yeah, my mom really likes that show."

What did you study at MICA?

I spent all my time in high school painting and thought I'd go to school for that. However, my parents were very influential in wanting me to get an education in something I could get a job with, and in the end I chose graphic design. In college I lost interest in painting but gained an appreciation for design.

What's your favorite art project that you've done?

After I graduated I made a magazine called *Junior Varsity Dangerous Sports Club*. (Because I ended up making only one issue ever, I like to think of it now as more of a book.) I made 150 copies, which included screen-printed covers and letterpress inserts, and had it distributed in eight different cities across the country. The book was a documentation of projects spearheaded by Heidi Gustafson (Ben Turner's fiancée) that were about group and individual activities full of thoughtful (dangerous) play that didn't involve money, competition, perfection, or power.

93

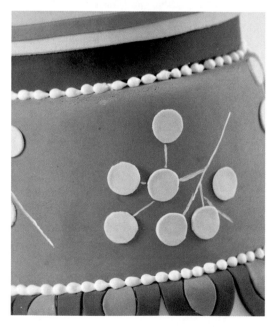

Does your background in art carry over to your work at Charm City Cakes?

Definitely. My experiences with painting in high school and learning about design in college help me be a successful cake maker. I actually really appreciate that cake making has combined those two skills, which never coincided beforehand.

What was your culinary experience before CCC?

None. It actually surprises people that aside from Duff, none of his employees has any culinary training.

What advice do you have for aspiring cake decorators?

Make cakes for your friends all the time! Who doesn't love cake? And most important, when things go wrong (which they will, and often), it's always really important to take a minute and remember, *it's just cake.*

BEHIND THE CAKE

See her story in
ACE OF CAKES episode 103,
"Wedding Cakes and Headaches"

DOROTHY SELESKI

There's nothing more meaningful than making a special cake for someone who has lived almost three times as long as I have. Dorothy didn't want any fuss to be made over her eightieth birthday because her husband had recently passed away, and she didn't feel up to having a party. But when her daughter Peggy told her that she could have her very own birthday cake made by Charm City Cakes, that clinched the deal. A year prior, Dorothy had loved the Australian-themed cake we'd made for Peggy and her twin sister's fortieth birthday.

Dorothy and her daughters spent many hours deciding what her birthday cake would be and came up with the idea of a 1960s-style hat that had been one of Dorothy's favorite Easter bonnets. Dorothy loved her hat collection, and back in her heyday she had owned more than twenty-five hats, with an individual hatbox for each. The good news was that Dorothy still had an old hatbox that we could replicate, plus she knew exactly what she wanted it to taste like: carrot cake, her favorite flavor. The bad news was that there were no photos of her wearing her favorite Easter bonnet, and we had to sketch the hat entirely from Dorothy's and Peggy's memories. So we went back and forth with sketches of different variations of hats until we got it right. We covered the hat with handmade flowers and created a green-and-blue-striped hatbox with pink tissue paper made of fondant, and we added a big bead on the hatbox of the letter "D."

When I delivered Dorothy's cake, I'll never forget her reaction: she had a flash of recognition, and then her eyes welled up with tears. She was speechless. I told Dorothy to start thinking about what kind of cake she wants for her ninetieth birthday party, because I'll be there.

We later found out that Dorothy saves the gum paste hatbox lid in a special trunk of keepsakes—and she still loves to talk about her eightieth birthday, where we helped bring back to life a long-lost favorite possession from decades earlier.

MARY SMITH Decorator

Hometown: Brogue, Pennsylvania, and Smithtown, New York

Favorite movies: *The Jerk, The Princess Diaries, Billy Elliot, The Life Aquatic, The Rundown*

Favorite hobbies: Baseball (Yankees and Os), air saxophone, stupid human tricks

Favorite music: The Zombies, The Stones, Belle and Sebastian, Brian Jonestown Massacre, Stiff Little Fingers, Creedence Clearwater Revival, The Dropkick Murphy, Oxymoron, Bobby Darin, Louis Prima, Jacques Dutronc, Creation, T. Rex, Long Live Death, power ballads

Favorite books: *The Universal History of Numbers: From Prehistory to the Invention of the Computer* by Georges Ifrah, *The Family of Richard Smith of Smithtown, Long Island: 10 Generations* by Frederick Kinsman Smith

Favorite nondessert dish to create or eat: Broccoli, kimchee, mac 'n' cheese

Fun fact: Katherine wrote a musical adaptation of the story of Baby Jessica.

In her own words . . .

In 2003 my friend Debbie's mom was turning sixty. In Argentine culture, when someone turns sixty it's a really big deal. So she and her sisters knew they had to go all out for their mom's party. Debbie was in charge of the cake, and she told me she'd read about this guy who made eccentric cakes. She went to the bakery—and I use that term very loosely, because Duff was still working out of his house—and he designed a purple cake with fiber optics coming out of the top. From then on I knew I wanted to work for him.

A year after Debbie's encounter with Duff I went to a party in Charles Village. Earlier that day I was hanging out with Anna and Katie, and Anna was telling me about how she wanted to intern with Duff and Geof. Coincidentally, that night Sherri was at the party and introduced me to Geof. I grilled him about the cakes, asking millions of questions, and told him that he really should let Anna intern with them, when secretly I wanted to work with them. I told him about cupcakes she had made for our friend for a Secret Santa present, and how awesome and creative they were.

Anna finally got the job, which, I'm fairly positive, my recommendation had nothing to do with. I was finishing up school, working with an interior designer, and waiting tables part time at a local restaurant/coffee

a better job. I told them to tell Duff I'd work for free. Duff agreed to have me come in.

I thought my visit to the bakery that day was just going to be an interview, but Duff threw me into the mix of it right away. I shadowed Geof while he fondanted, and then worked with Anna and Sherri while they worked on cakes. Soon they had me airbrushing flowers.

> **TIP** *Art courses are very helpful if you want to learn how to do what we do.*

Nowadays, everyone has pretty specific jobs at the bakery. Anna is in charge of all the figure making, along with painting with Katie Rose. Katherine and I do all the piping, and she does food replicas while I get stuck with a lot of purses, luggage, stilettos and such. And of course Elena gets all the dark, morbid cakes. But in the old days the bakery jobs were less specific. Generally no one person was put in charge of any of the cakes. I remember, though, how I started piping. I kind of knew how to pipe before I started working there. I bought a copy of the Martha Stewart holiday cookie magazine and learned how to make royal icing, and got a rough idea of how to pipe from that. Then for years I would make elaborate holiday cookies for my family and friends. But one day at the bakery Duff was piping a mehndi cake for his friend's wedding. He piped the first tier and then got distracted by something else. Having nothing to do at the time, I just started replicating some of the designs onto the table next to the cake, and came up with new patterns. When Duff came back I asked him if I could try my hand at the cake, and he agreed. Needless to say, I blew him out of the water! From then on I was pretty much stuck doing all the piped cakes.

Soon I decided I loved the job so much that

shop. I felt like I was stuck in a rut, and made a decision to apply to FIT for the fall and finish out my bachelor's in interior design. It was July of 2005, and even though I have been casually inquiring about employment opportunities at the bakery over the past year, I was really starting to hassle Geof and Sherri about it now. I didn't want to move to New York City and wait tables at another restaurant, and I thought this would give me another skill to find

I put my New York plans on hold and became a decorator full-time, around the same time there was talk of a reality show being filmed at the bakery. I really didn't want to do the show at first, but Duff made me feel comfortable about it. The first season focused mostly on Duff, Geof, and Mary Alice. They were sort of the guinea pigs—but when the show started to air and we all saw how it was put together, I became a lot more comfortable with having the camera crews around.

For this book I made several cakes, including the multicolored piped henna cakes, but my personal favorite is the cuckoo clock cake. We had a cuckoo clock at the bakery for a while, and I thought it would make for a really adorable cake. And since one of my favorite bands, Belle and Sebastian, has a song called "I'm a Cuckoo," I thought it would be cute for them to come out instead of a generic Bavarian band.

TIP *If you want to write out a message on a cake, find your midpoint and go from there out, and then go back and find the middle and extend backward toward the beginning. This keeps your message straight and centered.*

WHY CAKES SUCK

"Talent is a lightning rod and America is a thunderstorm. You go running around like crazy, you get soaked, your arm gets tired holding that damn thing up . . . and still, lightning, all too often, strikes half a block over, electrifying someone else."
—STEPHEN KING

Hmm, that's not really accurate; maybe I should call this chapter "why cakes are a pain in the ass" or "why one would have to be insane to choose cake decorating as a career" or "what the hell was I thinking when I opened my own cake shop?" I don't actually think cakes suck, of course—but it does illustrate a lot of the trials and stress and problems that need to be overcome in order to decorate a cake.

Let's start with the basic elements of cake: it's porous, it goes stale quickly, and it's not easy to sculpt. First off, and most important, it has to taste good. You have to think about the people eating it—whether they'll be pleased by the flavor and texture. That may seem obvious, but think back to how many weddings you attended where the wedding cake was beautiful but tasted like crap. There are a few reasons for this, but the main problem is that whoever made the cake didn't make flavor and freshness a priority. Maybe that cake was sitting in a freezer for a month, or worse, sitting in the fridge for a week. Perhaps the cake was made from a mix and the icing was pure hydrogenated oil mixed with sugar. Or it could be that whoever baked that cake just didn't know what he or she was doing.

Cake can go stale really quickly, that we know. So here at Charm City Cakes we make a point of planning the decoration before we even turn the ovens on. For example, why would we bake a cake and then sit around for three days making sugar flowers for it? Since the flowers and decorations are less delicate than the cake itself, why not create them first and then bake the cake, apply the flowers, and deliver the cake? If you go with option A, you'll have a cake that's been sitting around losing moisture and protein structure while you made flowers. If you choose option B, you'll have a cake that's fresh and moist inside—and looks just as good as option A. You just have to use a little common sense, and above all, you need to care!

MAKING A CAKE, STEPS A THROUGH Z

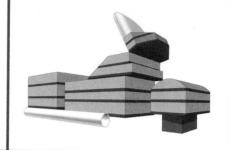

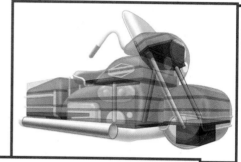

Here's another example: let's say we're making a cake in the shape of a car. First, we research the shape and individual parts of the car. Then we draw a diagram of how the cake version of the car will be put together. We draw templates so that we know what size cake to bake and what shape to carve into it. Then we list all the parts to make.

Now we're ready to get our hands into it. First we make all the gum paste pieces: wheels, tires, windshield, decals, license plates, headlights, people, and so on. Next we figure out how big of a base to make for the car and, using our diagram, figure out the wheelbase, wheel height, and length. Then we cut out a hardboard or foam base for the cake to sit on, cut and shape shocks to hold up the floor of the car, and build the whole base assembly. At first some people thought I was showboating by using power tools on cakes, but it's really not the case. I use power tools for the support of the cakes. I cut the floor and the shocks with a band saw or a scroll saw, and I screw the whole thing together with wood screws and a power drill. A cake's skeletal structure simply must be sturdy, and if you're open-minded about the tools you can use, you're likely to achieve better results.

Even with a custom-built platform for the cake to sit on, we're still not ready to bake. Next we decorate our sugary figures with clothes and hair and sand down the gum paste so everything

has a nice machined edge—no sloppy knife marks here! Then we color the pieces either with edible paint or with airbrushing (which takes me right back to my graffiti days), pipe the license plate and decals, and color the fondant to have ready for the car.

Now we can start on the cake. First we assemble a block of cake layers to fit the size of our sculpture, and then we chill it for an hour or so to make it easier to carve. As Picasso said,

"Art is the elimination of the unnecessary," and that's exactly what we do.

After laying the template on the block of cake, we carve away on it until it is the shape of the car. Then we apply a crumb coat of whatever flavor buttercream the clients asked for, chill the cake again to secure the crumb coat, and apply the fondant. We may give the car a metal-flake finish using pearl dust before the final step of putting the cake on its base, and then comes the fun part—applying all the details we made at the beginning.

Voilà! Awesome! We now have a beautifully detailed car that's ready to be presented and served. Even though it took a week to make, the cake is only a day or two old, because we planned the whole thing out before we even touched a grain of sugar. Beautiful cake *and* fresh and delicious! You *can* have your cake and eat it too.

THE SCIENCE OF BAKING

In order to work with cake successfully, you need to consider its physical makeup. Cake is basically flour, butter, sugar, eggs, and, in most cases, a leavening agent such as baking soda or baking powder, mixed together and baked. While the cake is in the oven, that baking powder turns into carbon dioxide, which causes the cake to rise and makes those little air pockets. So you have all these little baking powder grains that

are kicking out this gas (CO_2), and then you have a web of protein created by the gluten in the flour, which traps these little bubbles of gas and then expands. Because the oven is hot, the protein structure at this point is gelatinous, kind of stretchy.

When the cake comes out of the oven, it isn't done. It still has to cool. Let me say that again: *It still has to cool.* Chemically, cooling is just as important as baking, because that stretchy web of gooey gluten needs to solidify to keep your cake inflated. Otherwise it will fall and become a pancake with the consistency of a hockey puck. So here's another reason cakes are a pain in the ass: they're never static!

A bagel really doesn't change shape once it has cooled, mainly because it's made from a high-protein flour that makes really thick, strong gluten. The result is nice chewy bagels. That's all well and good for cream cheese and lox (with a slice of purple onion),

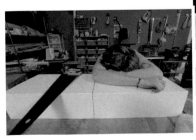

study your cakes and see how they react over time. How much do they settle? How much do they move? Once you've determined this, you can take steps to outwit your cake. I've dealt with plenty of cakes with minds of their own, believe me! Get a few steps ahead of the cake and put yourself in a position so that by the time the cake is displayed, it's perfect. Just like George Costanza, cakes are subject to shrinkage. For example, when you enrobe a cake in fondant or marzipan or modeling chocolate, you need to realize that tomorrow your cake will probably be ¼ inch shorter, so when you trim the bottom of whatever you are using, trim it a little high so it doesn't buckle under. That way the fondant will stay smooth and tight.

NEVER TRUST A CAKE

Don't forget that cakes are little bastards—not to be trusted! Don't think for a second that a cake will support any weight or empty space. Imagine, for example, a cylinder. Now, if that cylinder were made entirely out of cake, it would eventually settle, buckle, crack, and become a big mess. So what you do is cut that cylinder in half and make the bottom half cylinder out of Styrofoam and the top half cylinder out of cake. Now that thing won't go anywhere. A cylinder is a simple geometric shape; apply the same rule of physics now to something more complex.

When you have a daunting cake to make, break it down into simple shapes first to make the task much more manageable. Take, for example, a cake of a dog sitting upright. First figure out how big you want to make your dog. Draw a diagram of the setup you'll use to support the cakes. When we make a dog, we usually make a cantilevered skeletal system built out of wood, screwed together with a separate piece of wood on top cut to the exact shape of the

but can you imagine a cake with the texture of a bagel? *Yuck!* That's why when you're perusing the baking aisle at the grocery store you see the terms pastry flour, cake flour, all-purpose flour, high-protein flour, and others on the packages. All those different kinds of flour really are for different purposes, depending on what you're baking. Cake flour has a relatively low protein content and thus makes a fragile structure.

So at Charm City Cakes we need to take into account that cakes are never one shape. They settle, and the starch molecules push moisture out as the cake gets older—they actually *never stop moving*! When you're baking at home,

dog's head. We also use sheets of floral foam from the craft store and glue the foam to the dog's belly. When the glue is dry, we gently sand the foam down to the shape we want, cut thick dowels for his front legs, screw them to the belly and then to the board, and then screw down the bottom cantilever. Now you have a system that won't shift (three points make a plane; remember your high school geometry class?), and you can bake your cakes, insert them into the cantilevers, put his head on, and carve the cake away until he looks right.

Next you need to crumb coat the whole thing, wood and all. Chill it, cover it in fondant, airbrush it, or use a clay gun and extrude fondant "hair," add ears, a nose, eyes, a collar, and so on. If you want to make a tail standing up like a happy dog's, don't even think about using cake. Good old half-inch refrigeration copper pipe screwed to the base and covered in modeling chocolate and rolled fondant will hold its shape just fine. Now you have a cake that is solid, fresh, and easy to serve once you instruct the bewildered caterer how to take it apart!

If we could just start out with a block of cake and carve away like carving ice, no sweat, but since cake is so fragile and sensitive (like me), you have to go through this process of construction before you can even get into the kitchen. This is really when you have to get your craft right to get your art right.

THE PERILS OF DELIVERY

I do want to say a quick word about shipping cakes, which people ask us about all the time. The answer is simple: don't do it. You've worked too hard and someone has paid too much money for your art to be put into the hands of some delivery guy who's going to throw that box around like your latest eBay purchase. Though I do know a few decorators who have found ways to ship cakes, the methods are convoluted and expensive, and there's always too much risk involved.

But how do we get our cakes from bakery to event? We use big cargo vans with extra AC to keep them cool, but not so cold that the cakes get damaged by refrigeration or condensation (more on temperature in a bit). Anything with four tiers and over we build on-site so the cake isn't subjected as harshly to the laws of gravity and inertia while inside the van. Also, for any cake four tiers or higher, we use wooden dowels and plastic plates to support the cakes from tier to tier. For three-tier cakes and smaller, we use foam core and wide plastic straws to support the weight—sometimes with a single dowel extending through all three tiers and continuing straight down into the base itself to keep the cake together as one unit and solid to the base. We always bring a patch kit with us to fix any stress fractures or bumps that may occur en route. It's not too difficult as long as you have everything you need.

mertime, it's not only hot but humid as well. Cakes are very sensitive to the climate, especially humidity. A cake that is covered in fondant can deal with high heat, but humidity can ruin it pretty quickly.

Here's the thing: fondant is primarily made of sugar. Sugar is *hydroscopic*, meaning "water-loving." Sugar will draw the moisture out of the air around it and eventually become liquid itself, which is a disaster for fondant. If you airbrush color or brush paint onto fondant and then the cake becomes too wet from humidity, that color will run and ruin your work. If a cake is too cold when you cover it in fondant, the moisture in the air will condense on the cake, and the only thing to do is to get that cake in front of a fan as quickly as possible. That should keep it dry until it can slowly return to room temperature.

We also have a little dehydrator that we use to dry out gum paste pieces quickly in the summer. If you have to roll out a large piece of gum paste and let it dry, you have to use a porous surface, such as wood, to hold it. Then, when one side is dry, transfer the piece to a wire rack (dry side down so that you don't leave indentations) and let the piece dry evenly from both sides. If you can get a fan on it, even better.

Most important, remember that while all this is going on, you're making food, not just art! So you need to keep your entire area clean and neat.

So what makes delivering a cake suck? The exact same thing as riding a motorcycle: it's not *you* you have to worry about; it's every other idiot on the road. Bad drivers, traffic, rain, snow, excessive heat, humidity, unprepared locations, you name it. Timing is everything, and there are literally thousands of things that can screw up your delivery—but you need to know how to deal with all of them as they happen. It ain't no cakewalk!

Baltimore was built on a swamp. In the sum-

> *So much of the art of cake making is being able to think on your feet. You never say no, you can always do what a client wants, even if you've never done it before—so you say, "Sure, I can do that." Later, you figure out how.*
>
> —DUFF

THE MYTH OF THE EXPLODING CAKE

We're incredibly critical of our work, and we make cakes that we like, even if they're not what everyone else considers "normal." I like using motors in cakes to make moving parts. I like using lights. Dry ice is always fun. I like welding custom frames and stands for cakes.

Here's a misconception a lot of people have about me. "Hey! You're the guy who blows up cakes!" Not true. Yes, I love using pyrotechnics in a cake sculpture, but what's the point of blowing up a cake? Then you don't get to eat it! Sure, one of our cakes may shoot fire, but it's still edible. First we design the cake and what parts that will discharge an explosion, then we build a system of food-grade PVC pipe and line the inside of the pipes with aluminum flashing to absorb the heat. And then we build the cake around the system. That way, you can fire off as much ordnance as you want and then slice the cake.

Now, I make cakes that fire projectiles only for friends and TV. No insurance company would even consider covering me for actually selling a cake that shoots fireworks. But they're fun to make. I'm still five years old at heart, and what little boy doesn't like fireworks?

The thing to remember when making a cake that shoots out pyrotechnics is SAFETY FIRST: *know what you're doing!* If you don't understand how these things work, *DON'T DO IT!* Fireworks can be dangerous and even lethal if mishandled, and lethal isn't fun. Be safe if you want to make a pastry of death. Always have a fire extinguisher at the ready, and make sure that you yourself are igniting the fireworks. You built it, you know how it works, and you should know what ordnance you have and what it does. Yikes, I almost sounded like an adult there, sorry.

OKAY, CAKES DON'T REALLY SUCK

Cakes rule. They're fun, intellectually challenging, creatively stimulating, and oh, yeah, yummy. Never lose your joy, even when you're immersed in a cake disaster or another stressful situation. And don't be afraid to reinvent the wheel. We've gotten where we are by decorating cakes the way we feel they should be decorated.

Some people give us a hard time because of the way we do things (yeah, we read the message boards, cuddlemonkey217). Decorating cakes is a creative process, but it's not only the decorating that's creative; it's also the overall process we use. Some call it thinking outside the box, but I call it just plain thinking. We come up with some pretty wild designs and then have to find a way to make those designs work. Progress is achieved not by doing things the way they're supposed to be done but by finding new ways to overcome artistic problems—and coming up with original cakes to do in the first place. This philosophy can be applied anywhere, not just to cake design. Maybe I'm onto something—or maybe I just want to justify "blowing up" cakes.

> *Cake makes everything better.*
> —DUFF

Baltimore is Best

KATHERINE HILL Decorator

Hometown: Hurricane, West Virginia
Education: BA in studio art, Goucher College
Favorite hobbies: Balloons, thank-you notes, human pyramids
Fun fact: Ben used to be an aggressive in-line skater!
Favorite movies: *The Arrival, ABBA Gold, all Miyazaki movies*
Favorite books: *Vitamin D: New Perspectives in Drawing, Franny and Zooey*
Favorite music: Ann Peebles, Fever Ray, Stephen Strohmeier, Growing

In her own words . . .

Baltimore is best. There's such an incredible group of people full of creative energy and excitement here. It's cheap living in the city, so you have the opportunity to take time to play music, make art, write plays, or even start selling cakes out of your kitchen! It's a really inspiring place to be, and everyone encourages each other to do what they want to do. It's somewhat of a never-never land—a place where I now find myself playing with sugar every day.

After graduating, I decided to stay in Baltimore because of the family of friends I'd acquired. I'd known about Charm City Cakes for a while; occasionally Mary Smith or Anna would show up at a friend's party with some amazing pink-and-purple unicorn cake, and I'd say, "That's incredible! I want to make unicorn cakes!" After I said it enough times, Mary encouraged me to come in and meet Duff. We got along and I started interning in April 2006, and by the end of that summer, I had a full-time job.

When I was an intern, I heard about the possibility of a Food Network show being filmed at the bakery. The thought of being on TV seemed unusual, but ultimately I wasn't surprised by it all. *Ace of Cakes* itself is like having professionally produced home videos of all our days here at the bakery. I actually don't have cable, but I like knowing the show is there, and that it's going to be a good way to reminisce about what we've done here in

the past couple years. Having the film crew here with us has actually been an incredibly smooth transition. We're all really laid back and ready to have fun and the crew just fits right into that atmosphere. The best part is that no one here takes themselves too seriously. I think that's the reason Charm City Cakes is such a special place to work.

My decorating jobs at the bakery range from piping delicate wedding cakes to making fondant look like bacon. Food, especially fast food, lends itself to looking very cartoony, and with fondant's similar potential, they're a perfect marriage. When it comes time to make food that looks like other food, Duff frequently assigns that task to me—so for the book, I thought I'd take three "cool foods"—a hamburger, hot dog, and french fries—and stack them up. I've previously done all three individually, but this time around I wanted to try something a little more visually interesting. You never get to see an

actual meal in this configuration, so I thought it would be really nice and complete.

Wedding cakes are a refreshing break from some of the stranger and more complex cakes that we make. Sometimes picking a nice color with bold accents can really make a traditional wedding cake stand out. Seeing a black-and-white polka-dot ribbon at a fabric store inspired me to push for a more modern look for my wedding cake design.

By far the most satisfying part of our job is making cakes for friends. It's good to be free to create whatever you want to create for someone you love. There are no rules! Last spring Anna, Katie, and I each made a little cake for our friend Russell's birthday. Anna made onion rings, Katie made an adorable four-inch-tall three-tiered cake, and I made Russell's favorite candy bar: a giant Snickers. He said it was like a dream come true—even though he was a little hesitant to cut into them.

Cake is impermanent. It's an edible gift, meant to be enjoyed visually and then eaten. I think this excites some creative freedom in me. For lots of people, art is something to be treasured and preserved. Cake doesn't take itself so seriously. It takes hours of very difficult and

TIP *Clean hands make a clean cake!*

TIP *If you're really excited about having some sparkly elements to your wedding cake, then go ahead and do it—but only just a little. Pick one thing to shimmer (such as a light golden fondant), but keep everything else matte (piping, flowers, and ribbon). Too much can be completely overbearing.*

delicate work to create some of the sculptures we make, but I'm happy that each one will be cut into and used up by a group of merry people.

Working with sugar can be limiting at times, though. You'll be brainstorming about a design and think, Oh, and then I'll cover it in sequins, only to remember that sequins are inedible and some people may not like having them all over their dessert. There are certain things sugar just won't do, and that's when you fully realize the difference between creating art in a kitchen or bakery versus creating it in a more traditional studio.

Here you're making a product for someone, being challenged in ways you wouldn't normally think of and using materials that aren't always ideal (to say the least).

It can be frustrating at times, but the challenges we face are what make this job exhilarating—and I'm grateful to work with such intelligent and talented people. We're constantly pushing ourselves to think of new designs and better, more efficient ways of doing things. There are always great ideas floating around in conversation, and we all turn to one another for critique and advice, and of course lots of jokes:

What did the zero say to the eight?

Nice belt!

TIP *When you receive a cake and it's perfectly amazing and all you want to do is look at it and treasure it and save it forever, don't think twice—just take a bite right out of the side.*

ON *ACE OF CAKES*

Jacob Strauss, editor-in-chief, foodnetworkaddict.com

Ace of Cakes is one of the best shows on the Food Network, and I should know—I'm the Food Network Addict. On my blog, foodnetworkaddict.com, I uncover the latest news and gossip on all the celebrity chefs and shows on my favorite channel, Food Network. Duff, Geof, Mary Alice, and the rest of the crew at Charm City Cakes are big faves on the blog.

I didn't really know what to expect back in 2006 when the first commercials for *Ace of Cakes* began to air. Here was some bald guy rocking out on the guitar and blowing a cake up in his face. Huh? If I didn't know what to expect, I'm sure the diehard cooking-shows-only-please Food Network audience was totally confused—and maybe a bit frightened.

Luckily, there was nothing to fear. The show is less about explosions and more about Duff's real-life bakery in Baltimore and the talented staff of artists, painters, and sculptors he employs. Regular viewers like me instantly loved Mary Alice's awesome, quirky style, Geof's laid-back, effortless humor, and Duff's amazing ability to keep his cool and problem-solve, even in the most stressful of situations—and *Ace of Cakes* is chock full of 'em. Will they finish in time? Something just broke! How can they fix it? Oh no, the cake doesn't fit in the van!

Through it all, the cakes always seem to be delivered in perfect condition to a beaming, grateful client. Although they are made to be eaten, we still cringe at the sight of the inevitable knife turning what once was a personalized Jeep or tequila bottle or Scrabble board into a pile of stray crumbs and icing globs. They're not just cakes; they're truly works of art.

My first few posts about *Ace of Cakes* generated a huge response. I could instantly tell the show was registering with Food Network's longtime viewers, while simultaneously attracting a whole new audience to the network who had previously dismissed the programming as, well, just cooking shows.

On my blog, I started the Mary Alice Fan Club and was totally taken aback when Mary Alice herself emailed me to let me know how honored she was. Since then, I've had the great opportunity to meet her—and Duff and Geof—in person and can honestly say that these funny, quirky people we see on TV every week are just as funny and real and generous and grateful and . . . gorgeous (will sucking up get me a free cake?) in person.

The Clients of CHARM CITY CAKES

BENJAMIN TURNER Decorator

Hometown: Derry, New Hampshire

Education: BFA, Maryland Institute College of Art

Favorite hobbies: Falling down hills, endangered species, and water crafts

Fun fact: Mark Muller wrote a five-page paper about Anna Ellison for an Asian American Studies class without her knowing it.

Favorite movie: *The Idiots*

Favorite books: *If . . .* by Sarah Perry, *The Contemporary Picturesque* by Nils Norman, *Off the Books* by Sudhir Alladi Venkatesh, *The Bloody Future* by Heidi Gustafson

Favorite music: Bill Wells, Brian Eno, J Dilla, Group Inarane

Favorite nondessert dish to create or eat: Wood-fired brick oven pizza

In his own words . . .

Although I was born in small-town New Hampshire, which makes me a Yankee by birth, I've been transformed by Baltimore into a wild southern spirit! By attending the Maryland Institute College of Art (MICA), partaking in a wild music scene, and making great artwork, I finally become part of Charm City Cakes. And as if making outrageous cakes weren't enough, working daily in a reality television show is both captivating and bizarre.

I can't say enough about the people I've met in Baltimore, especially my peers, who have been a huge part in making it an incredible place to be. My relationship with cake making began with a phone call from Anna Ellison, a college friend of mine, asking if I would like to work at Charm City Cakes. My only experience making cakes up to that time was during a few days' internship at Charm City a year earlier, but having had my fair share of waiting tables and prep cooking I took her up on her offer.

My first day at the bakery started with me carving a three-foot-tall teddy bear out of foam, which as you can imagine was an incredible way to start. Since then the projects have only gotten bigger and more complex: edible motorcycles, ships, castles—I've built them all. Although we all wear multiple hats here at the bakery, one of my specialties is to make sure the large cakes are structurally sound. I also do a lot of the

Young Ben

nonedible sculpture work that may be necessary to make a client's cake perfect. We occasionally have cakes that require specific adornments that can't be created from flour, sugar, and butter, and we also get a lot of clients who request display cakes that won't rot.

My first impression of Duff actually came a few years before I started working at the bakery. Anna had put together a magazine called *Junior Varsity Dangerous Sports Club* (which I was a part of), and we needed a big enough venue for the magazine's launch party. Duff was cool enough to let us use the bakery, so we cleared out the whole room and had free use of all the materials needed to make the party come to life. It was incredible. Although at the time I had met Duff only in passing, he struck me as a genuine, nice, trusting, and down-to-earth guy. All of which makes working for him a real privilege. As a boss, Duff gives us complete freedom over how our jobs are structured: the time we work, the time we eat, when we leave, the list goes on. The amazing atmosphere makes Charm City Cakes a unique place to be.

I think having a TV show as part of my daily routine is something I'll never get used to. It's

> **TIP** To make a smooth pour-in (when you use royal icing to fill the base around a cake), mix the royal icing to the desired consistency, set the mixer to its lowest setting, and let it mix for five minutes. This will get rid of any bubbles and inconsistencies.

TIP *Think outside the box. (Please—I'm very serious about this.)*

just as surprising today as it was when I was first introduced to it, and I'm glad to say the only thing that's changed is that I now have a great relationship with the people behind the camera. The TV crew have become a part of our work staff, with our decorators working around them, in front of them, against them, behind them, and sometimes with them—even when there seem to be more camera people than cake decorators. They've really become part of our team, and now I can't imagine Charm City Cakes without them.

The cakes I created for this book are a reflection of my favorite cake concepts. I enjoy the cakes that become very specific for an individual, both because of their expressive individuality and for the challenges they often present. On the one hand, they can make for a very unexpected cake, but on the other, combining an aircraft carrier, a dog named Randolph, and a left-hand turn signal into one cake can be a daunting task. If anything, my job gives me the chance to steal a secret glimpse at the fascinations of the human psyche: we're always discovering something new. Everyone is looking for their dreams, and what better surprise than to find they are real, crumbly, sweet, and covered in fondant icing!

One thing I'd love to take this opportunity to address is the fact that most people think we're always eating at the bakery. Though it's true we might have a nibble of cake here or a slurp of icing there, I never eat the raw materials! I don't want to lose the respect of my amazing fellow decorators or, worse,

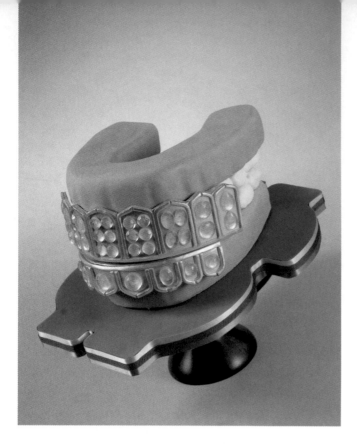

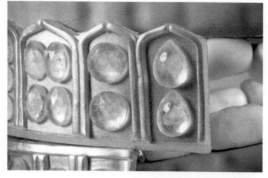

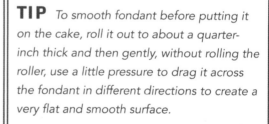

rot out my teeth! In the bakery we often talk about our tendency to have "cake dreams"—well, I keep having a recurring dream in which I have a set of invincible golden teeth that allows me to eat cake and icing all day long without ever brushing or flossing . . .

. . . so what does *that* say about me?

> **TIP** *To smooth fondant before putting it on the cake, roll it out to about a quarter-inch thick and then gently, without rolling the roller, use a little pressure to drag it across the fondant in different directions to create a very flat and smooth surface.*

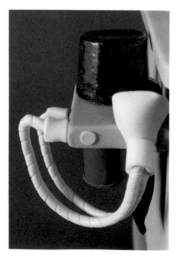

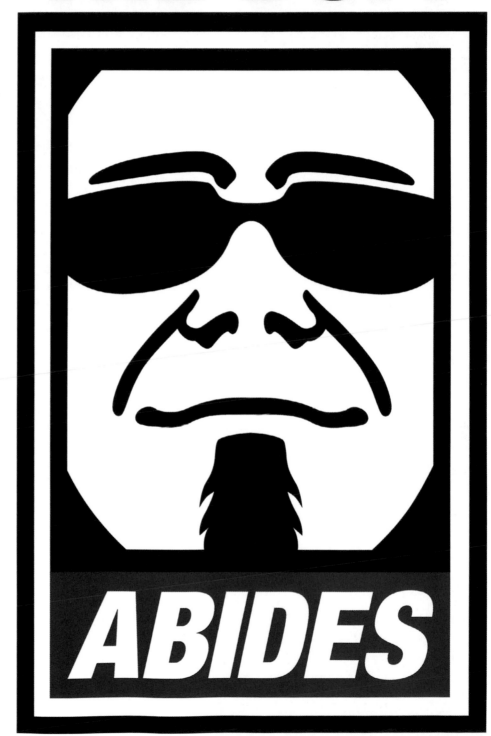

AN ORAL HISTORY OF ACE OF CAKES

In an exclusive conversation, we talk to the following Food Network executives:

Brooke Johnson,
President, Food Network

Bob Tuschman,
*Senior Vice President,
Programming and
Production*

Allison Page,
*Vice President,
Programming*

Charles Nordlander,
*Vice President, Program
Development*

Susie Fogelson,
*Vice President,
Marketing and Brand
Strategy*

Carrie Welch,
*Vice President,
Public Relations*

Brian Lando,
*Director,
Programming*

Katie Ilch,
*Consumer Marketing Director,
Advertising and Branding*

Lisa Krueger,
*Director,
Public Relations*

Here, in their own words, is the story of how *Ace of Cakes* landed on Food Network.

After Food Network was turned on to Duff by fellow cake decorator Colette Peters, he popped up as a competitor on *Food Network Challenge*.

Page: I met Duff in Sea Island, Georgia, when we were filming Food Network Challenge in 2005. The episode was the Spooky Cake & Candy Cook-Off, and Duff definitely stood out among the competitors. He didn't look or sound like any cake baker I'd ever met. My first thought was that this guy looked tough, but then he opened his mouth and that characteristic, disarming laugh came out, and I knew he was a softie on the inside. He was filled with this spirit of fun, and it was infectious!

Johnson: I had seen Duff on Food Network Challenge and thought he was an unusual-looking and unusually engaging personality. He was so far outside of what you would normally expect a baker to look like that I was very struck by him on that series.

Tuschman: Duff was instantly memorable—his rocker look, his offbeat style, his slacker humor—not to mention his amazing vision and technique in cakes.

Ilch: We'd set out to do an ad campaign for Food Network Challenge and needed someone to make us some outrageous cakes. Programming recommended a distinctive character in the show, Duff Goldman. Duff actually ended up making two cakes, one of Styrofoam and one real. He did more than make the cakes—he helped us make the ad come to life.

Krueger: I was in Phoenix, where we were shooting several episodes of Food Network Challenge. Duff and Geof were competing in the mystery cake challenge and were working on a hilarious cake that eventually fell apart. Instead of leaving an empty table, Duff made a big showing of carrying a small fondant fish to the table as their finished product, and the whole spectacle made me laugh so hard I had tears in my eyes.

Fogelson: Duff was made for reality TV. He and the crew are wildly entertaining characters and some of the best reality TV out there. Geof and Mary Alice are just gold.

When Food Network was first presented with the idea that a docusoap centered around cake decorating would be a good match for the network, the reactions ranged from enthusiasm to hesitation.

Nordlander: Well, I had come to Food Network from A&E, where we were having a lot of success with character-driven reality shows like *Growing Up Gotti* and *Dog, the Bounty Hunter*. I loved the idea of bringing that kind of series to Food Network, especially since one of the main reasons I was hired was to develop new programming that was different from traditional shows on the channel. And a reality series starring Duff was definitely not going to be traditional!

Johnson: I liked the idea. We had wanted to do a culinary docusoap but had never found the right environment. Duff's rock-and-roll bakery seemed like it might just be the environment we had been looking for. One of the architectural advantages is that there was some inherent drama about how and when and if the superelaborate cakes would be successfully completed. Another plus was that cakes are probably the most visually exciting element in the world of food, so this was a great subject for television.

Welch: I thought, great! Then, wow, this is going to be really different for Food Network. We had just started to get into the reality realm with *The Next Food Network Star* around that time, so it was really exciting to know we would go even further.

Page: My first thought was: that's a show I would love for Food Network to do and that I would personally love to watch.

Tuschman: I thought if anyone could pull off a reality series set in a bake shop, it was Duff Goldman. I always say, "Duff marches to the beat of his own mixer."

Krueger: I thought it was a great idea. Our audience has always loved cake shows and Duff has a really fun energy, so he seemed like a natural fit.

Fogelson: I was told there was a show called *F—— You Let's Bake* being pitched, and the pilot was circulated around Food Network. The lead was a guy named Duff, and he was a baker who did awesome cakes and was in a rock band.

The original pitch presentation for a Duff-centric show included a five-minute demo, or sizzle reel, which helps give networks a visual idea of the tone the producers had envisioned for the potential series. Taking a cue from Duff's earlier stage show, the sizzle reel retained its edgy title, *F—— You Let's Bake!*—a style that was certainly different from existing Food Network programming.

Nordlander: It was the summer of 2005, and I'd been at Food Network for just a couple of months, working as their first-ever VP of program development. Authentic came in to pitch me a reality series starring Duff and showed me the five-minute demo for *F—— You Let's Bake*. This was the first time I'd ever seen or heard of Duff, but others in our programming department knew him from his participation in a couple of cake competitions on Food Network Challenge. And those who knew Duff liked him a lot, describing him as talented and funny, with a great personality.

I thought the sizzle reel was amazing—really well produced and hugely entertaining. But here's the ironic part: even though this demo sold me on trying to do a series, the approach it took was completely not right for Food Network. Duff was pretty much portrayed as a badass dude, and I seem to remember a lot of obscenities—beginning with the title, of course! Not that all of this wasn't hilarious to watch, but there was no way on earth that the G-rated, family-friendly Food Network was going to put something like this on the air. But it was clear that Duff and the gang at Charm City were great people/characters whom I wanted to watch. With that kind of foundation, I never doubted that we could come up with a great show that was right for Food Network. I just didn't know at the time what it would be.

A funny anecdote about that demo: I was at a big executive meeting in FN's boardroom one day after the series was in production but still didn't have a final title. The room was packed, and I'd forgotten that many if not most of the people there weren't from programming, so they didn't know that the demo was titled *F—— You Let's Bake*. But as I was speaking to the group about the series, I kept referring to it by that name, and when I noticed the stunned look on their faces I realized they had no idea why I was dropping F-bombs left and right. It was embarrassing but pretty funny, and I quickly explained the situation.

Ilch: I was excited about the possibility of the show but was nervous about how audiences would react to the non-G-rated content.

Welch: I remember being called over to the desk of someone in marketing who'd gotten a copy of the *F—— You Let's Bake!* DVD. It gave quite a look into Duff's fun, weird world that I'd never seen before. I wanted to go hang out with them!

Page: It wasn't a piece that Food Network could air, but it proved that Duff was multifaceted and one of the more intriguing people we'd ever come across.

Johnson: I thought the sizzle reel was hysterical! We all thought the tape was the freshest and most unusual thing we had seen in the culinary world in many years.

Tuschman: Though I saw the potential for Duff to reach a wide audience, it wasn't through this tape. It emphasized a darker, heavy metal, angry rocker side. What I always loved about Duff was that behind this rock-n-roll baker was an incredibly sweet, funny, slightly goofy guy.

Welch: I still think about it! It's not the average Food Network sizzle reel, and it really got everyone talking in the cubicles here. People were passing it around, saying, "Did you see this?" and "Can you believe they're thinking about making it into a show?" It was exciting!

Despite the enthusiasm, Nordlander did encounter some resistance.

Nordlander: I have to give props to my boss at the time, Kathleen Finch, who is now head of the DIY Network. Kathleen was fearless and really encouraged me to go forward with developing the show, even though a reality series like this was a big gamble. We didn't know if viewers would like or accept a show that was so different from FN's usual programming, plus it was much more expensive to produce. Over time, we developed the idea of each episode being a week in the life of Charm City Cakes.

Season One debuted with six episodes, but the network was still unsure how the show would be received.

Tuschman: We called it the Zen Bakery. We simply realized that *Ace of Cakes* was unlike any other reality show. It was fun, unpredictable, and quirky. It worked on its own terms.

Nordlander: The series was a hit right from the start, and there's nothing like great ratings to help a network feel good about a new show.

events, and they're from all age groups, backgrounds, regions. . . . They're so enthusiastic and dedicated to Charm City Cakes, it's really fun to see.

Aside from a business perspective, many executives had their own personal reaction to the show as well.

Johnson: I think my reaction was very much in line with most of our viewers' reactions. I loved and continue to love the quirky characters in Duff's bakery and how they interact together. The process alone of building these incredible cakes would be terrifically compelling, but the magic of the show is the addition of the baker-artists who work with Duff.

Page: From day one it was obvious that our audience loved the show as much as we do.

Fogelson: *Ace of Cakes* brings in a younger demo for Food Network. It's an edgier show for us. It's perfect for the direction we want to take prime in that it has very compelling characters and big food and is story-driven.

Welch: The real story is how the audience grew so steadily and captured its own loyal fans. I've seen fans of Duff and the show at

Tuschman: Personally, I love watching it at home for the same reason everybody else does—it's a funny, unpredictable experience with distinctive characters who are also incredibly talented.

Nordlander: I've been with Duff in public a couple of times, and it's amazing how fans just keep coming up to him. I also think that for a lot of people, Charm City Cakes represents the sort of workplace they fantasize about having. And the show is inspiring for people—Duff has built a successful business playing by his own rules and never forgetting about fun.

I've really loved *Ace of Cakes* from the first episode. Of course, the fact that I love a show doesn't necessarily mean a thing

when it comes to ratings, so it's especially nice for me to see the show succeed. I also have to acknowledge the outstanding job done by Kelly McPherson and Authentic in producing *Ace of Cakes*.

Fogelson: I love the show and always laugh when I watch it. That's not something you can always say about Food Network shows. I mean, I enjoy our programming, but I'm not often caught laughing out loud. Geof's reactions are the best. His chemistry and the way he plays off of Duff's personality is my kind of humor. And Mary Alice is so smart and capable that she could literally do anything (run for office?), plus she is one of the most sincere and gentle souls I've ever met.

Lando: I really understood how much people liked *Ace of Cakes* when Steve Carell was visibly nervous to meet Duff. When giant movie stars are starstruck by you, you've made it big.

Welch: I think people react to how lovable and just plain nice everyone who works there is. And it's the real deal—anyone who has met them knows that Duff and team are legit!

Page: I'm really proud to have *Ace of Cakes* on our air. It's the kind of show that makes me love my job. It's so well produced, and the people at Charm City are clever, funny, and genuine.

Ilch: I haven't met one person who doesn't like *Ace of Cakes*. It always seems that they have a favorite character, whether it's Geof, Mary Alice, "The Girls," or Duff. The cast of characters offers something different for everyone. The breadth and diversity of the fans is so great—from little kids writing in asking to meet the cast to all my friends wanting Charm City Cakes to create their wedding cake, to all the aspiring bakers who have submitted their cake photos to FN.com's "cake community."

Has the success of Ace of Cakes changed anything about the way Food Network now develops and/or produces new shows?

Nordlander: Apart from showing that the right docuseries could work on Food Network, I think *Ace* helped pave the way for considering other new types of formats for the channel. It helped to demonstrate what was possible when you had the right mix. That last part is especially important. Keep in mind that Food Network has always been driven by its on-air personalities, much more so than any other network. Plus, shows and specials that focused on cakes generally rated pretty well. So, by bringing together great personalities and amazing cakes in a docuseries, we were giving viewers what they wanted, but wrapped in a new kind of format.

Page: *Ace of Cakes* raised the bar and opened our minds to new kinds of programming.

Welch: *Ace of Cakes* came at a time when we were starting to get into the reality realm, and its success has only shown that we can and should explore the genre more.

How do you think Ace of Cakes compares to other shows in the genre?

Page: *Ace of Cakes* is real reality! There are so many "reality" shows on TV that have nothing to do with reality. It's made me dislike the term, because it has no meaning. The beauty of Charm City Cakes is that what actually takes place at this bakery is so compelling that there's no need to construct anything to make a good television show. That's a rare thing indeed.

Johnson: Many reality shows feel stagey, artificial, and forced. *Ace of Cakes* feels just the opposite—real, fresh, understated. Additionally, many or most reality shows have an undercurrent of meanspiritedness, and *Ace* is again the exact opposite of that.

Tuschman: *Ace of Cakes* has definitely set a new template in the reality world. There's no forced drama, no trying to make heroes and villains, no trying to manipulate audience reactions.

Nordlander: "Real" reality shows, to be honest, can often be very boring to watch. Trust me, I've seen it. So reality shows are often produced to deliver more conflict, drama, and sense of competition. But Duff and the Charm City gang had no interest in becoming your typical reality show stars—in fact, I think the latter was their nightmare. Ironically, producing a docuseries that's genuine and honest is a whole lot harder than producing one where you manipulate the characters or action to get what you want.

Ilch: It's unlike *The Girls Next Door, Big Brother*, and *Living Lohan*, where their reality is anything but. It's just fun. And I think if everyone had a little more cake in their life, their lives would be too.

Fogelson: It never feels contrived. Since I've been to Charm City Cakes twice, I can attest to the fact that it's pretty much what you see on air. The first time I went there I was struck by how quiet and mellow the environment was. The air smelled like sugar, and despite Mary Alice's fast-paced juggling of the front desk, it was pretty relaxing and cool. A bunch of artists at work, really, creating magic from sugar.

Lando: More than other docusoap show I've seen on TV, *Ace* does not have any hint of manipulation or contrived drama. It's as if the staff of Charm City invites you to hang out with them as they really are during a pressure-packed week.

Welch: *Ace of Cakes* has great drama—Will they get the cakes done? Will the cake make it in one piece? Will they get there in time?—with genuine, fun personalities. The show is honest, with no negativity infused to get the drama across.

Krueger: Viewers can tell when people are being fake on air, so the shows that tend to be successful for us stem from the hosts or casts being true to who they are day in and out.

Do friends and family offer up any stories/ comments of their own when they find out your involvement with the show?

Tuschman: I'm always struck by the amazing amount of affection people have for this show.

Ilch: Inevitably someone I know, unrelated to my job or the food world, will mention thatl they know someone that Charm City Cakes has made a cake for—a fire engine, a dog, so random. Still, I often wonder how they heck they get all those cakes done.

Page: Mostly, when people find out that I work at Food Network and that I know Duff, they tell me I'm incredibly lucky.

Nordlander: People want to know one of three things: first, are the characters really the way they seem on the show? Second, how can they can get a job working at Charm City Cakes? And third, could I call Duff and ask him to make a cake for them? By the way, the answers to those questions are: (1) Yes, absolutely. (2) Move to Baltimore and go to art school. (3) Yes, if you'll to drive to Baltimore to pick it up with serious cash in tow.

Lando: Before the show aired, I would tell people that I was working on a show about a really cool bakery in Baltimore. Their initial reaction was generally "That sounds kind of boring." Then the show aired. Those same people came to find me to apologize and say, "I totally get it now."

Welch: For me, it's just constant "Oh, my god, I love that show!" every time I tell someone that I work on it or that I know Duff. Everyone loves Duff.

Do you have a particularly favorite cake, episode, or Duff story?

Ilch: For the Season Two launch, we worked with Duff and team on our second ad campaign. The concept of the TV spot was this: the local clowns were launching a campaign to put the *Ace of Cakes* out of business because he'd been infringing on their party appearance territory. No one wants clowns anymore; they all want the Ace of Cakes and his amazing cakes at their party. It was a freezing day outside Charm City Cakes, and the shoot lasted until about 4 a.m. Duff and the team were good sports and really got into the shoot. In one scene, the clowns were running off after vandalizing the Charm City Cakes van. Totally off script, Duff hands off the cake he is holding, bolts down the street after the actor/clown, and tackles him. The guy didn't know what hit him, the crew was dying with laughter, and we got the shot that made it into the commercial. It was a great night.

Welch: I've worked with Duff since the show's launch and enjoy everything about him, especially his phone calls, where I usually end up spending over an hour talking and laughing with him. Duff stories? How about the time he pranked my assistant Nils by prending to be a stalker viewer. . . . The time Duff made a cake for an event in New York City, and after a superlong night with the event ending at 2 a.m., he went outside only to discover his van had been towed. . . . And the icing on the cake, if you will, was

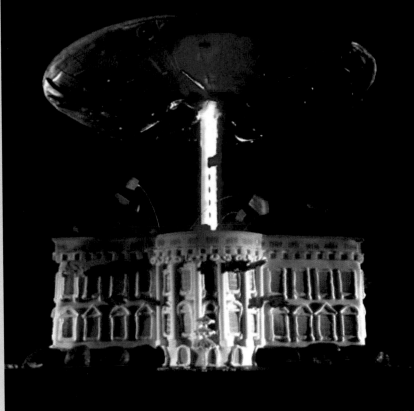

This cake depicting a scene from Independence Day features a specially constructed illuminated tube that also acted as support for the cake on top.

standing in the Mall of America watching Duff and Geoff decorate the World's Largest Cupcake by throwing silver candy at it. They'd been gracious enough to make the cake and break the record for our charity Share Our Strength, which was hosting the largest bake sale ever for their Great American Bake Sale childhood hunger relief effort. Oh, and then Duff lit the cake on fire. He had only hinted to me that there might be some pyrotechnics inside that very large candle—and you should have seen the reaction of mall security . . .

Nordlander: My favorite cake had two parts to it: one part was shaped like a Netflix envelope and the other looked like a Chinese food container filled with noodles. While it wasn't the biggest, fanciest, or most colorful cake, the execution was really flawless, and it was one of those simple but brilliant ideas: who can't relate to a night at home with Netflix and Chinese takeout? My favorite episode included the cake shaped like a beaver for a family with that last name. I saw the rough cut, before it was heavily edited to meet Food Network's G rating, and I laughed so hard I cried. Duff and the Charm City gang did every beaver joke imaginable, but they did them all as clever double entendres delivered with a straight face. It was genius.

My favorite Duff memory occurred when I traveled down to Baltimore to take out the cast and crew for a celebratory dinner to thank them for all the hard work. I was there with my daughter, Chloe, who was fifteen at the time, and we went to One-Eyed Mike's in Fells Point. Chloe was a big fan of the show, so she was very excited to be there at dinner with Duff and the rest of the Charm City gang. While sitting at the table, she called her friend on her cell to give her the play-by-play when Duff looked over and asked, "Do you want me to talk to your friend?" Two seconds later, Duff had Chloe's phone and was chatting away. It was a really cool thing for him to do, and my daughter loved it, of course—she's never forgotten that night.

Page: My favorite Duff memory . . . that's tough! Meeting him for the first time when he competed on Food Network Challenge was a very special moment for me. I realized in an instant that this guy lived his life in the present. He wasn't wondering who would win the next day or how he would look on TV or how he could get his own show (ironically). He was there to make a spooky-looking cake and to have fun doing it. He wasn't trying to be compelling. He was just being the beautiful, hilarious, inspired, crazy person that is Duff.

Lando: My favorite cake so far is the Exorcist cake Duff made in the fourth season. It's not every day that you turn on the Food Network to see a figure with its head spinning around 360 degrees while spewing green vomit.

The funny thing is, I'm sure that disgusting-looking cake actually tasted great.

Fogelson: The most memorable cake, not necessarily my favorite, was the cake made to look like a Campbell's soup can. We shot Duff for a paid media campaign and featured this cake (Campbell's was an on-air *Ace of Cakes* advertiser). The gist of the spot was that Duff was stealing the thunder of, and upstaging, clowns on the party circuit. Duff had to beat up a bunch of clowns in the spot, which he seemed to enjoy a little too much. *Yes!* Also, the Super Bowl cake was a mind-boggling marvel of cake.

Krueger: My favorite Duff memory is of when he competed on Food Network Challenge in the Mystery Cakes episode. From building a runaway boat to naming it the SS *Colette*, to presenting a fondant fish as the finished product, he was hysterical to watch!

Johnson: I like the Wrigley Field cake episode, when Duff says, "Look, they made a stadium that looks like my cake!"

If you could have Duff and Charm City Cakes design your ultimate dream cake, what would it be?

Johnson: A piano the size of a toy piano. Playing the piano is my hobby, so a Charm City cake shaped like a piano would play very beautiful music indeed.

Ilch: Big Fat George, my orange-and-white cat, sleeping on his back on the couch.

Welch: A big tennis court with Monica Seles hitting a winner against Steffi Graf. I've played tennis since I was five and never quite got over Seles losing the number one ranking at the height of her game because that random guy stabbed her with a kitchen knife.

Krueger: I'm a big Patriots fan, so maybe a life-size Tom Brady cake?

Nordlander: You know, I do think I sense a wedding cake in my not-too-distant future, and when the time comes, I'll be giving Duff a call.

Page: Duff would come up with something far more interesting than I could ever imagine. My dream cake would be whatever he wanted to make.

Anything else you'd like to add?

Johnson: We at Food Network so appreciate the work that Duff and his team do for the show. It's been a tremendous addition of our prime-time lineup, and I know it's not always been easy to have cameras and crews in the middle of their business and work environment. More important, we appreciate the opportunity to showcase such culinary artists and to allow our viewers a window into their fascinating world.

Fogelson: I'd like to see Duff eat more cake. I never see him eat cake.

Lando: I think it's refreshing how much Duff has stayed the same through it all. Here's a guy who owns a successful business, stars in a hit TV show, and makes cakes for some of the biggest events in the country yet is still happiest when he gets to act like a kid. He had a good time at the Harry Potter premiere. He enjoyed making a cake for the Super Bowl. But his smile was never bigger than when he got to press all the buttons in a fire truck.

Tuschman: I was blown away by the Harry Potter cake. The skill and technique needed to recreate Hogwarts out of basically flour, sugar, and eggs is just unbelievable.

Krueger: Duff and the team at Charm City are an incredibly talented bunch of people, and I hope they keep creating unique and fabulous cakes that we can capture for years to come!

Welch: They're such a wonderful, hilarious, smart group of people to work with and have as part of the Food Network family!

> *People say all of the time, "Oh, man, I couldn't do what you do!" You can, you really can.*
>
> —DUFF

the "ADAM" cake

SHYLOCK

GOLDY

ADAM GOLDSTEIN Baker

Hometown: Charm City
Education: BS in psychology, University of Maryland, College Park
Favorite hobby: Playing with Shylock, the wonderdog Boston Terrier
Fun fact: The "Adam" cake featured on the Charm City Cakes website was my wedding cake.
Favorite movies: *Talkies*
Favorite books: *Harold and the Purple Crayon, Titus Groan, The Emigrants*
Favorite music: Pavement

In his own words . . .

Ace of Cakes/Charm City Cakes: You don't have to be a philosophy major to understand that the necessary and sufficient feature of both these phrases is *cakes*. Without it you're merely left with a city's sobriquet or half of a godforsaken nineties band. Yet watch an episode of *Ace of Cakes*, and you'd think these tasty, sweet confections were magically transmogrified through the bakery walls or whipped up by those creepy baking elves in their hollowed-out oak tree sweatshop across the street. No. These cakes are not simply conjured up at a moment's notice, ready to be covered in fondant and bejeweled with shiny dragées. Someone is in the bakery at 4:30 in the morning, creaming butter, slinging batter, and whipping up gallons of ganache. Hi. That would be me.

I first met Duff years ago, when I had a job in the produce department of a gourmet store here in Baltimore. Duff was a personal chef and frequently came to the store to purchase his ingredients. Carrying around a clipboard and wearing an immaculate chef's coat and shorts, Duff strutted through the produce section like a hipster version of Emeril or Wolfgang. Of course I had to give him a hard time, and we soon became friends. Eventually, though, we lost touch.

In a strange twist of fate, I met up with Duff again a few years later when my soon-to-be wife and I were shopping for our wedding cake. She dragged me to some odd-looking bakery in the middle of nowhere that she had heard did amazing things with cake. You

Young Adam and one of his first cakes

Preparing
samplers for
new clients

guessed it: Charm City Cakes. I soon realized that the owner of this place was none other than Duff Goldman. A couple of weeks later, when we came back to sign the paperwork and finalize the cake design, Duff offered me a job. How could I possibly turn it down? My wedding cake was now free.

The original bakery was nothing like the sleek, expansive, colorful building we now occupy. Put simply—it was a dump. Since I had no formal culinary training and very little experience with large-scale baking, it took me a while to get into the swing of things. Fortunately for me, when I started, the notion of TV crews, cameramen, and fanfare was inconceivable. In the beginning there were stretches where customers were sparse and cake orders were few. This gave me a bit of a learning curve and enabled me to experiment with various recipes and baking techniques. Now, with close to fifty flavors available and scores of clients knocking down our door, I am grateful for those early days when I was able to learn the ropes. We must be doing something right, because our cakes always get rave reviews from even the most die-hard foodies.

But in order to prove to people that I'm actually on *Ace of Cakes*, I have to record the show and play it back in slow motion, frame by frame, constantly rewinding and pausing as if I were dissecting the Zapruder film—just to maybe catch a glimpse of my shadow in the far corner of the

Adam with Charm City Cakes intern Joseph Weinstein Avery

Adam's Baking Tips

+ To avoid catastrophe, store eggs and butter at 38°F. To avoid a "caketastrophe," allow them to come to room temperature before mixing.

+ To restrain hair without the stigma of a hairnet, wear a beanie.

+ Do not leave cake unattended around vultures, jackals, or underpaid art students.

+ If your cake turns out a little dry, try eliminating an egg white or two next time.

+ If your butter cake turns out rather heavy, chances are that you didn't cream the butter and sugar long enough—at least five minutes is a good rule of thumb.

+ To take your chocolate cake to the next level, try adding brewed coffee to the mix.

+ If your recipe calls for baking soda, make sure there is an acidic component (buttermilk, vinegar, citrus) in your ingredients as well—unless, of course, you're going for the always popular soap-flavored cake.

+ Preheating your oven is not optional in baking.

+ The toothpick test is still the best way to determine if a cake is done—give it a poke in the center, and if the toothpick is clean, you're good to go.

+ For perfect, easy-to-spread ganache, use slightly more (by weight) cream than chocolate. So if you have 1½ pounds of chocolate, use about 1¾ pounds of cream. And make sure to allow for ample time for the ganache to set up.

+ When making a meringue, it is better to underwhip your egg whites a little than risk overwhipping and drying them out.

+ When whipping egg whites, make certain that your bowl is clean and that you haven't gotten any yolk in the mix. Fat spells doom to light, fluffy meringues.

+ Restrain yourself—or have someone else restrain you—from cutting into the cake until it is completely cool. If you plan to ice the cake, this is particularly important.

Clients receive a sampler of potential flavors from which to choose.

screen. The high point of my television career occurred not long ago, when I was recognized at the grocery store. So what if I was dressed from head to toe in Charm City Cakes garb and the woman insisted on calling me Geof?

As the baker of Charm City Cakes, I can't tell you how many times I cringe when I hear the same statement over and over: "Sure, they look cool, but there's no way they can taste any good." As I said, we've got almost fifty flavors and they're all delicious. There's no way we'd still be in business if the cakes didn't taste good. Trust me. I know. I bake Charm City's cakes.

Now, unfortunately for me, I'm the only member of Charm City Cakes without even the faintest whiff of artistic ability. Sadly, my art skills peaked in the third grade, and it's been downhill ever since. As a result, I'm banished to the kitchen—the belly of the beast—and rarely

venture out into the artistic hive of the decorators. I'm just waiting for that one costumer who wants her wedding cake bedizened with turkeys that look like hands. That's right in my wheelhouse— my potential big moment in the spotlight. Until then, I'll remain in the background, behind the mixers and cake racks—out of sight, out of mind.

Just remember, though: all those elaborately painted frescoes, ornithologically accurate birds, and intricately piped curlicues festooned on the cakes won't amount to anything if it doesn't taste awesome. It all starts and ends with the cake.

WHAT'S IT LIKE TO BE ON TV?

*"We must be willing to get rid of the life we've planned,
so as to have the life that is waiting for us."*
—JOSEPH CAMPBELL

At this point I could write a whole book called The Guide for Normal People Who End Up on Television. Okay, so let's be honest, when we were all first approached about being on TV, everyone was weirded out. We've all seen all those train wrecks of shows that glorify mediocre people whining and screaming a lot. *Ace of Cakes* was never intended to be a "cooking" show. It was never intended to be some scripted faux soap drama. It was always understood that our show was about how we go about the daily routine of doing something amazing. And now I marvel at what they capture, the same way I marvel at all the bakery's completed cakes every Friday night. I step out of my own skin and see, really, as an objective observer how incredible the people around me are. The film crew, the production team, the network, and my staff are some of the best artists I'll ever know. My spidey sense is always tingling with joy at this incredible collection of people we're on this incredible adventure with.

I love my staff, I love our work, and I really do love our how. But no one can really prepare you for being on television. How can I describe being a normal, everyday working

cook who's suddenly on TV, under a nationwide microscope? Imagine having every word you speak, facial expression you emote, and action you take suddenly recorded for all to see. I've always had cake nightmares, usually about once a week, but now I have microphone nightmares. I wake up thinking that everything I've said has been recorded (which is actually mostly true). When I get to work, there's a little wireless microphone that I have to stick to my shirt, and two audio operators can hear everything I say. Then the cameras are primed, tapes are put in, and my whole day is recorded. Imagine that every day for nine months out of the year.

Now, I know what you're thinking: boo-flippin'-hoo, anyone fortunate enough to be in my position should be thankful every single day. Believe me, I am—it's an opportunity a lot of people would kill for. But right now it's just you and me talking. I'm not complaining, but everyone's always asking me what it's like—and the simple answer is that the entire experience is a little unreal. Make that *very* unreal. Just today when I was designing cakes for clients, I saw people stop outside the bakery and pose for pictures. When this first started happening, I was mystified, but now I just smile. How cool is that? Our fans will come from all over the country and take pictures of *my bakery*! I guess I might eventually get used to it, but it hasn't happened yet—and don't plan on it anytime soon.

> If someone wants it hanging from the ceiling with motors in it and spinning around and shooting out bottle rockets, we'll figure out how to do that.
>
> —DUFF

*Cameraman Mark Lafleur
captures Erica and I discussing
her cake design for the book.*

Fun is our goal. How can you make nice cakes and entertain millions of people if you're *not* having fun? I've seen people try to entertain when they're not having fun, and man, is it obvious! How about some highlights? Here's an abbreviated list of some the fun things we've experienced while making the show:

- ✦ We got to go to the Super Bowl (and while there I gave one of our directors, Brandee, a mohawk and got knocked out by our sound guy). We also swam with dolphins!

- ✦ We made a cake for Jay Leno, and I was a guest on *The Tonight Show.*

- ✦ We went to Lebowski Fest, and my band got to play with Mike Doughty.

- ✦ We made a cake for the premiere of *Harry Potter and the Order of the Phoenix,* walked a real red carpet, saw the movie, and met Daniel Radcliffe and Rupert Grint at the Potter-themed afterparty.

- ✦ We made Macy's 150th birthday cake!

- ✦ We got to make a cake for a shark ray named Sweet Pea and scuba dive with her, her boyfriend, "Scooter," and their friends—a bunch of sharks.

- ✦ I fell off a stage while lighting fireworks for the Washington Monument.

- ✦ We got to make the cake for the premiere of *Get Smart* and hang out with Steve Carell, the coolest guy ever.

- ✦ I got to snowboard down Federal Hill in Baltimore and fall on my face.

- ✦ Geof and I saw a billboard of ourselves in Times Square in New York City.

- ✦ We made a cake for the premiere of *Kung Fu Panda* and got to meet and rub the belly of one of my personal heroes, Jack Black.

Celebrating with the cast and crew of King of the Hill during the show's final table read.

Celebrating the 100th episode of Lost with the show's cast.

✦ I got to dance with a bunch of Rockettes at Radio City Music Hall—good thing I can decorate cakes!

✦ We got to make the cake for the premiere of *Hairspray* and meet John Waters, Adam Shankman, and the cast.

✦ I got to run the firefighters' challenge course, which consisted of hauling several pounds a firefighting gear through one hell of a gauntlet.

✦ I got beat up twice on the ice by the legendary Hanson brothers of *Slap Shot* fame, as part of Hockey Fights Cancer's fund-raising effort.

✦ I got to ride in a tank and present a cake on the field at Camden Yards for the Army's birthday.

✦ I attended a fund-raiser with Tony Hawk, another personal hero.

✦ I got to help raise money for the Howard County Fire Department and the Johns Hopkins Children's Cancer unit.

✦ I voiced an animated version of myself with Geof on *King of the Hill*.

✦ We fought hunger issues with Share Our Strength and Meals on Wheels.

✦ I saw myself and my staff replicated as puppets.

✦ I flew over Oahu in an Army Black Hawk.

✦ I heliboarded in Alaska.

✦ We were joined by Jorge Garcia as we made a cake for the 100th episode of *Lost*.

✦ I met several New York Yankees, including Derek Jeter and Yogi Berra, with Mary Smith and Geof at a celebration of their new stadium.

But the most amazing thing for me is not all the crazy stuff but all the incredible emails, letters, photos, pictures, and drawings we get from viewers. We've received pictures of little kids dressing up as *us* for Halloween. We get drawings from other artists, young and old, from all over the world. Wherever I go, people show pictures of cakes they've made and tell me how inspired they are by what they see us do on the show. I've said it before, but we have the best fans on the planet. I don't know what draws them in so much—maybe it's nice to see something positive and fun on TV; maybe our fans just like to see us working under deadline

and getting the job done and laughing a lot in the process; maybe they just like cake. Whatever it is, it's overwhelming and humbling.

Maybe we really are funny and entertaining. But truth be told, we really are who you see—we're not rehearsed personalities. That's the best part. We're real human beings who go to work, play in bands, go to shows, and hang out around town. Maybe it's our accessibility that people love—that we're the same people on camera as we are off; we're the same people as you!

I love the variety in our fans. Kids like us, adults like us, guys like us, girls like us—it's incredible when some crazy tattooed biker-looking guy says, "Hey, man, love your show!" Cops like our show, the military likes our show! I think maybe people see us overcoming obstacles while creating art out of something as fleeting as cake, and they *relate*! They get it!

{Again, it's not the fancy stuff, but the millions of people we reach and inspire or entertain that

*Assisting
Ace of Cakes
director
Matt Carr
in shooting
the Schofield
Barracks
Family Day
celebration
Blackhawk
Cake, on
location at
Wheeler Army
Airfield in
Oahu, Hawaii.*

makes this whole thing so cool. For example, as I type this Geof and I are flying to Los Angeles to be guest voices on *King of the Hill*, but before we do we're spending the day with a kid from the Make-A-Wish foundation—but then have to race back and create a cake for the Girl Scouts

of Maryland. Hollywood stuff is fun, but making cakes for and with kids is not only amazing but also inspiring. We see ourselves reflected in their eyes, and it helps us keep a perspective on the journey we've all been so fortunate to take.

> *You have to remain open while creating a cake. You want it to look like your original concept, your drawing, but you can't get stuck in it. Sometimes the cake is going to go a different way, and you just have to let it.*
>
> —DUFF

SQUAAKS!

ROCK CONTROL

10S BLACK

ELENA FOX **Decorator**

Hometown: Babylon, New York

Education: BFA in graphic design, SUNY New Paltz, New York

Favorite hobbies: Playing music, running, collecting toys, spoiling my cat rotten

Fun fact: I can walk on my hands.

Favorite movie: *Carrie, Star Wars: Episodes IV, V, VI, Raising Arizona*, most comedies from the 1980s with preposterous plots

Favorite books: Anything by Christopher Moore, most things by Kurt Vonnegut, *Maus 1* and *Maus 2* by Art Spiegelman, *The Very Hungry Caterpillar* by Eric Carle

Favorite music: Everything from Patsy Cline to Van Halen, but The Beatles, The Kinks, The Pixies, and Pavement are among my top faves

Favorite nondessert dish to create or eat: Anything on a barbecue in the summertime

In her own words . . .

I'm the youngest of four children and grew up in the seafaring town of Babylon, on the south shore of Long Island, New York. We lived in a small house positioned snugly between two boatyards on a street that ended with a canal. My mother is an elementary school art teacher and my father builds machinery that I've always liked to refer to as his robots. My parents are some of the biggest artistic influences in my life; my mom is also a painter. Realizing that I loved to draw and paint from a very young age, she was always very encouraging, and we spent a lot of time doing art projects together. And my dad and I were always creating some crazy cartoony world on a giant piece of paper.

My siblings range from between six and ten years older than me. I always wanted to hang out with them and their friends, go to rock concerts, stay up late, wear "cool" clothes, and so on. I was fortunate that they made me feel as if I were one of

the big kids, rather than a tagalong. Aside from art, my siblings are also responsible for some of my earliest musical influences: they exposed me to a lot of seventies classic rock and heavy metal, as well as a lot of eighties new wave and postpunk—all of which would later resurface as influences in a band of my own, The Squaaks.

I'm not sure that there was an exact point of my life when I said, "I'm going to be an artist." My whole life, even today, has been a constant battle between my desire to create visual art and my desire to be a musician. As a child, I excelled as a flute player, and I was determined to go to Juilliard and play with the New York City Philharmonic. Of course this all changed the day I picked up a guitar in my sophomore year of high school. Like most teenagers, I was *not* listening to classical music, and when I realized I could actually play the very music I listened to, my focus changed from high school band to extra-extracurricular rock band. This actually freed my schedule enough to allow me to take more art classes.

Around this time, I joined the set crew of my school's drama department, where I constructed and painted all sorts of props, from five-foot snakes to building facades. By graduation, I had my sights set on art school, figuring, If I'm going to be a musician, I'm going to play in a rock band. Successful rock bands don't come out of music school; if anything, they come from art school . . .

At college I dabbled in many different artistic fields, including sculpture, drawing, and painting, before finally settling on a degree in graphic design (which I was told was the only art degree that would yield any future jobs). I graduated with a BFA and four years' experience playing bass guitar with various friends and bands.

After school I had few jobs as a graphic designer in New York City and quickly decided it wasn't for me. I simply felt there was nothing more boring and creatively stifling than sitting in front of a computer all day—which had me really freaking out, seeing as how I'd spent the greater part of five years building a portfolio that was now completely immaterial. In the midst of my freak-out, I realized that if I were to be some sort of creative professional, I needed to have an open mind about what I was going to create professionally.

In the two years before I moved to Baltimore, I had some other jobs that I absolutely loved, such as being a makeup artist, a toy designer,

and a Halloween costumer—but I also did my fair share of bartending and waitressing to make my hideous Brooklyn rent. During this time, a friend of mine (a recent graduate of the Maryland Institute College of Art) asked me to play bass in his Baltimore-based rock band, which would later become The Squaaks. We spent some time playing shows up and down the East Coast, mostly between Brooklyn and Baltimore, before finally deciding that we'd like to stay in Baltimore, because most of our connections and fans were in Baltimore and we spent most of our time in Brooklyn avoiding eviction.

When I first moved to Baltimore in February 2006, I worked as a bartender at a popular restaurant in the art museum. One evening, a wedding planner came by with a very peculiar but awesome groom's cake: a perfect large-scale replica of the Yellow Submarine from the Beatles movie. It was huge and bright yellow and made the whole bar smell like vanilla. It completely blew me away, especially since I'm such a huge Beatles fan. I immediately thought, Whoa! That's somebody's job to make that? I could totally make that! Of course I had to know who'd made the cake. To my surprise, the wedding planner told me that Charm City Cakes was

only about two blocks away from us, so I went on a recon mission to scope out the bakery. I had to figure out some other way to nose around in there—and, with any luck, get hired.

Coincidentally, my boyfriend, Virat, got a phone call from an old friend of his named Chris. Chris had been working at Charm City Cakes

Sketching her cake design first helps Elena visualize the completed concept.

155

as a cake icer for Duff for quite a while and was looking to make a career change. He called to ask Virat if there was any availability where he worked as an architectural model builder. Virat said yes but also asked if perhaps I could take his place as an icer. Chris asked Virat if I could ice a cake, and Virat, not really knowing what that might entail, said, "Sure." So I got an interview—I couldn't believe it. (That's definitely a lesson to be learned: just say yes, no matter what.)

My interview with Duff was definitely the strangest I've ever had—but also easily the coolest and least stressful. All the decorators were quietly working at their stations and listening to some sixties pop music. Duff introduced me to everyone and showed me what I'd be doing, all of which took about five minutes. For the remaining fifteen minutes, he showed me the music room where he and his band practice, and we had a good conversation on the finer points of bass playing. In the beginning of the interview, Duff said, "It really is this

chill in here." I smiled and thought, Yeah, right! No workplace is this chill. But in hindsight, he was totally telling the truth!

Of course I had iced a cake before—my mom used to bake cakes all the time, and I would often slap the frosting on them for her—and so I started at Charm City Cakes as an icer. But though it sounds simple enough, icing a cake professionally is a whole other story. I'd seen fondant before on wedding cakes, but I never thought about the physics of how it actually stuck onto a cake or what the hell it was actually made of. I thought fondant worked like that chocolate Magic Shell syrup—you know, it goes on wet and dries instantly around whatever you pour it on to form an airtight chocolate helmet. I had no idea that it's the icing underneath that's crucial for making a fondanted cake look like a smooth, pristine cylinder.

My first day at the bakery was extremely intimidating. I was the new girl, walking into a place where all the employees are a tight-knit family of close friends with years of experience working with one another as well as the medium. Aside from the social awkwardness, what was even more frightening was the realization that

I pretty much, uh, had lied about being able to ice a cake. This was *so* not slapping the frosting on Mom's birthday cake. Cakes don't come out of the oven and get stacked into perfect tiers. If you look at the sides of any cake, there will be a lump here and an indentation there, and all these things need to be fixed with the right amount of cutting and spackling with buttercream.

I spent my entire first day trying to ice a single six-inch tier of a four-tier cake. Duff would come by to check on me, size up my wobbly tiers, and say, "Nope, not yet." Finally, after hours of toiling, I emerged from the kitchen covered in buttercream and holding my very first perfect-ish six-inch cake. I excitedly showed it to Duff, and he said, "Yer slower than a molasses goin' uphill in a snowstorm." I was a little disappointed, but I couldn't help but laugh. He said what he had to say to encourage me—he's obviously a funny guy, and for some reason, he had confidence that I would eventually get the hang of icing . . .

. . . and I did.

TIP *If you feel as if you're going to fall backward, resist the urge to put your hands out behind you; you could break your elbows or wrists!*

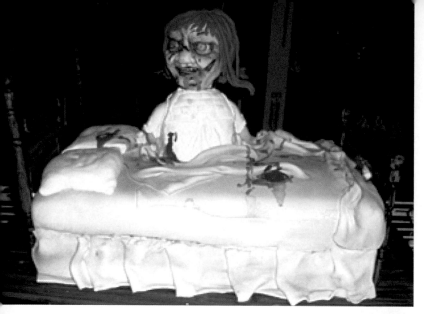

Elena's Exorcist *cake*

TIP *When icing a cake for fondant, always make sure your buttercream is well beaten and warm.*

worst thing that could happen would be that I just ended up icing cakes, which is nice work if you can get it. A few months later I got my first cake to decorate: a gothic-style Sweet Sixteen cake.

People may notice a trend in the kinds of cakes they see me doing on *Ace of Cakes*. Usually, I'm in charge of the most eccentric cakes: often gory horror-themed cakes, sci-fi cakes, or cakes that look like animals. I love Halloween—it's by far my favorite of all holidays. I love everything about it: the costumes, the fake blood, the candy. I also really like horror movies, especially old ones. As far as the animal cakes, well, it's no secret that I'm an animal lover, especially when it comes to cats! And although I have a reputation as the sci-fi girl, I think I kind of got the short end of the stick here, because these cakes tend to be really difficult—usually some kind of *gigantic* spaceship! One of the first things that Duff and I really bonded about, besides music, was how awesome the original *Star Wars* movies are. I love *Star Wars*, but not to the extent that some die-hard fans do. Somehow this translated to Duff and my coworkers as "Elena's a sci-fi expert, and henceforth she shall decorate all the cakes categorized thereunder." I honestly really do enjoy making the sci-fi cakes, it's just that sometimes I feel guilty when I have to research the original cast of *Star Trek*, being an "expert" and all.

It's hard for me to pick a favorite cake that I've created. I'd say it's a toss-up between the *Exorcist* cake and the piped five-tier wedding cake I made for the guitarist of my band. For those who haven't seen the episode, the *Exorcist* cake was a moving confectionary illustration of the famous scene where Regan sits up in bed and blows pea soup chunks from her rotating head. The wedding cake was a favorite because I *finally* got to do a pretty, piped cake for a change—and it was for a good friend.

One of the other most memorable cakes for

And now, here, I'd like to make a confession: when I got hired at Charm City Cakes as an icer, I had an ulterior motive: I really, really, *really* wanted to be a decorator. So I figured I'd do the best job I could at icing and then stick around during the week so I could do little jobs for the decorators. My plan was to get more and more opportunities to show my talent. I thought the

me personally is one that wasn't on the show (thankfully). It was easily the most heinous idea for a cake I've ever heard, and it made everyone in the bakery both laugh and cringe with utter disgust. It was a cake of a physician's model of an old person's derriere, complete with bedsores (let me type that again in case you missed it: B-E-D-S-O-R-E-S). This cake was presented at a proctologist's convention, so I guess in that context it makes sense—still gross!

When I first started work at Charm City Cakes, they'd just wrapped the first season of *Ace of Cakes*. I knew about the show but hadn't seen it, and I didn't think they were doing a second season, because nobody had mentioned it. Then one day out of nowhere, the camera crew came back, and suddenly I was wearing a mic and talking to a guy with a camera. Being filmed felt really weird at first. I felt as if everything I said was completely nonlinear and silly, and I spent a lot of time blushing. But by the end of my first season, I started to feel quite comfortable with the production team. This was largely because the guys and girls on our film crew are some of

the coolest people I've met since moving to Baltimore. They're all around the same ages as us, and we have a great time together. The bakery is much more of a party when they are around.

Never in my wildest dreams would I have thought I would end up on a reality show about making cakes. It's totally surreal to see yourself on TV, just being yourself at your job. It's like there's a fly on the wall with a webcam strapped to his head. However, being on the show has been one of the most fun things I've ever done. I'm kind of one of the lesser-known "characters" on the show. I didn't really appear regularly until at least the middle of the third season, so unless I'm in Baltimore and someone is a superfan of the show (or I'm standing next to Duff in an airport), I don't usually get recognized. In any event, the show's success has done awesome things for the popularity of my band.

One of the greatest things about my job is that everyone gets along really well. We all share the same twisted sense of humor and have no problem helping each other out when we hit

TIP *Never put limitations on yourself! Try everything you want to, even if you think you have no experience. The only thing worse than failure is never to have tried. Remember: fake it till you make it!*

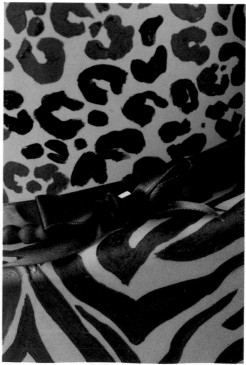

Elena forces fondant through an extruder to replicate hair.

the inevitable cake pitfalls. Whatever problems arise usually get extinguished shortly; then we can get back to pelting each other with balls of fondant.

As you may suspect, Mary Alice, Jessica, and Adrienne get tons and tons of emails about the show every day. Some of them are from people who say they never see us wash our hands and think we're disgusting and filthy and should be banned from television. But I'd like to say that *we all wash our hands at least twenty times a day, if not more, depending on how many hours we put in. So please stop calling the health department.* Every time I handle a different color of fondant, I have to wash my hands, or else that yellow rubber ducky will have a green dye splotch on his head!

Hi I am Selah. I am 6 yearsold. My bruther duse not lieke you. My dad nhats you. My mom likes you. But I love you.

I woch you When I cah and I am haveing a Ase of cakes BirthDay

Duff Goldman

Baltemore Maryland

Charm City Cake

Flipover

Gingerbread Man with Flame throwers By ZOE B

CHARM CITY CAKES

food

ACE OF CAKES FACTS

1. The *Ace of Cakes* crew shoots roughly 120 hours of footage a week for a single episode. That 120 hours is then cut down to a twenty-two-minute show.
2. The show is shot on Panasonic DVX100 cameras. We use five cameras for filming each episode.
3. Since we began filming *Ace of Cakes* in 2006, the show has had five directors.
4. All our interviews take place in Duff's basement, a space formerly used by Anna Ellison for her graphic arts business.
5. The *Ace of Cakes* crew is Los Angeles–based, but they live in Baltimore nine months out of the year for filming.
6. The production crew drains fifty to sixty lithium batteries every week. More than 130 Alkaline batteries are consumed a week.
7. The *Ace of Cakes* crew plays more than ten hours of Frisbee golf, or "Frolf," every week.
8. The farthest the *Ace of Cakes* crew has traveled from Baltimore to accompany Duff on a delivery is Los Angeles—for both the *Harry Potter* and *Kung Fu Panda* premieres and for Duff and Geof's voice work on *King of the Hill*. A cake for *Lost* was created on location in Hawaii. And a small crew accompanied Duff on a "research" trip to Alaska.

SOFIA RODRIGUEZ Decorator

Hometown: The beautiful town of Annecy, France

Education: University of Chambery, International Business and Languages

Favorite hobbies: Spending time with my friends; eating good food and drinking good wine; running in the woods; going to the movies; observing my cat, Margot, doing cat things

Fun fact: I'm trilingual: English, French, and Spanish

Favorite movie: *Women on the Verge of a Nervous Breakdown, Some Like It Hot, The Godfather Parts I & II, Zoolander, The Madness of King George, La Gloire de Mon Père*, anything from the Coen brothers, *The Science of Sleep*

Favorite book: *Lamb* by Christopher Moore, *Le Rouge et le Noir* by Stendhal, the *Griffin & Sabine* trilogy by Nick Bantock, *Perfume* by Patrick Süskind, *Letters to a Young Poet* by Rainier Maria Rilke, *Iberia* by James Michener, and *Larousse Gastronomique*—any questions you have about a cheese dish, you'll probably find the answers in there

Favorite music: Radiohead, The Beatles, Tom Waits, Led Zeppelin, Serge Gainsbourg, Ella Fitzgerald, Nina Simone, Janis Joplin, P. J. Harvey, Patsy Cline . . . and these are only a few of my favorites

Favorite nondessert dish to create or eat: My mom's red wine/garlic mussels, her couscous, and her Galician octopus

In her own words . . .

I was born in Annecy, a very pretty town in the eastern area of France, the youngest of five children. My parents gave my siblings and me our love for food. Both my parents are excellent cooks, and eating is one of the most important things in our family. It seems that we're always planning the next meal, even as we're enjoying the current one. My parents are from northern Spain, and my dad was known in town for his paellas. People would request them for parties, weddings, and other celebrations. His paellas were always prepared on a wood fire, and watching him preparing this dish was amazing—he was so intense about it. It became a Rodriguez family tradition, and now all my siblings and I have proudly carried it on.

*Young
Sofia*

As a child I was pretty shy, and I'm glad I grew out of that. I liked playing outside, and climbing trees and going into the woods in search of treasures were probably my favorite things to do, as well as making my friends laugh. I couldn't wait for summer vacation, which meant I could visit my sisters in the United States. I have wonderful memories of the United States from before I lived here full-time, so when I decided to move to Baltimore in 1994 it was really only one of my dreams. I wanted to experience a different culture.

How did you first meet Duff?

I'd thought about moving to the United States for a while, so after attending college I moved to Baltimore, where one of my sisters lived. Originally my plan was to stay for a year, travel, and then go back home, but that changed and I've been living here since 1994. Many years later, when I was working in a bakery making bread, a friend started telling me about this guy I should meet named Duff. So one day here comes Duff walking into the bakery, going up to my boss, and asking if he could spend the day in the bakery making bread and hanging out (with me). Not the usual "let's hang out with friends and have a drink," much more original and unexpected—just like Duff. I have to add that the thought of baking bread was very attractive to Duff as well (was it me or the bread?).

So here I am working hard pulling loaves of breads out of a burning oven while Duff is making the coolest challah breads shaped like a star, braided and twisted. It was right before Thanksgiving, so you could say we were a little busy. The whole time we were laughing and playing loud music in the bakery (bakeries and music go very well together). At the end of the day Duff handed me this beautiful loaf of bread made especially for me: a crazy Aztec sun-shaped challah. It was one of the most adorable things ever, and he looked so cute . . . so now, eight years later, here I am working at the bakery, icing cakes and dabbling in decorating.

The first incarnation of Charm City Cakes was Duff doing everything out of his apartment. Then he moved into a house, and more and more orders came in. Soon, "Cool Hand" Geof started working for Duff, baking, icing, decorating, deliveries—the two of them did everything. The town house was incredible, I would walk in and the sweet smell of cakes was ev-

erywhere! I still enjoy the smell walking into the bakery every day. I would go to the studio and say hello, and here they were decorating away in a nice, relaxing atmosphere. I'd grab a seat and chat with them; sometimes there would be some things to cut out or paint, and I would help out a little. Their schedule was very different from mine, and they would work until they were done, very late.

I started doing deliveries on weekends when Duff and Geof were buried. What a frightening responsibility! Moving precious "cargo" on the streets of Baltimore can be quite a challenge—there's no duplicate in case something horrible happens, so you drive very, very slowly and ignore the curses coming your way from other drivers. Now, if something happens, you do have to fix it, so you have to make sure you have your delivery toolbox and enough time and do whatever you have to do. We are professionals, after all. One of the best things about a delivery is the response from the clients. I've had a couple of deliveries from hell—one involved me driving out to a dock and jumping on a boat

ride to another boat, where the wedding reception was taking place—and, in the middle of the party, reattaching the cake topper, which was the groom holding his bride above his head like a cheerleader. Thank God now we have a delivery crew to handle most of the orders.

So now we're in this amazing space. I officially started working at Charm City Cakes as a cake icer in June 2007. All cakes are iced before anything else happens to them, as the first part of the week is dedicated to the icing and helping our awesome baker, Adam. The rest of the time I get to decorate, and this is what's so great about Duff: if you show any interest in something, he'll give you the tools the time and independence to try it.

Sofia and Anna check out a shot with cameraman Justin Gurnari

What did you think when you first heard they were going to be making a reality show in the bakery?

It was surreal; I was not crazy about the idea; why would anyone want to watch people working in a bakery? Granted, cake decorating is a fun job, but really, I thought the TV show would be more of an inconvenience than anything else. Could one work, be creative, and enjoy their jobs with cameras on all day week after week? Well, I guess the answer is yes, after a little adjustment.

As a matter of fact, the reason filming goes so well is that the crew is who they are. I can't imagine working with a different group. They're kind, smart, and talented—what else could you ask for? Over time, we've developed a good relationship, where you feel you can be yourself. I would say that if someone has to put a camera in my face, I'd prefer it be a friend!

Are the staff all really friends the way it seems on TV?

I consider everyone in the bakery a friend. Now, does that mean we have to hang out every day after work? No, we would kill each other. There's a common desire to work together in a pleasant atmosphere, which means laughing as often as possible and listening to music as much as possible. We do get along pretty well; a lot of people were already friends—or friends of friends—so it looked like a good recipe. We bounce off one other quite well, from the back of the bakery, where Adam starts all the cakes, to the front, where the commando girls keep the bakery in line, or try to at least.

What is your dream cake?

I'm still thinking about a dream cake. This week, for example, I have time to work on a dummy cake, and it seems that the possible dream cake will involve a lot of colors and flowers.

TIP *Icing can be very frustrating. Sometimes it's like doing surgery, so always have these four tools: a well-greased wheel, a medium Slimfit, a taping knife, and lots of patience, and voilà!*

What's the story behind the cake you created for the book?

I wanted the cake to be elegant and Art Deco inspired. I chose to do a three-tier square cake, with a burnt orange color and black piping, deep red flowers, and little separations between each tier. I liked the shadow effect the half-inch separation makes. This cake is the first one I decorated, and it was a little more challenging. I like cakes that are pretty traditional—it must be because I'm French. I like it when simple is beautiful.

THE BUSINESS OF CHARM CITY CAKES

"Making money is art and working is art and good business is the best art of all."
—ANDY WARHOL

One of the best pieces of business advice I've ever gotten from my dad was also the simplest: Work hard, and work smart. Running a cake business, or any business for that matter, means you're taking risks and making hundreds of decisions every day. You're responsible for your product, paying the bills, minding health code regulations, taxes, payroll, vehicle maintenance, property maintenance, mortgage or rent, staff morale, customer service, and a million other things that come at you all the time. Overthinking will make you crazy, but I try to live by a few really simple rules, and the rest just seems to work itself out.

RULE 1: Have fun. If you're not having fun while you decorate a cake, it shows. I've seen miserable people making cakes, and they pour all of their misery into their work and you can really sense it. I think that's true about everything creative, really.

RULE 2: Make nice cakes.

RULE 3: Be nice to people.

That's it. If you do that, the rest will come as it comes. Sure, sometimes you'll lie awake at night figuring out cake designs or pondering a business move. Sometimes you'll even have a cake nightmare—I know I do, usually about one a week, but then I wake up and realize that everything is okay. In fact, if you don't have cake nightmares, you might want to ask yourself how much you really care about cakes. I like to think that having cake nightmares regularly means that I still love my job. And I do.

With our dad at the Super Bowl

I have no academic idea why my business works; I do everything a Harvard MBA would tell you not to do. I never worked in a cake shop before I opened Charm City Cakes, so we do things our own way. Everything we do we've learned through trial and error (sometimes too much error) and from the help of much more experienced cake decorators. I don't presume that what we do is *the* right way to do things, but it works for us.

There are two questions we're constantly asked. The first, "How come I never see you wash your hands on *Ace of Cakes*?" has a very easy answer: We don't. Kidding. As I've mentioned, we shoot more than three hundred hours of footage every week, and with so much to choose from for a twenty-two-minute episode, the boring stuff—like washing hands—ends up on the cutting room floor. The second is "How much do your cakes cost?" A simple question, and believe it or not, simple enough to answer: How much you got? Hah! Again, kidding.

People assume our cakes must be expensive, but that's a generalization based on the three cakes the producers of *Ace of Cakes* decide to feature on TV, not the up to thirty-seven *other* cakes Charm City Cakes is creating that week. Here and on our website you'll see an incredibly wide variety of cakes—ranging from a traditional three- or four-tier white wedding cake to those much more complex in execution and design. We do everything from a basic square sheet cake to an array of fifty minicakes suspended upside down from a ballroom ceiling.

Most bakeries have what they call a "per slice" fee, which means they charge for as many people as the cake needs to feed. The cost of our cakes is determined by a variety of factors: the complexity of the design, the materials involved, the number of decorators, the amount of time involved, and so on. You want a regular cake? One hour. Boom! Done. We can do it, have done it, and continue to do it—and it keeps our prices on par with bakeries nationwide. But obviously prospective clients don't come to Charm City Cakes looking for a square cake with *Happy Birthday Joe!* written on it. They have a special event: a wedding, a special birthday, a Bat Mitzvah, an anniversary, a party, a graduation, a retirement party, a product launch—and they want something special to commemorate that event. That's what we like to do—we specialize in special.

What makes Charm City Cakes a successful business? The simple answer is this: people want our cakes. But how we got to this point is a much more complex story. Fifty years ago there couldn't have been a Charm City Cakes as it exists today, simply because there wasn't a large market for highly unusual cakes crafted by a team of bakers, decorators, and artisans. The American economy has allowed many people to afford more specialty goods—everything from a second car to a designer handbag to even one of our cakes.

An entrepreneur is a business's leader—the person who combines labor, management, capital, supplies, marketing, plus other factors into making and selling a product. Here's where I display effective but sometimes unusual ways of doing things.

MY STAFF

One element of our success and the success of Charm City Cakes is the fact that we believe in what we do. I was a history major in college—not an MBA. I didn't know how to run a business. Show me an artist who does. All I know is that by believing in what I do and believing in what I see, whatever the business guys say, I'm doin' it my way: I praise my staff, and I'm not afraid to defer to them when I feel the need. And of course I reward them accordingly—after all, I was the one who hired them in the first place, right? Of course I give vacation time,

but I also take them on vacation with me! We have fun together, let down together, hang out together—probably the opposite of most workplaces, where everyone can't wait to get away from one another.

Of course, mixing friendship with business is risky—because close camaraderie among management and staff can complicate hard business choices. Yet somehow we've been able to make it work in most cases. We're all friends who enjoy applying their skills to cake decorating, and the staff is well paid, complete with two months' paid vacation annually. Treating everyone the best you can instills a loyalty that contributes to the collective success of the business. For example, one of our interns was accepted to a culinary school, but it was financially beyond her reach. I contacted the school and worked out a deal to do guest lectures in exchange for a scholarship.

GIVING CREDIT WHERE CREDIT IS DUE

You can achieve a lot more if you're not interested in claiming all the kudos for the accomplishments of your business. It's important that everyone at the bakery receives acclaim for their work. Charm City Cakes isn't just me, it's a family of skilled artists, musicians, chefs, and likeminded creative individuals: Anna may have a better sense of color, Geof usually has the best construction and architecture techniques, and Mary Alice certainly has the better customer relations skills. For me personally, it's important to acknowledge what I've learned from others. Though I may be comfortable with my own abilities as a decorator and entrepreneur, it's really credit to others who have taken a chance on me and believed in everything I thought Charm City Cakes could be.

MARKETING

Before the worldwide audience of *Ace of Cakes*, Charm City Cakes had one of the simplest, oldest, and best forms of marketing one can have: word of mouth and free cakes. The very first Charm City Cake was made for free for the wedding of Mary Alice's brother, Neil. The cake was a hit, and guests at the wedding began spreading the world locally about this wild and fantastic-looking cake they'd seen at a recent wedding. One guest told two others, the two others told four more, and word of our unusual cakes spread around Baltimore.

Moreover, Baltimore residents are renowned for their strong sense of community and love to give back to the city they call home. One time, with the batter mixed, the fondant rolled, the icing bought, and the oven still warm, I decided I wanted to bake a couple more cakes, so I donated them to the local Meals on Wheels organization. Their reaction halted me in my tracks—I simply couldn't believe how happy they were to receive a couple of fresh cakes. It was then I realized that no matter happened with the business, I had to make my love for Baltimore a part of the future of my business. I decided Charm City Cakes would continue the tradition and donate as often as we can. The result was twofold: formidable exposure in the community and positive word of mouth, both key ingredients for any small business trying to start out.

It wasn't until a little while later, when the business was still in its embryonic form, that a single article about this "crazy Culinary Institute–trained baker from Baltimore" appeared, which begat a few more articles—which then caught the eyes of a few local, then national magazines. The media was beginning to take notice.

LONG-TERM DECISION MAKING

As corny as it sounds, there's a lot of truth in the adage that "if you fail to plan, you plan to fail." We need to remember to buy enough eggs for the cake batter, heat our buttercream before spreading, and measure the inside of our delivery van to see if it's tall enough to support five-foot flamingos (see episode 105), among countless other things. Planning is essential in trying to start a small business—and decreases the need to continually revisit problems. As we were growing, one of our first decisions was where to find a new bakery—something better than the kitchen in my apartment. While that seemed to do the trick for a while, what with the business growing and a neighbor who had the health department on speed dial, it became clear it was time to move. The first big move was the rental of a small commercial bakery (ironically, this is where the *Ace of Cakes* pilot, or "sizzle reel," was filmed). However, an expanding business, even more troublesome neighbors, and the looming possibility of a television show meant a risky business decision had to be made: should I roll the dice and purchase an even bigger building, or was it time to hedge the bet and try and make do with another rental location? After much trepidation, I decided to go all in. I secured a small-business loan and purchased an old church building that seemed primed for transformation.

CUSTOMER SERVICE

There's no secret that the customer is king is a must for most businesses. Charm City Cakes takes tremendous pride in the design, delivery, and taste of every single cake that goes out our front door. On the rare occasion that a customer is unhappy, even unreasonably unhappy, we usually offer a refund or another cake on a future date or work out some other solution. No one, and I mean *no one*, wants to be responsible for upsetting a bride on her wedding day. But you can't always predict people's reactions—there was one client who ordered a wedding cake shaped like a toilet bowl, and though she and the entire wedding party were thrilled with it, we found ourselves at the receiving end of one angry mother who couldn't believe we'd put her daughter's wedding into the crapper!

With most of the events we deliver to, there's an air of excitement but also anxiety and tension, as caterers, party planners, parents, and other relatives pinball about, scrambling to make sure everything goes off without a hitch. Moreover, upon delivering to a function such as a wedding, where non-cake-related problems can arise (and they always do), we do our best to volunteer our time and expertise in decorating, arranging, servicing, or, hell, even cooking, to make sure the special day remains special.

BRANDING

Another part of the bakery's success has been our ability to define a "Charm City Cake" in the eyes of the public. Some view our cakes as a luxury brand, similar to how they'd view a fancy watch, dressy shoes, or an expensive car. Some customers are willing and expect to pay more for one of our cakes than another cake from somewhere else. When I began the business, I was hoping to be able to sell cakes at $6 per slice. Now on some occasions we can receive much more than that. It's simply a matter of supply and demand, as now we find ourselves actually turning down orders because we're booked. With customers ranging from a nearby Remington neighbor to local politicians to a faraway movie studio, there's increased demand for a specially crafted cake to spice up a celebration.

SELECTIVE EXPANSION

Given this excess of demand, Charm City Cakes has had many opportunities to expand, both physically and in branding. One of our favorite offers was from a financier in Dubai who insisted we open a branch in the Middle East. Though all opportunities are flattering, most are turned down because we don't want to dilute the quality of our cakes. The responsibility for every creation that leaves the bakery lies with all of us—it's our name and reputation on the line up to forty times a week. As much as word of mouth has helped Charm City Cakes, it can easily have the opposite effect. If you open a franchise somewhere and you're not there to supervise, you get the blame when something goes wrong. Though we'd love to expand and there may be a way to do so in the future, it's important for us to be selective.

We once considered selling large numbers of standardized cakes at lower prices. Though this certainly could have been profitable, it would have involved our spending our limited time supervising a typical bakery instead of pouring our energies into making creative cakes. That said, one area of business growth we have adopted is the selling of ancillary products such as Charm City Cakes–branded hats, T-shirts, aprons, and other similar items. Once the original designs are approved, our further involvement is minimal.

From, Carole?

I have little to offer you in terms of convenience or cash...I do have two beautiful teenage daughters who will be ready to date (legally) in about 4 years.

Hi my name is Sandy and I am a 45 year old **mail**

I'm turning 20 and I am completely obsessed with My Little Pony. Specifically Fizzy...the green one who blows bubbles out of its unicorn horn.

tijdschema

I am your biggest fan with a capital I...

I sent email to Ellen Degeneres also busy. So, you are my last chance of fame (LOL).

FAIL

schreibtisch

Can send **pitcher.**

I am the Maid of Homor for my sister's wedding.

Scrapple, this letter is about scrapple.

There is some chance, however, that HB 315 will <u>not</u> be brought to vote in the House of Delegates, and that the legislation may be quietly placed in a drawer. If that happens, there will be no State Dessert named during the 2008 legislative session.

ally offer a refund or another cake on a future date or work out some other solution. No one, and I mean *no one,* wants to be responsible for upsetting a bride on her wedding day. But you can't always predict people's reactions—there was one client who ordered a wedding cake shaped like a toilet bowl, and though she and the entire wedding party were thrilled with it, we found ourselves at the receiving end of one angry mother who couldn't believe we'd put her daughter's wedding into the crapper!

With most of the events we deliver to, there's an air of excitement but also anxiety and tension, as caterers, party planners, parents, and other relatives pinball about, scrambling to make sure everything goes off without a hitch. Moreover, upon delivering to a function such as a wedding, where non-cake-related problems can arise (and they always do), we do our best to volunteer our time and expertise in decorating, arranging, servicing, or, hell, even cooking, to make sure the special day remains special.

BRANDING

Another part of the bakery's success has been our ability to define a "Charm City Cake" in the eyes of the public. Some view our cakes as a luxury brand, similar to how they'd view a fancy watch, dressy shoes, or an expensive car. Some customers are willing and expect to pay more for one of our cakes than another cake from somewhere else. When I began the business, I was hoping to be able to sell cakes at $6 per slice. Now on some occasions we can receive much more than that. It's simply a matter of supply and demand, as now we find ourselves actually turning down orders because we're booked. With customers ranging from a nearby Remington neighbor to local politicians to a faraway movie studio, there's increased demand for a specially crafted cake to spice up a celebration.

SELECTIVE EXPANSION

Given this excess of demand, Charm City Cakes has had many opportunities to expand, both physically and in branding. One of our favorite offers was from a financier in Dubai who insisted we open a branch in the Middle East. Though all opportunities are flattering, most are turned down because we don't want to dilute the quality of our cakes. The responsibility for every creation that leaves the bakery lies with all of us—it's our name and reputation on the line up to forty times a week. As much as word of mouth has helped Charm City Cakes, it can easily have the opposite effect. If you open a franchise somewhere and you're not there to supervise, you get the blame when something goes wrong. Though we'd love to expand and there may be a way to do so in the future, it's important for us to be selective.

We once considered selling large numbers of standardized cakes at lower prices. Though this certainly could have been profitable, it would have involved our spending our limited time supervising a typical bakery instead of pouring our energies into making creative cakes. That said, one area of business growth we have adopted is the selling of ancillary products such as Charm City Cakes–branded hats, T-shirts, aprons, and other similar items. Once the original designs are approved, our further involvement is minimal.

POSITIVE ATTITUDE

As much as I can, I try to be highly optimistic and seek out the positive in situations. I like to think I have a thick skin and try my best to let most irritants roll off my back. When others push the envelope by trading on our name and/or creations, we all take note but are generally too busy to be worked up over it. There are so many successful happenings at Charm City Cakes and on *Ace of Cakes*—why be bothered with a few small negative issues?

THE CAKE-DECORATING COMMUNITY

According to the Culinary Institute of America (my alma mater), the number of student applications there and at other culinary schools is rising. Though we in no way take credit for this, we're proud to shine a spotlight on the culinary arts and hopefully inspire others who may not have thought of trying this area before.

Bakers around the country have written in and said they've been inspired and empowered by the success of our show and cite it as proof to their own clients that there really can be almost no limit to what a cake can be. Though we certainly weren't the first bakery to create wild cake designs, it's rewarding to hear of customers entering local bakeries and ordering an *Ace of Cakes*–style cake. Bakers also tell us that the show helps clients understand the amount of work and creativity that go into creating and decorating their custom creations—which in turn allows them to sell more and, in many cases, justify increased prices for the more extravagant customer demands.

Others tell us they've learned from the techniques employed on the show. Our website receives thousands of hits daily, many from other bakers looking for a particular cake design. We care about the industry and delight in helping it reach new heights either through our show or by answering questions from other bakers. We also refer a tremendous amount of business to other bakers, both locally and nationally.

THE EFFECT ON FOOD NETWORK

The very first episode of *Ace of Cakes* aired on August 17, 2006, and received a strong rating for the series premiere. A single national rating point represents 1 percent of households with television sets (share is the percentage of television sets in use tuned to the program). That weekend, the very same episode was rebroadcast on Sunday, and the rating actually *increased*, a rare feat for any show, let alone a cable-based reality program. As the second, third, and fourth episodes debuted, it quickly became clear that Food Network had a hit on its hands.

Food Network's gamble had worked. As word of mouth grew, those early episodes came close to reaching one million viewers (a number actually achieved in later seasons). And not only that—the show was bringing in a younger demographic, an audience that's the prime draw for advertisers. Following the first six-episode season of *Ace of Cakes*, network executives told us that it's rare that one single show can change the way they look at a network—but that is exactly what it had done. The same way MTV broadened its reach beyond music videos and into original programming, *Ace of Cakes* helped energize Food Network's development of a new class of culinary-based entertainment programming.

ON *ACE OF CAKES*

Brian Ford Sullivan, editor in chief, thefutoncritic.com

Ace of Cakes falls into the rarest of all reality television genres. No one finds a wife, wins a million dollars, or eats a bug (unless he wants his cake to look like one of the above). Instead it's a window into a world in which genuinely creative people do genuinely creative things. Duff Goldman, then, is our Willy Wonka to the Chocolate Factory that is Charm City Cakes in Baltimore. Each week Duff and company try to convert anything you can think of—from pinball machines to frogs to even the Millennium Falcon—into please-can-I-reach-through-the-screen-and-eat them cakes. They are tasks that involve feats of engineering, mountains of fondant, and healthy doses of wit from Geof, Mary Alice, and the rest of the Charm City Cakes staff.

What really sets Ace of Cakes apart, though, is how it brings a fresh perspective to what reality television can do. This isn't *The Hills*, where quasi-scripted "events" inform the lives of quasi-celebrities. This isn't *The Real World*, where twentysomethings give confessionals on the horrors of twentysomethingness. And it certainly isn't *Survivor* or *Big Brother*, where the participants lie around and obsess over what alliance they can form or strategy they can apply in playing "the game." Furthermore, Duff and company aren't setting out to be celebrities. They don't have their own fashion or makeup lines. They aren't inviting some gossipy magazine over to do a profile on their homes. And they certainly aren't going to show up on *TMZ* in a drunken tirade. Nope, the Charm City Cakes crew has the audacity to just want to make cakes.

Leading the charge then is Duff himself—part philanthropist, part rock star, part mad scientist, and all kid in the proverbial candy store. Quite simply, he's just as excited to see how things turn out as you are. These are aspects that have somehow sharpened—not diminished—with success. To this day, you can't go a week without seeing Duff clear his schedule for a local charity, fashion some sort of contraption to get a particular order right, or marvel at the work his coworkers have achieved. He's a genuine artist giving us a tour of his craft on a weekly basis.

It may seem impossible, but *Ace of Cakes* manages to make you laugh, be amazed, and get hungry—all at the same time. And that's what I call great television.

From,
Carole?

I have little to offer you in terms of convenience or cash…I do have two beautiful teenage daughters who will be ready to date (legally) in about 4 years.

Hi my name is Sandy and I am a 45 year old **mail**

ZOMBIES!

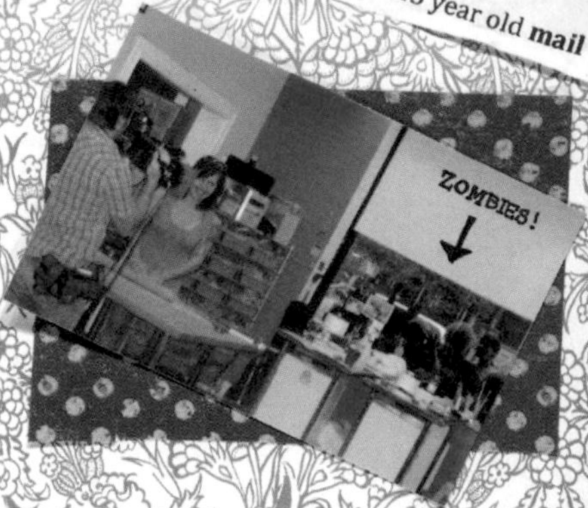

I'm turning 20 and I am completely obsessed with My Little Pony. Specifically Fizzy…the green one who blows bubbles out of its unicorn horn.

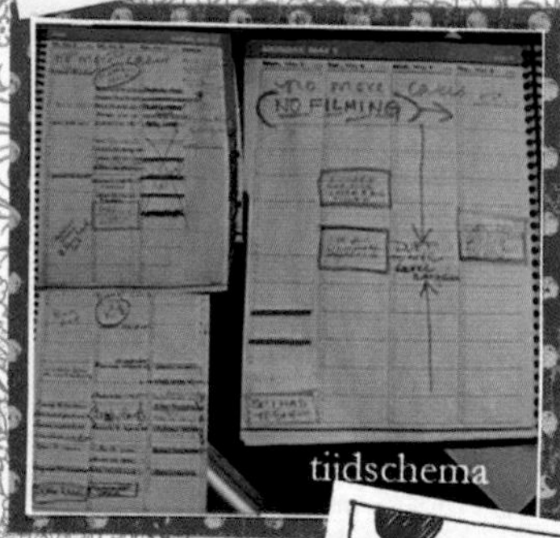

NO FILMING
tijdschema

I am your biggest fan with a capital I…

I sent email to Ellen Degeneres also busy. So, you are my last chance of fame (LOL).

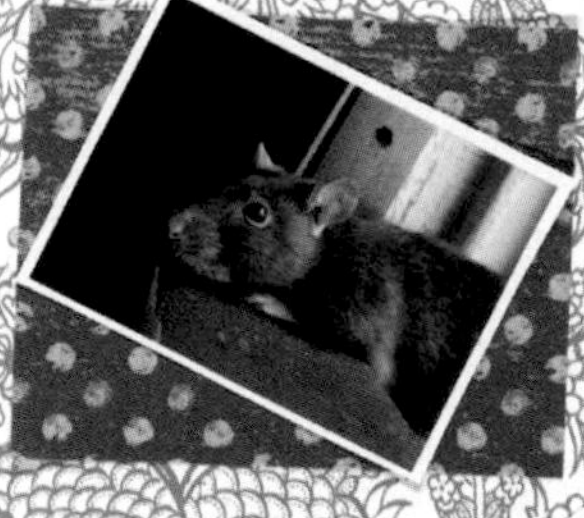

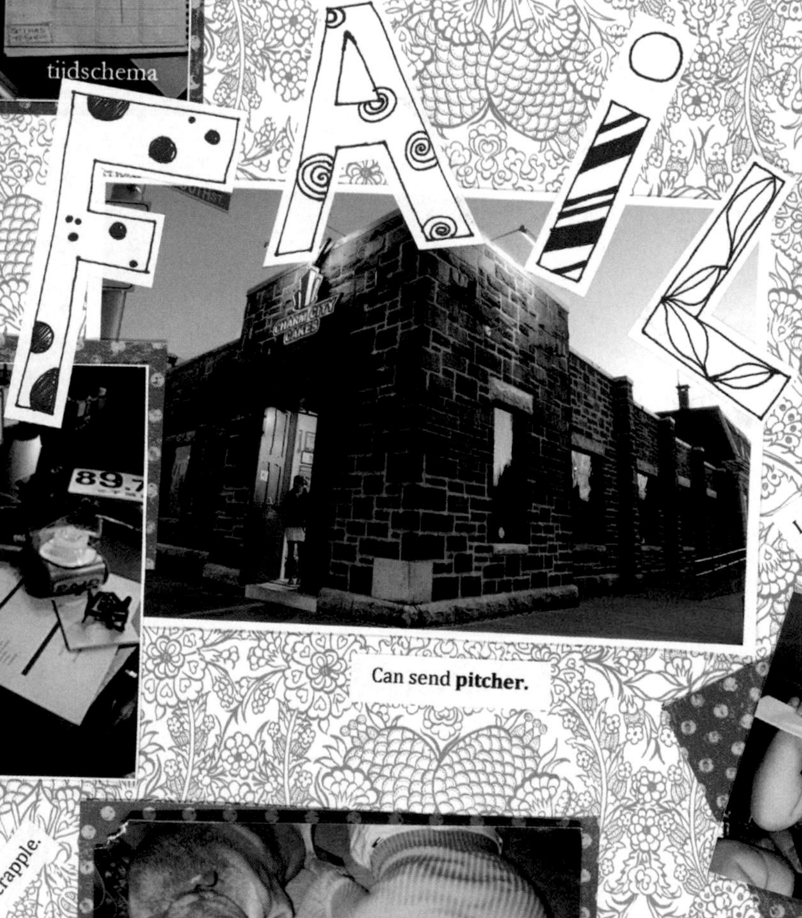

FAIL

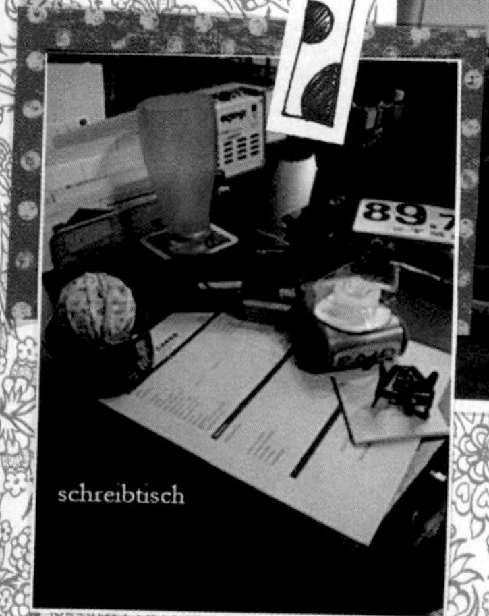

89.7
schreibtisch

I am the Maid of Homor for my sister's wedding.

Can send **pitcher.**

CHARM

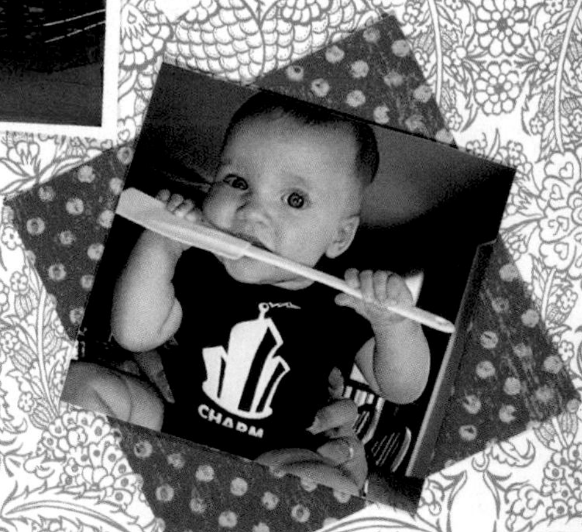

Scrapple, this letter is about scrapple.

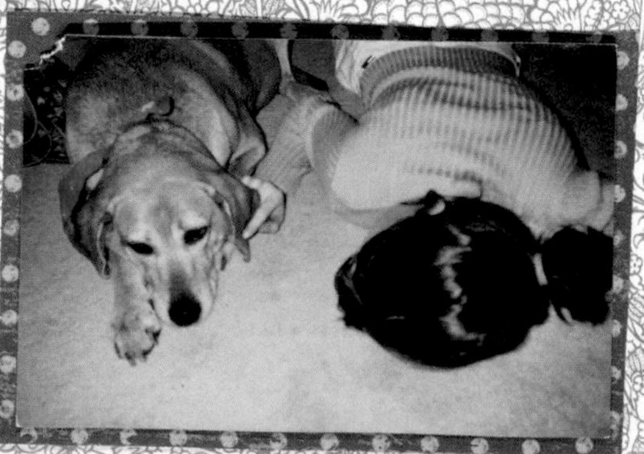

There is some chance, however, that HB 315 will <u>not</u> be brought to vote in the House of Delegates, and that the legislation may be quietly placed in a drawer. If that happens, there will be no State Dessert named during the 2008 legislative session.

JESSICA CURRY AND ADRIENNE RUHF

Job Title: Everything Else

Hometowns: Union, New Jersey, and Columbia, Maryland (Adrienne);
Waldorf, Maryland (Jess)

Education: Towson University (both)—BS in anthropology (Adrienne), BS in women's studies
and cultural studies (Jess)

Favorite hobbies: Reading, music, hanging out with Cotton and Kira, my dog and cat
(Jess); crafts, ethnography, exploration, notes, ratties, tattoos (Adrienne)

Fun facts:

Adrienne: Altogether, I have had sixteen rescued rats (no, I don't mean rescued from the
street, there are small animal rescues). I have a rat tattoo. I can do obstetric ultrasounds. I
volunteered with an sea turtle project in Costa Rica. At my other job, I'm a research assistant for public health and drug abuse research studies.

Jess: I have more than fifteen nicknames for my dog and cat. I was a Junior Olympian in
race walking.

Favorite movies:

Adrienne: *4 months, 3 weeks and 2 days; Amélie; The Battle of Algiers; Big Fish; The
Devil's Backbone; Land of the Dead; Millions; Salt of the Earth; Sunshine*

Jess: Many kinds

Favorite books:

Jess: Some of my favorite authors are Raymond Queneau, Vladimir Nabokov, Toni Morrison, Georges Perec, Salman Rushdie, Joan Didion, Italo Calvino, and Clarice Lispector

Adrienne: *In Search of Respect* by Philippe Bourgois; *Pathologies of Power* by Paul
Farmer (and everything else he's ever written); *Slaughterhouse-Five* by Kurt Vonnegut;
Never Suck a Dead Man's Hand by Dana
Kollman

Favorite music:

Adrienne: Covenant, Gogol Bordello,
NIN, Saul Williams, Son of Nun, VNV
Nation, and things of that nature

Jess: Old folk songs

**Favorite nondessert dishes to
create or eat:**

Jess: soup!, baba ghanoush, muffins

Adrienne: Michael Chisari's fried zucchini
with rosemary and garlic sauce

Jess and Adrienne

A: The first time I ever came to the bakery was when I was living down the street and we were making cookies for our patients at the clinic where we were both working.

J: Yeah, I remember. I think I was working part-time at the bakery then. I don't remember my first bakery visit. Unlike most people here, I actually came to Charm City Cakes under pretty normal circumstances—Mary Alice needed help, and I needed a part-time job. I started off working nights after I got off at my day job to answer emails, process contracts and payments, and so on. *Ace of Cakes* began airing on Food Network around then, so pretty soon I was needed full-time.

A: And then things got even busier and you needed help, so I came. I don't think I was ever specifically hired. The first day I was here Duff walked up to the desk and said, "Who the f—— are you?" And I said, "I work here now." And that was kind of my official introduction and welcome to the job.

> **TIP**
> *Always drink plenty of water.*

JESS AND ADRIENNE'S DUTIES

Respond to emails (this is really a full time job by itself)

Answer the phones

Give price quotes

Process all mail (bills and fan mail)

Process contracts and handle order logistics

Gather and organize design and reference materials, which includes frequently reminding some our clients to please take a picture of their house, dog, husband, or whatever so we can start their cake!

Manage the cake calendar, calendar of events, and appearances

Process all payments, receipts, and reimbursements for the bakery

Fix spelling errors on the contracts (Jess is so crazy about this she sometimes retypes them. This really could be a full-time job itself)

Pay the bills

General accounting (also really a full time job)

Merch, merch, and more merch: oversee CCC merchandise: processing, inventory, shipping, ordering (yup, that's another full-time job)

Send out donations

Coordinate schedules with TV production

File everything

TIP *Be resourceful. The Internet is an amazing research tool. If you haven't already, check out the search engine called Google. It's incredible. All you have to do is type in a keyword or a phrase, and all these Web pages containing information will appear magically. So instead of calling Charm City Cakes to ask for a fondant recipe, ask Google.*

J: There's not really a formal process of introduction to this job.

A: Or a concrete job description, for that matter.

J: How would you even describe what we do during the day?

A: I spend a lot of time on email. Well, we all do. But I specifically spend a lot of time letting people know what we can't do. I say "no" a lot in a day. Charm City Cakes may be well known, but we're still a pretty small place.

J: What's your *favorite* part of the job?

A: Telling people no. Just kidding. I mean, what's your favorite part?

TIP *There's also this very cool place called the library. You can check out books for free. Really, it's true. They can help you find books specifically on cakes, and they even have computers for you to use! These are great ways to educate yourself about cake-decorating techniques.*

J: Nothing. [Pause.] Kidding . . . we don't really have interesting or glamorous jobs. Unless you consider reading weird emails interesting.

A: It is interesting to an extent. We get a lot of emails that commit one or more of the following:

Adrienne

✦ What we call "dropping emails." These are the ones where the entire email has very little to do with an actual cake order. Types of dropping include, but are not limited to, life histories, experiences of disease, famous connections, and anything else unusual, unfortunate, or tragic.

✦ Fan mail and love letters (e.g., "Is _____ single?"). We will tell you now, no.

Jess

✦ "Creative" advertisements and business propositions. And by creative I mean scary.

✦ Answers to anything we've ever asked about on the show. We received a lot of disco balls, dried sage, glue recommendations, ideas for how to pleat a cake, and so on.

TIP

Remember the three Rs in all communication: be reasonable, rational, and respectful.

✦ "Can I get a cake in [insert some faraway state]?" There's this magical idea created by the show that we can transcend time and space. But in reality, we are located in Baltimore. California is really far away, and it costs a ton of money for us to drive a cake there.

J: What's been your favorite piece of mail, Adrienne?

A: We got a coupon from McDonald's, written in Korean, for a chicken sandwich addressed to "Bok-Bok" (the name of a chicken cake on our website).

J: Yeah, that was a good one. What else do people ask us?

A: What's it like to be on TV?

J and A: We're not on TV.

A: How are you affected by the show?

J: Mostly by visitors to the bakery.

A: I have completely started regarding visitors as zombies. It gets really scary outside!

J: Sometimes they don't go away—they hang around outside peering in the windows, pulling on locked doors, and generally freaking out—that's why A calls them zombies.

A: Fortunately, there are plenty of fun things to do in Baltimore, like looking for other famous people, such as Michael Phelps or Jenna Bush.

J: Museums, restaurants, art galleries . . .

J: Adrienne, what's one thing you want people to know about the bakery?

A: We generally get one to three hundred emails per day during the week and between three and five hundred over the course of a weekend. We're seriously busy! I wish people wouldn't write us a book where a sentence would do. I promise, if I can do it I will. If I can't, the rest of the story is just going to make me really sleepy. Unless it includes pictures of animals. What do you want people to know?

J: We keep a file of all the weird and embarrassing emails we receive. It's our next book idea . . .

A: Best book ever. Do we sound really bitter?

J: No way, we love it.

TIP *Pictures of your cute, shelter-adopted pets are a much better way to grab our attention and bribe us. Sorry, the kids, wrecked cakes, and wedding pictures don't do it for us.*

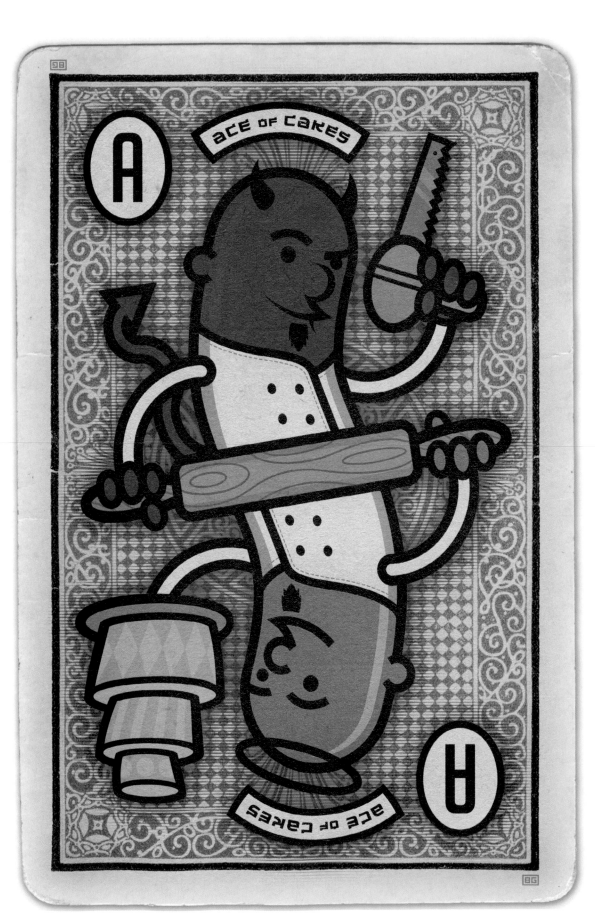

The Weddings of CHARM CITY CAKES

KATIE ROSE **Decorator**

Hometown: Overland Park, Kansas
Education: BFA, Maryland Institute College of Art
Favorite hobbies: Bookmaking, printmaking, photography
Fun facts: The first time Anna met Ben, he was wearing nothing but a paper bag for a Halloween costume. The bakery has named the smaller of our two airbrushes "Turkey Jones."

In her own words . . .

I first learned about Charm City Cakes from Anna, when we were living together. I think one of her teachers introduced the bakery to her, and then soon after Anna showed me the website. I had no idea I would end up there. I really needed an internship to graduate, and Anna was already working at CCC. She made the suggestion, and then Duff was nice enough to let me intern, even though I'm not sure if at the time they really needed an intern. Anna must have talked me up.

I'm not on *Ace of Cakes* very much and I don't have cable, so I rarely see myself on TV. It's easier for me to be filmed and to do my job and to not have any embarrassing mental images of myself on TV. So far I haven't been recognized. At first I was wary of the television show. I felt as if the camera crew was going to come in and create a lot of artificial conflict. It's truly been the opposite, and if anything they've given us space during any non-cake-related disputes or personal issues. I consider the crew my friends, and often it's more fun when they're around. They bring a different dynamic to the bakery.

My favorite cake I've decorated was for my friend Laura's wedding. She came up with a simple, beautiful design, and the results were exceptional. Mary, Anna, and I all contributed, using each person's strength. My job was to make

TIP *When making colors for fondant, I almost always use a little bit of brown or black to dull the color a bit and give it another dimension. I usually never use straight colors from the bucket unless the cake specifically calls for it.*

the flowers out of gum paste. I'd always wanted to attempt flower making, but I'd never had the opportunity. Since this cake was for a special occasion, I put in some extra time and was able to develop the skills for creating flowers.

Everyone at the bakery has such a good sense of humor. I'm frequently being entertained or made to laugh. When Sofia and Ben get at it with each other, they take it to another level. I enjoy watching their disagreements unfold into something amusing and ultimately distracting.

I made three cakes for this book. The brown Woodland Creatures cake was inspired by traditional Scandinavian art and design—it makes me think of folklore and fairy tales, and I wanted to capture that in a cake.

TIP *When designing a cake, simplicity is always best. One idea or element is always better than trying to make two or three ideas work on one cake. A cake doesn't need to represent every aspect of you—just pick one.*

With the Gray Painted cake, I thought it would be nice to use a grayish color, something more muted and simple that you traditionally don't see in a wedding cake. I never really used my painting skills in a design before, as usually I'm just painting landscapes on a cake, so for this I wanted to create a unique pattern that you might see in wallpaper or nicer fabrics. I really just wanted to show how painting could be used for a traditional wedding cake, since usually people prefer piping and it's not that common to see painted cakes. With the Square Tree cake, I was just experimenting with stencils and highlighting a way I could overlap color. It was more of an experiment in technique than anything else.

CELEBRATION CAKE*
CONSTRUCTION KIT • FULLY EDIBLE • AGES 2 and UP

Charm City Cakes was started in March of 2000 when Chef Duff had tired of wandering the country and decided to settle in Baltimore. At first, Chef Duff was just making a few cakes for friends and family, but as word got out about his uncommon creations, business picked up fast. In March of 2002, Chef Duff was getting so inundated with cake orders that he decided to fling off the oppression of his day job and make cake baking his full time gig! He quickly outgrew his home kitchen and two bakeries; in August of 2005 he bought a 6,000 square foot cake compound in Remington. Today, Charm City Cakes has grown to a staff of eleven friends who make cakes, listen to music, and eat a lot of sushi.

Here at Charm City Cakes, we are motivated by constantly trying to outdo ourselves by making cakes that are beautiful, challenging, and as out-of-the-ordinary as possible! Our inspiration comes from everywhere: art, fabric, furniture, architecture, landscapes, science, music, anything! Most of all, our inspiration comes from you! Each cake is individually designed to match you, your personality, and the theme of the occasion you are celebrating.

We only have one rule at Charm City Cakes, and that is whatever we do, we must have fun! Charm City Cakes is a very relaxed, creative environment - and that spirit is reflected in every cake we bake. Our staff is a ragtag group of musicians, artists, and creative souls with experience in architectural modeling, graphic design, sculpture, painting, DJ-ing, coffee slingin', performance art, massage therapy, and waitressing. Our designs are unique, our flavors are unusual and delicious, and our demeanor is chill but professional. Our cakes are all individually baked to order, and every cake is always fresh, never frozen. We have over 40 flavors, and experiment with new ones all the time - - if you don't see it on our list, don't be afraid to ask, 'cause we can probably make it. You dream it, we'll bake it, you eat it.

There are no limits to what we can do here at Charm City Cakes. You dream it, we'll bake it, you eat it.

*fictional product, not for sale... yet.

ERICA HARRISON Decorator

Hometown: Dumfries, Virginia

Education: BA, James Madison University (double major: public relations and French; minor: studio art/pottery)

Favorite hobbies: Understanding the science of baking and pastry, cycling, tennis, perpetual student of the electric bass and hammered dulcimer

Fun fact: The two-owls "Erica" cake was created by the entire Charm City Cakes staff for my wedding cake.

Favorite movies: *Les Triplettes de Belleville, The Muppet Movie, Wallace and Gromit*

Favorite books: *How to Cook Everything* by Mark Bittman, *Fantasy Worlds* by John Maizels, *Salt* by Mark Kurlansky, *Charley Harper: An Illustrated Life* by Charley Harper and Todd Oldham, *Jim Henson: The Works* by Christopher Finch, *Busy, Busy Town* by Richard Scarry, *Ed Emberly's Drawing Book of Animals*

Favorite music: Stereolab, Yo La Tengo, Young Marble Giants, Morrissey, Pylon, Brian Eno, X, Nina Nastasia, Kraftwerk, Stephin Merritt, Björk, John Fahey, The Meters, Wire, Pixies, Gang of Four, Bedhead, Rose Melberg

In her own words . . .

It all started with the exploits of a little green frog. After decades of watching the magic of various Jim Henson productions, it was *The Muppets Take Manhattan* that made me wonder about the behind-the-scenes artistry that brought these amazing creations to life. While watching a particular kitchen scene that featured Rizzo the Rat skating around a frying pan, I fell in love with the idea of becoming the next person to create the small little butter pat ice skates prop used by the puppet. In that very instant, I was bitten by the production bug. During the day I was working at National Public Radio in Washington, D.C., but in the evenings and on weekends, I soon sought out various jobs that saw me dabble in costume design, design, puppeteering, and baking.

I began moonlighting in a few kitchens in northern Virginia. First I started as assistant baker at Common Grounds Coffeehouse in Arlington, Virginia, where I found myself up to my ears in gingerbread, apple upside-down cake, eclairs, chocolate mousse, carrot cake, and other neighborhood favorites. In 2004 I relocated to nearby Alexandria, where I applied for a part-time job at The Dairy Godmother assisting in baking nostalgic treats, including homemade marshmallows, shortbread, almond tuiles, macaroons, and dog treats shaped like squirrels.

TIP *When combining dry ingredients in a mixer, always start it on the slowest speed to avoid causing a snowstorm.*

Following a move to Baltimore in 2005, I decided to taste-test local bakeries in the hunt for a new part-time job, and there was one I kept hearing about: Charm City Cakes. But my husband, John, beat me to the punch: as a surprise birthday present, he secretly emailed Duff and Mary Alice. "Erica sent us the cutest handmade and hand-illustrated card asking to come help out at the bakery. It really stood out and showed her creativity! I knew she was a kindred spirit right away. Then when her husband contacted me and I realized it was the same Erica, I knew it was meant to be," remembers Mary Alice.

I was asked to come to the bakery in spring 2006 to help out by washing dishes and organizing the workshop's tools and supplies. Mary Alice recalls, "I remember one of the first things she did was to completely reorganize our shelves that hold sugar flowers, ribbons, and all kinds of decorating supplies. Erica shares my love of über-organization and tidiness—when I saw those shelves after she was done with them, I nearly fainted from joy! We instantly bonded over our shared passion for being crazy obsessive about organizing things."

When the producers of *Ace of Cakes* scouted the bakery, they couldn't have been more thrilled with the building's interior. There was just one problem: all the walls were white,

which translates into a nondynamic, flat, boring image when seen on TV. As my first official task, I was asked to hop up on a ladder and take down all the framed press clippings and pictures in time for the painters, who were on their way to give the bakery a makeover. It was on this ladder where I first met Duff, who walked in, saw what I was up to, and welcomed me with that bellowing laugh of his.

I soon joined the staff as a part-time decorator, working two nights a week, Thursday and Friday—the busiest nights for cake. Then, in January 2008, I decided it was finally time to pursue my love of baking, production, design, sculpture, and making cakes full-time. After a thirteen-year career at National Public Radio, I resigned from my day job and joined the bakery, full steam ahead. I took on a variety of decorating tasks, including working on transportation-related cakes involving wheels and axles: convertible cars, mail trucks, motorcycles, and bicycles. I also found myself developing decorative specialties such as creating gum paste animals; working on landscapes involving trees, rocks, and snow; coloring fondant; prepping cake bases and pans; crumb coating; and or-

ganizing tools and supplies. Even Duff was surprised how fast I picked everything up. "Erica's a really fast learner, she never lets the pressure get to her, and she's always under a lot of it. I can give her as much work as I want, and she'll find a way to get it done," he said.

I especially like to experiment with shaping sugar and other unique baking and decorating techniques. I continue to learn from my friends' projects that push the structural integrity of sugar and other decorative edibles and practice my teensiest royal icing penmanship.

For the cake created specifically for this book, I decided to try out a few embossing techniques—a newly acquired skill I picked up

> **TIP** *Cakes don't like to travel in the front seat or backseat of the car or be held on someone's lap. I've learned that the hard way. Seats feel really slanted to a cake and can start to cause fissures in your fondant and structural problems in your stacked tiers. The best place for a cake en route is on a completely flat surface in the cargo area of a van or in your trunk— without your luggage, of course, and with the air conditioner on full blast.*

we really hadn't seen before at the bakery.

The pink-and-silver cake pictured here is actually the second version of this design I had worked on. I was unsuccessfully trying to lay the fondant down in clean vertical strips, and Duff recommended I do some more research on other techniques and give it another try. Then I applied an idea that Anna had, which is to cover each tier in one whole sheet of white fondant and then delineate the sections by embossing with a roller tool and highlighting the divisions by painting them with copper luster dust. Then I mixed the colors with lemon extract instead of the traditional vodka, which gave a higher iridescence and brighter color sheen as the alcohol evaporated.

I was excited when I first heard about a possible Food Network show featuring Charm City Cakes. It's really

from her Charm City Cakes colleagues—and applied several bright, iridescent colors to rounded corners. I recently came across a print by Charley Harper entitled "Grand Canyon." His juxtaposition of the bright pinks and oranges in those geometric shapes really struck me. Pairing brilliant colors side by side in such a way that it nearly tricks your eye works well with sculpted cakes. I wanted to design a cake that showcased the combination of colors that aren't normally paired together: oranges and pinks with copper and silver. I thought it would have a cool effect on the shape of the tiers and would be something

and hand-printed in our kitchen for our wedding invitation. To see Anna artistically interpret a two-dimensional piece of work into a three-dimensional cake so well was really inspiring.

Another cake the entire bakery all pitched in on was a massive box of sixty-four crayons created for Crayola's official fiftieth-anniversary celebration. I think everyone in the bakery, including Duff, has such incredibly fond childhood memories of that box, with its wide range of colors and all the possibilities they presented us with in recreating it in cake. We even made the little sharpener on the back.

For the cake itself, my primary task was to replicate the wrappers on the crayons and make them edible. First I figured out the precise curve of the black swirl on the top of each wrapper, and then I created a template for it. Then I helped Mary press the fondant into a special mold in the shape of the crayon tips. It was great because each person on the staff worked on mixing colors to represent all of the crayons in the box—and then we planned how all the crayons would fit inside the box, just as they do in the real flip-top

exciting that there's a TV show that explores the many positive and creative aspects of life in Baltimore. People may think they know our city already from visiting the Inner Harbor as a tourist or from watching other television shows or reading novels. But there are so many interesting sound, art, community, and architectural expressions happening right now, and our show explores those as we travel out of the bakery to meet our clients and our neighbors.

As for the impact the show had on my life outside the bakery, I don't get recognized too often, but more often than not I am stopped and asked if I've ever seen the show *Ace of Cakes*, and before I can answer, next comes "Because you look like you could be Mary Alice's sister." Maybe it's because we used to have similar eyeglasses or something.

One episode of the show stands out for me and my husband, John. My favorite episode was in Season Two, "Four Weddings and a Rat," because it featured my wedding cake of the two owls. The inspiration for the cake was a linoleum-block print that John and I designed

> **TIP** Ideas for cakes come from everywhere, not just from cookbooks or baking magazines. Keep a paper or electronic reference file of shapes and colors and designs from everyday things and events that inspire you. Music, fabrics, stationery, flowers, animals, clothing, and architecture inspire me.

TIP *Handle tiny beads and dragées with care, and especially don't spill them onto the floor. Enough said.*

box—we even had to get on stepladders to assemble the massive cake sculpture. To work on a project of such large scope was intense—but it represented such a foundation of memories from our childhoods that everyone got a huge kick out of working on it. By the time we were all done, the cake was huge! I loved it!

Though my attention to detail and work ethic aren't always picked up by the *Ace of Cakes* camera crew, one person in particular has

noticed: Duff. "Erica is one of the first people here, and time and again is the last to leave. She's a smart worker, and her work is always amazingly clean and incredibly tight. As such a genuine superhappy person, she's always a joy to be around." Mary Alice adds, "It's hard to believe Erica came to us with no formal art training at all. She's gone from cleaning out our shelves and washing our dishes to becoming an incredibly talented decorator in her own right. She has a true natural talent, and it shows. She's also one of the kindest, sweetest people I've ever met. She brings an air of thoughtfulness and quiet determination to the bakery."

Behind the Scenes of ACE OF CAKES

THE PRODUCTION STAFF OF
ACE OF CAKES

Our lives have been drastically altered, we have to schedule our work to include TV cameras in our face daily, and we get all the fun stuff that comes from living under the microscope. But our TV crew are not just a bunch of nameless, faceless Hollywood types—they've become a part of our lives and our friends. When we go on location, we hang out together, and often all go out after a day of taping in Baltimore. They come to see us play music. We even vacation together. We miss them when they're not around, and though sometimes I've gotten so frustrated with them that I've thrown my microphone across the room (yes, I've done that a few times), we really enjoy Matt and Daniel, Nick, Mark, Duffy (we have a sound guy named Duffy, weird, huh?), L'il John, Joey, David, Skip, Justin, Jimmy James, the siblings Peters, Rev. Cheney Moon, Jeff, Josh, Kelly Mac, and the many others who have become our muses. We love them for watching what we do and putting up with our nonsense, but most of all we love them because they respect us. Just from watching ourselves on TV and knowing what footage they *didn't* use, I know they're an awesome bunch of people who don't get nearly as much credit as they should. Same thing goes for the editors, Grace and M. J., and the writers, Miriam, Jen, Heather, and Kelly. Think about it this way: for every one of us you see on TV, there are about five people you don't see trying to make us and our cakes look good. Here, in their own words, the crew of *Ace of Cakes* talk a little about what they do for us.

WILLIE GOLDMAN, co-creator and co-executive producer

DANA LEIKEN RICHARDS, co-creator and co-executive producer

LAUREN LEXTON, co-creator and executive producer

TOM ROGAN, co-creator and executive producer

KELLY MCPHERSON, executive producer

MATT CARR, director

JEFFREY R. DANIELS, director

HEATHER MITCHELL, writer

MIRIAM LEFFERT, writer

JEN WISE, writer

GRAYCE LACKLAND, supervising editor

M.J. LOHEED, editor

DANIEL HOPPS, supervising producer

DUFFY NAGLE, audio

NICK RUSH, audio

CREATING AND PRODUCING *ACE OF CAKES* (Part One)
Willie Goldman, co-creator and co-executive producer

I first met Duff when I was twenty-two . . .

. . . months old.

They say anyone who claims to remember anything from when they're that young is lying, but there was a day shortly after he was born that I can recall perfectly—and as fate would have it, this memory revolves around food. Of course, I wasn't old enough to understand the concept of what the hell a brother was—all I knew was that for almost two years of my life there had been one of me, and now there was another. Who was this other one? Was it a new pet? Should we put batteries in it? Why was it peeing on itself?

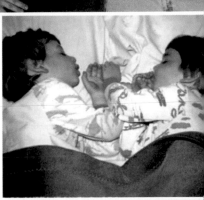

As I stood there at the side of this thing's crib with my bare feet *buried* in this pink-red plush shag carpeting, only one thought went through my head: what does he have that I haven't got? And then I saw it: a big old bottle of milk—and let me tell you, I wanted that milk.

And I was bigger.

So I took it.

Snatched my little newborn brother's milk right out of his hands.

I didn't feel bad at all; I didn't even understand the concept of feeling bad about something. I was two. I was unspoiled by the ways of the world (and girls). Thinking back on it now, how my new little brother cried and cried and cried as I took and drank his milk, I kinda feel (somewhat) guilty—but at the time, whoa, was that ever a eureka moment. From that day forward, this new thing, this new "brother," would provide for me—be it extra milk, more candy, extra allowance, etc. Already at two years old I somehow figured out how to profit off my baby brother . . .

. . . and then he grew up to be talented—and I grew up to be a television producer.

Thirty years later I was halfway around the world doing research on a Navy ship for another TV project, when I got a call from one of my producing partners back in Los Angeles, Dana Leiken Richards. She said there was a production company interested in looking at some of the footage we had of Duff, and if they liked it, would we be interested in teaming up on a potential series? Now, for the past seven years I had worked

on the show *ER* in a variety of positions, so my main specialty was TV drama—but here was not only an opportunity to work in a new genre but a chance to turn Duff into my own personal ATM machine.

I was on the next helicopter out of there.

The producing and pitching of the pilot were relatively straightforward. When I returned to L.A., Dana and I met with Lauren Lexton and Tom Rogan at their production company, Authentic Entertainment. They liked the footage we had but figured the best way to pitch the series was to put together a sizzle reel—a quick five-minute presentation of what everyone envisioned the show to be. Now, to me, as a TV drama writer, this concept was relatively new; the majority of projects pitched in Hollywood either come from the page or are simply verbally pitched. But we're working in a visual medium—so what better way to convey an idea to a group of executives than to actually show them what you're asking them to take a chance on?

So Authentic sent a two-man crew to Baltimore—Jeff Daniels on directing and camera and Josh Spector on audio and everything else. Their mission was to follow Duff around for two

weeks and return to L.A. with all the footage. Once they did, Authentic cut a five-minute presentation that became our pilot, and it was time to "go out" with it (present it to perspective networks). Oddly enough, though Food Network was the obvious home for the show, at the time they were known for less expensive in-studio shows. To produce a docusoap like ours would require sending a field crew across the country, putting them up for months on end, and filming around the clock, six days a week—all while the show's producers, editors, writers, and support staff worked tirelessly from L.A. In its own way, it's like a small military operation—but with better food.

So as the show was pitched to pretty much everyone—HBO, The WB, TLC, Bravo, Discovery, and so on—Food Network was the one place that didn't initially get a copy. At least officially. Somehow, some way, the assistants at the network managed to get a copy, and they loved it. So much so that they found a champion in one of their bosses, Charles Nordlander, vice president of program development. And he saw it and loved it. Fully aware of the fiscal realties of trying to sell the idea to his coworkers at the network, he encountered some hesitation, if not all-out resistance. But the assistants' champion soon became ours, and Charles managed to secure us a commitment of a short, six-episode "cycle" that would serve as our first season. Duff couldn't have been more thrilled, as he had a long affinity for the network, and of course, as he said, it just felt right. Within weeks we were crewing up. Soon after that I found myself on a plane to Baltimore with seven strangers, completely unaware that not only would we become family, but that (cue dramatic music) things were about to change for us all . . .

Aaaand . . . here's the big dramatic part that couldn't be easier to fast-forward through: we shot the show in Baltimore, edited the show in Los Angeles, delivered the show to New York (technically Knoxville), Food Network aired the show nationally, and you watched it in your homes, and now, well, now my "little" brother has become the Chuck Norris of cake decorators. With its hip, Willy Wonka, record-store-meets-surf-shop-meets-bakery vibe, *Ace of Cakes* was a hit.

As for the physical production of the show itself, there is a team of guys and girls who work their asses off to make sure the laid-back, fun-loving atmosphere in the bakery is delivered to your screen: the crew of *Ace of Cakes*. It isn't just the skills they bring to their directing, writing, editing, sound, and so on that make our show what is, but their dedication. Even though the majority of their work takes place behind the scenes, in the end we can all see it come through on screen.

Speaking of people, one of my favorite quotes is from the French writer and aviator Antoine de Saint-Exupéry, the author of *The Little Prince*, who said, "There is no hope of joy except in human relations." Wow, he nailed it. For me personally, the greatest joy I take from *Ace of Cakes* is exactly that: the people I get to

With our mom in Southern California

meet, work with, live with, and celebrate with. And not just our incredible crew but our fans, the bakery's clients, the team at Food Network, our representatives in L.A., and of course our cast, the staff of Charm City Cakes.

One of the key elements behind our show's success is the fourteen people viewers see on screen each week. Be it Duff's adrenaline-fueled, rock-fury attitude, Geof's easygoing, laid-back demeanor, Mary Alice's spunky, spirited gate-keeping sass, or the rest of the staff's unique sense of baking, artistry, and fun, we seem to relate to them because we are like them. And although they're incredibly diverse, if there's one thing the cast members of *Ace of Cakes* have in common is that they're genuine—and this honesty comes across on-screen. One of the reasons for the popularity of reality TV is that viewers are able to look at the people on screen and usually find a little bit of themselves. All too often "reality" shows are anything but—and feature

Ace of Cakes co-creators and co-executive producers Dana and Willie have been friends since high school

format adapted perfectly for reality TV.

Which brings me back to my brother and one last story we didn't catch on tape. There was one extremely late night over Thanksgiving break when the TV crew had gone home, the bakery staff was done, and it was just the two of us alone in the bakery. I had some paperwork to complete, and Duff had one last cake to finish. We were up all night, working away, and when he was done, the cake just blew me away. So much so that it *had* to be part of the show. With the crew gone and no one to operate all the gear, I had Duff bring the cake down into the base-ment where we shoot the hero shots. I set up the lights, grabbed a camera, and did my best to capture his creation on tape. Now, though my footage turned out to be pretty much unus-able, for me it was that moment—Duff on cake, me on camera—that became an almost living metaphor for the collaborative effort that is *Ace of Cakes*. When you're a kid, it's hard to com-prehend the influence your upbringing has—but looking back on it now, it all makes perfect sense. It's in our DNA. Our father is a hard-core businessman, our mother is a passionate artist—and somehow, some way, we found a way to do business by creating art.

people none of the rest of us can relate to. Luck-ily for us as producers, our on-screen personas had already been "cast" by Duff long before we showed up with our cameras. And once we did, what we discovered was a group of people as real as one could hope for on TV.

And from a creative point of view, there was something I didn't pick up on until after the show started to air. Most screenwriters are well versed in the three-act structure—a narrative paradigm with roots as far back as Aristotle (ap-parently I *did* pay attention in English class). And even though films have ninety minutes or more to tell a story, in half an hour divided by com-mercial breaks we establish a world, confront a challenge, and end with a climax. A storytelling

Oh, and Duff, I really do feel bad about the milk.

I've known Duff and his brother Willie since I was fifteen and we were all classmates at McLean High School in the suburbs of northern Virginia. We were surrounded by the sons and daughters of congressmen, but it was clear that Duff was different. Before Duff was the "Bad Boy of Baking," before Duff was a "rock star," he was a meathead, a jock whose favorite class was metal shop. Duff wasn't remembered for being brilliant, and he wasn't remembered even for being good at sports. The most remarkable thing about Duff was his laugh.

Duff's laugh is truly unique, a throaty chuckle that is simultaneously lovable, grumpy, endearing, and full of mischief; if we could, we'd trademark and patent that sucker tomorrow. When it comes to Duff and his crew of talented cake

decorators, what you see is what you get. Part of Duff's endearing star quality is that, in spite of the success of *Ace*, he's remained wide-eyed and humbled by his success. Who would have thought that his artistry, charisma, and contagious laughter would be the driving force behind a hit TV show? Certainly not his high school teachers! But some of us knew it even then . . .

I got my start in the business from Duff's brother Willie. We had no particular connections, but luck struck and Willie landed an internship at NBC in Burbank. Six months later he called to say that he had finished his semester-long internship and that he had referred me to the "powers that be." The next day I packed my bags and headed for the West Coast, imagining palm trees, white beaches, and Hollywood Boulevard. Willie helped me get my foot in the door in Hollywood, and I'll always be grateful to him.

The fifty-year-old NBC page program is meant to be a stepping-stone to better jobs and higher wages in the entertainment industry, and with a little bit of luck and some hard work, I ended up with experience on shows as divergent as *The Tonight Show*, *Life Moments*, *Battlebots*, and *It's Christopher Lowell*, an interior design show.

I hadn't talked to Duff much after coming to California, but through Willie I knew he'd started a small, profitable bakery and that he had some celebrity clients such as Al Gore and Alice Cooper. When Willie sent me a link to the Charm City Cakes website and I saw Duff's cake creations, my jaw dropped! I immediately recog-

With Dana at the bakery

nized that Duff was not your average cake decorator. These cakes were edgy, unique, and beautiful. On a whim I dialed Charm City's number, and Duff himself answered. We caught up on old times and new, and then I asked him if he'd be interested on being on the Christopher Lowell show. Duff was revved up and ready to be on TV, and he gave me the lowdown on his cakes, his training, and his power tools. (Fortunately, my experience on *Battlebots* had prepped me on the importance of power tools.)

I decided to pitch an idea for a feature field piece on Duff showcasing some of his cakes along with his wizardry with power tools in the kitchen, and thankfully Christopher Lowell liked it. I had no idea that Duff's appearance on the show would become his breakthrough into television.

We aired a three-minute piece on Duff that was lighthearted, funny, and fluffy, and it was clear that Duff's larger-than-life personality offered TV something new. He was both a bad boy and a baker! He was a guitar-playing, chainsaw-wielding maniac who didn't speak with a French accent. And he was a natural—comfortable on camera, something that all aspiring actors, TV personalities, and presidential aspirants are desperate for, because you can't fake it. So I embarked on a journey to create a show around this wild, edgy, and incredibly talented guy.

What I didn't know was that it would take four more years to write, pitch, and sell a show with Duff at the helm. Willie and I worked closely together and wrote up a show treatment that was based off one of Duff's pet projects, an underground live baking comedy show in Baltimore called *F—— You Let's Bake*. Just try to imagine our bad boy whipping, chuckling, baking, and brimming in a late-night show format. It would be interactive, just like the *The Rocky Horror Picture Show*—but with baking and more fun!

Eventually, through the help of my colleague and friend Elayne Sawaya, we were able get the treatment and Duff under the noses of Authentic Entertainment, a production company that was willing to think outside the mainstream.

During the four years that it took to get *Ace of Cakes* on the air, I continued working in Hollywood, then with *Best Damn Sports Show Period*, and finally to MTV, where I've been producing dating reality shows for two years. I'm responsible for many of the episodes on the pop-culture phenoms *NEXT* and *Exposed*. And yes, for those of you who have been my victims (being tackled by police dogs or wrestling in a vat of pudding), I proudly take responsibility for coming up with those crazy date activities! But helping to create *Ace of Cakes*—well, it's the buttercream icing on the red velvet cake!

Favorite show moment: The Wrigley Field moment with the eighty-year-old Cubs fan touches a soft spot in my heart because of my dad and Grandpa Ben. They are true-blue Cubs fans (so am I).

Favorite episode: The Super Bowl special. To this day it still blows me away that the NFL asked Duff to make the official NFL Super Bowl cake. That's when I knew Duff had made it.

Favorite cake: My own wedding cake topper (which traveled from Baltimore to Los Angeles and made it to my wedding safely), a Greek-inspired rendering of the blue-and-white church domes found on Santorini.

Favorite flavor: It's a tie: pumpkin chocolate chip (which was also my wedding cake topper) and red velvet with buttercream. I love anything with buttercream.

Favorite show titles before we ended up with *Ace of Cakes*: *F—— You Let's Bake*, *Eat Me*, *Charm City*, and *Doughboy*.

I hear pitches for new TV shows every day. But it's not often that I'm sitting in one of those pitch meetings, watching video of a live audience shouting "F—— You Let's Bake! F—— You Let's Bake!" as they throw eggs at a chef-hatted, goateed young man who has just shown them how to make the perfect soufflé. But in March 2005, that's exactly what I was doing.

"There's *something* there," I said to the people pitching the show—Elayne Sawaya, who made the introductions; Willie Goldman; and Dana Leiken Richards. "I don't know what, and I certainly don't know who we can sell it to, but

there's *something* . . . " Several weeks later, as soon as my partner, Tom Rogan, and I met Duff in person in L.A., I knew that *something* was Duff. Within weeks we sent a crew to Baltimore to film "a week in the life" of Charm City Cakes. The idea was to put together a sales tape. It's very difficult to walk into a network and say, "I want to do a show about a baker in Baltimore with a great personality" without visuals. And nothing can describe how amazing Charm City's cakes are as well as seeing the cakes themselves.

We edited the sales tape and called it *F—— You Let's Bake.* We knew the name wouldn't stick around, but it was a good way to get the attention of networks we were pitching to. In the footage we shot, Duff didn't hold back with his "Bad Boy of Baking" persona, and Geof was brilliant in his "Geof" way. The funny thing is, we didn't even know about Mary Alice's charms— she played a very small part in the tape—so her fantastic personality was an incredible surprise when we went back to Baltimore to start filming the series.

We made the rounds of networks, tape in hand. TLC loved the show and was currently in production on *Miami Ink*, so the idea of another "docusoap" really appealed to the people there—they were definitely interested in ordering a pilot. The funny thing is, we never even pitched it to Food Network, as we thought it was too edgy for it. Then one day, Food Network called and asked to see the tape. Within days it had made an offer for six episodes. This was just the type of thing it was looking for to change its image, and Charles Nordlander, who had just started at Food after developing shows at A&E, was incredibly excited and supportive.

Director Matt Carr and producer Lauren Lexton set up the hero shot for the main title sequence.

Lauren Lexton, Kelly McPherson, and Heather Mitchell

We hired the veteran producer (and funny guy) Kelly McPherson to run the show. Suffice it to say that this was one situation where the stars just aligned—more than in any other show we've ever produced. The bakery staff, the producing team, and Food Network all had this incredible synchronicity, with mutual respect for all of our individual talents. Duff and the team at Charm City respected us as producers, Authentic respected the whole team there as great artists, and the network respected that, together, we were going to deliver a great show. And by gosh, we did.

The one last thing I'll say is how much I respect the commitment to helping people and the community that I've found at Charm City Cakes. Because that has been the greatest gift—to be able to bring to the TV-viewing public episodes that feature organizations such as Make-A-Wish Foundation, Habitat for Humanity, and so many other charitable concerns in such a fun, edgy, and entertaining way. Duff Goldman, you have made a difference. And I think that's all you really ever wanted.

215

Our first reaction was that a raucous live baking show would be a tough sell, but as we talked to Duff and got a better sense of who he was, and as he told us more about his bakery and the type of people who worked there, we thought there might be another approach. We floated the idea of a docusoap and arranged with Duff to send a crew to his bakery for a few days.

Deciding whether or not to risk money on a "pitch tape" is always difficult. When you're trying to sell a show, having tape for a network is almost mandatory, especially if the show is personality-based, as this one was. But as engaging as someone may be in person, you never really know how he or she will come across on tape. The fact that we'd never been to the bakery or even met any of Duff's staff didn't make the decision any easier.

I was iffy on sending a crew. I felt there were only a few places to pitch a show about a guy who bakes cakes, no matter how interesting he was or how elaborate the cakes were. But it's hard to let a unique personality like Duff go, and Lauren was convinced that Duff would be great on camera, so we decided to go for it.

We shot for only a few days in the bakery, and when we got the tapes back the footage was better than we'd expected. Duff was a natural on camera, and the interaction between Duff and his staff was engaging, unforced, and, most important . . . funny. But as good as it was, I still had my doubts: would any network really buy a show with no conflict whatsoever, where the central story element is baking cakes?

Once the pitch tape was complete, the pitching process began. In a decision that seemed perfectly rational at the time, we pitched the

Appropriately enough, I first met Duff in a kitchen.

It was the kitchen of our office, which doubles as a conference room. Duff was there with Willie and Dana, and they'd come in to pitch *F—— You Let's Bake* to my partner and me. The finale of the show was Duff wearing a protective mask as the audience hurled raw eggs at him while chanting, "F—— you, let's bake! F—— you, let's bake!"

show to almost every network *except* Food Network. Based on what we'd seen, we figured the channel wouldn't be open to a pitch with Duff's power-tools-in-the-kitchen approach to baking . . . or with "F—— You" in the title.

Shortly after we pitched the tape around, I received a call from TLC: "This guy's *awesome*. We'll buy ten episodes!" It's extremely rare to get that kind of reaction from a network—it usually prefers to start with a pilot. Ten episodes seemed too good to be true, and unfortunately it was. The next day I got another call from TLC, this time telling me that though they thought Duff was terrific, people at the network had their doubts about a cake show, so they wanted to start with a pilot.

And that was it. We'd successfully sold the show as a one-hour pilot to TLC. All we had to do was make a great pilot, and with luck we'd go to series. Once we received the paperwork from the network, we'd sign on the dotted line and get started.

And that's when I got an out-of-the-ordinary call that started like this:

Dialogue:
Receptionist: Tom?
Me: Yep.
Receptionist: Kathleen Finch is calling for you.
Me: Kathleen Finch?
Receptionist: Yes.
Me: Kathleen Finch, the head of Food Network?
Receptionist: Um . . . she didn't say.

To give a little context here, it's very unusual for the head of a network to call out of the blue. Every network has a development staff, and they're usually the ones who do the calling (although even then it's usually the production company calling *them*).

Of course, the call was about *F—— You*

Let's Bake. Kathleen had heard about the pitch and wanted to see the tape ASAP. I told her we hadn't pitched the show to Food because of the whole "F—— You" thing, but according to her, the network was going in a new direction and this show could be the perfect fit. Sure enough, the next day she called back: "We'll go straight to series with six episodes."

And *Ace of Cakes* was born.

Of course, it wasn't quite that easy, and until the name was changed to *Ace of Cakes*, the process of getting the show off the ground led to some entertaining email subject lines, such as "RE: F—— You," "Several F—— You Questions," and "Where are we with F—— You?" But in the end, Food Network was very supportive of the show. Our executive there, Charles Nordlander (who, as it turns out, had been the driving force behind the call from Kathleen), saw the potential in Duff and his crew. If it hadn't been for his vision and support of the show, *Ace of Cakes* might never have made it to air, and we'll always be grateful to him.

I had no idea what I was getting into when I signed on to co–executive produce a reality show called *F—— You Let's Bake*. All I knew was that Duff Goldman was a funny, talented baker, prone to dropping cakes and F-bombs—sometimes simultaneously. I was intrigued.

Within six weeks of starting the job, the show's title had been changed to *Ace of Cakes*. By then, I was well versed in the ways of fondant, modeling chocolate, and gum paste and ready to call Baltimore my second home.

There's always laughter, lots of cake, and, from time to time, a little drama. I found that out during our first week of shooting at the bakery, as Duff and Geof prepared a fifty-pound cake for the Preakness horse race. Preparations went down to the wire, as Duff ferried the cake through a stable full of racehorses and across a track to the VIP tent—oh, by the way, he was

nearly run down by another horse. In the end, the cake was a big hit, just like the series.

My job is to oversee the day-to-day operations of the show, from picking the cakes and storylines we're following to hiring crew to working through story with the writers and editors. All of us worked very hard from day one to create a format and style that made the show feel unique. We wanted the show to have a bit of an edge but to be accessible to kids, adults, and, yes, hipsters. We want the audience to come away from watching the show saying, "I wish I worked at Charm City Cakes." My favorite part of the job is working with the editors in the bay to craft and shape the show to a tight, entertaining twenty-two minutes.

It's hard to say what my favorite episode is, because there are several: the premiere episode (for sentimental reasons), the flamingo episode (number 104), the Washington Monument lighting (number 208), and the episode in which we included footage from the early days of the bakery, including Mary Alice's first week on the job Anna at the bakery paid us the best compliment of all: she said it was as if we were making high-end home movies of everyone at CCC.

Working on *Ace of Cakes* is the best job I've ever had. Everyone on the staff spends much of their day laughing at Duff, Geof, Mary Alice, and the rest of the CCC crew. Sitcoms don't have anything on these kids. Ironically, some of my best times working on *AOC* haven't been at the bakery but rather at the office in Los Angeles, late in the day. That's when the phone calls come in from Baltimore—urgent updates from our director or field producer. For example: "The flamingo cake is too tall and won't fit into the van.

The very first day of production on Ace of Cakes *saw the crew shooting in a hotel room just before* The Tonight Show.

It's pouring down!" Or "Duff just fell off the scaffolding at the monument-lighting ceremony—but his cake was awesome." And finally, "A woman just ordered a $3,000 Spider Man cake for her kid's birthday, and she wants to pay Duff in marble because her check bounced."

My dream cake would be pretty much anything four tiers or bigger with sock monkeys dancing around it. My favorite cake I've seen on the show is Elena's Zombie Head or the Highland Cow that lost its hair. I also loved the beaver, because of all the jokes that came with it.

The best thing about my job is that I've had the chance to work with the funniest, nicest, and most talented people in the cake decorating/ television worlds. To anyone who disagrees with me, I say, "F—— you, let's bake!"

A while before production began on Season One of *Ace of Cakes*, Jeff Daniels and I were shooting a reality show that we hated on a Caribbean Island for a number of months. We talked often about what was wrong with it and how we would film it differently, and, more important, how *F—— You Let's Bake* was the best chance we'd get to prove that all these ideas we'd come up with could work. Jeff already had the job of directing it at the time (as the series was sold to Food Network based on the demo he shot and directed) and thankfully was able to lobby for me to be given the role of shooting it. I doubt that it was an easy sell to the powers that be; I was a B-roll guy. On that island my job was to shoot pretty palm trees, pretty sunsets on the beach, pretty animals, and various other pretty things. I loved being pigeonholed into to that position—I had a camera, a tripod, and an island to freely explore and quite honestly had no interest in shooting the reality portion of any reality show. Talking with Jeff and watching *F—— You Let's Bake* changed my mind.

I firmly believe that if anyone besides Jeff had made the demo called *F—— You Let's Bake* (and subsequently directed the first season), the show wouldn't have gone anywhere. People like Duff, Geof, and everyone else at the bakery aren't born feeling natural and comfortable as themselves on camera. It takes someone to bring it out of them, and if you've ever met Jeff you'd have that strange experience of talking to a total stranger as if he were one of your best friends within five minutes (if he wanted you to, that is—he's also one of the most odd, confusing, and hilarious people I've ever known). Watching that demo, an audience could feel a real connection to the people at Charm City Cakes *because* they were being themselves in front of the camera—more accurately, they were being themselves in front of the people behind the camera. It's this relationship between those in front of the camera and those behind it that we designed the look, style, and lighthearted feel of *Ace of Cakes* upon.

On a production such as *Ace of Cakes*, the job of the director begins and ends with the filming of the show. It's the producers and executive producers in Los Angeles, namely Kelly MacPherson, who decide what cakes or events

Young Matt with dad and cake

we're going to feature in the episode and how it's edited. He's like Miles Silverberg from *Murphy Brown*, except he's calm, bald, and filled with good-natured (and often a little dirty) Texan humor. *Sports Night* would be a good comparison as well.

The filming of the show is my playground. That's not to say Kelly isn't involved in the filming; if Kelly says "Jump," I say, "How high? But before I do, you should know my foot is hurting today—it's the one I broke, like, four or five years ago and cut the cast off myself after I got it wet and it was stinking up the room and everyone was looking at me but trying not to look at me—and what if you call and tell Duff to jump and I'll shoot it? It will be great! But I need another camera operator, a crane, and at least ten thousand live snakes." Kelly has a great

*Matt filming
the puppet
sequence on
location in
Hawaii*

laugh and a right hand in the field named Daniel Hopps (supervising producer) who makes sure I reach an appropriate and satisfactory vertical height.

We film the episode in Baltimore, , and send the footage back to L.A., where writers watch it and write a script of quotes from, and references to, the footage; editors get the script and footage and put together a rough cut; Kelly watches it and asks for changes; the editors make changes; Food Network executives watch it and ask for changes; Kelly and the editors make some of the requested changes (but not all of them, in order to preserve their creative integrity), Food Network puts the episode on the air; a fresh goat is sacrificed to the fickle deity Neilsen, the episode gets good ratings, we get more money, and we film more episodes.

We roll cameras Tuesday through Saturday for the most part—sometimes Monday through

Saturday and sometimes Sunday through Saturday. Whatever the week, my job as director is, simply put, to make sure that from the reality footage, the B-roll, the on-the-fly interviews, and the sit-down interviews, Kelly (with the writers and editors) will be able to construct a good story. The creative part of my job is in how each of those elements is crafted.

The *Ace of Cakes* crew on location at Charm City cakes consists of eight people, making up two units—the A crew and the B crew. There are two camera operators, including myself, two sound recordists, two assistant camera people, a supervising producer, and an associate producer. Perhaps the most important thing to note about how we shoot the show is that we shoot single camera as much as possible—with one camera operator and one sound recordist capturing scenes without the assistance of an additional camera. This isn't easy to do when

With Matt filming the opening credit sequence for Season One

you're shooting twelve to fifteen cake decorators working and talking to one another. The camera operator has to be right in the middle of it.

Ace of Cakes isn't shot through hidden cameras. It isn't shot from the sidelines to preserve a fourth wall, either. If I were to point to anything and pronounce it the secret of *Ace of Cakes'* success as a TV show, it would be this: the camera is just another employee of Charm City Cakes, and Duff hires only friends and friends of friends to work in his bakery. It's a very tight-knit group, and placing cameras on the periphery wouldn't work. We couldn't force our way in and produce things either, as Duff has an extremely keen sense of bullshit and wouldn't stand for anything of the sort (one of his best qualities). It's Duff's house and his rules, so being invited in meant that we were to be friends or we were to leave.

Mat with a Warhammer Squig

Reality blows. I stand in long lines at airports, I misplace car keys on a daily basis, I answer unwanted cell phone calls and struggle to pay the rent each month. Reality, my reality, would be a whole lot tastier served as thirty-minute appetizers made up of only the day's best ingredients. Sprinkle in a few whip pans, sound effects, speed ramps, and laugh tracks, and you have yourself "reality television"—the ultimate recipe for digestible reality.

It started with the demo known as *F—— You, Let's Bake!* I had to shoot the pilot to present to prospective networks, so I spent a week in Baltimore living in Duff's apartment, filming his daily routine at a bakery down the street. There were crazy cakes, awkward employees, loud music, and a red velvet curtain hanging from the front window. "This is the style of the show," I said to Josh Spector, the sound guy and sole member of the crew, and pointed to the curtain. "Take

that down and hang it from a C-stand." We spent the afternoon building a mock stage that would play host to the wild creations produced by Duff and his team. These "hero shots," captured with a handheld camera wide enough to include the lights, popping back and forth between focal lengths, and snapping in and out of focus would become the iconic look of *Ace of Cakes* and the backbone of the style used in the show. Theatrics was our muse.

A year later, Duff had a new bakery and the show was green-lit. We wanted to avoid shooting into the endless white walls of infinity and convinced Duff to paint his place. The color palette you see in the bakery today was extracted directly from the demo: red, green, and blue, complementary colors that appeal to the eye. I hired my friend and longtime colleague Matt Carr to come on as the director of photography, and together we created a light scheme that would provide our cameras with an all-access pass to the bakery. The first day of prep, we suspended twenty-five additional lamps from the ceiling and gelled down the windows to balance the blue daylight with our studio tungsten lamp light. With Duff, you never know what to expect, and you want to be there when it happens. With our 360-degree view of his playground, we were

sure to never miss a beat. The oven was hot, and our imaginations were cooking . . .

Some of our sweetest camera tricks were executed by our B-camera cinema star James Mann and usually involved strapping cameras to bizarre objects. One slow afternoon James spent his lunch rigging a camera to Mary Alice's pedal bike, and we filmed her riding down the neighborhood streets on her way to work. "If it's outrageous, let's do it," I would say every morning to Matt and James as the gear was unloaded. The two would mount cameras everywhere—inside the oven, high and wide on top of ladders, underneath the delivery vans—all in an attempt to complement Duff's wild and playful behavior. The day's tapes were sent overnight to Kelly and the postteam in L.A., who sprinkled the goods across the first batch of shows that would make up Season One. With the final ingredient now in . . . dessert could be served.

Reality is uncut, obtuse, infinite, and uncontrollable. But when I sit back and watch *Ace of Cakes*, I smile with delight. This reality tastes good! From Authentic Entertainment to the gang at Charm City Cakes to the red velvet curtain hanging in Duff's window, I congratulate them all on creating a deliciously entertaining, wildly digestible Food Network show. Long live *Ace of Cakes*.

225

WRITING *ACE OF CAKES* (Part One)
Heather Mitchell, writer

Like so many L.A. stories, my time at *Ace of Cakes* started with a call from a friend:

Kelly McPherson: "I've got a new show coming up. Wanna work on it?"
Me: "Eh, maybe."
Kelly: "It's called *F—— You Let's Bake.*"
Me: "When do I start?"

From this auspicious beginning came two of the most entertaining years of my life.

There's no getting around it: there's an aspect of creepiness to writing a reality show. Whereas scripted-TV writers work with characters who live only in their minds, reality writers spend their days watching real people they'll probably never meet.

Heather holds a sign made for her by Mary Alice

We live each week along with our "characters"— just one week after they lived it themselves. We're there for their jokes and their fights and their day-to-day lives, sifting through fifty hours of footage to tell a twenty-two-minute story.

By necessity, this professional voyeurism leads to a sense of dissociation between writer and subject—the "characters" stop being real people as soon as the tape starts rolling. But from the start, *Ace of Cakes* was different. Emails, phone calls, cross-country flights— within a few weeks we were all friends, albeit long-distance ones. When I went to Baltimore to visit the bakery, I was promptly put up in Mary Alice's guestroom—a friend from out of town, not a writer visiting a set. And we spent the weekend like girlfriends do—shopping, gossiping, just hanging out.

The world of *Ace of Cakes* is so real—not just the bakery but the stories behind the cakes and the people who receive them and the city of Baltimore itself—that watching the show makes you feel as though you're spending time in a real workspace. And I think what people love most about the show is the sense that if they happened to live in Baltimore, happened to go to art school, or just happened to have the good fortune of knowing Duff Goldman, they could fit right in.

What I hear most often from our fans is how much fun life in the bakery looks and how different it is from their own office culture. And they're absolutely right—anyone who gets to create something special with their friends for a living should feel lucky.

I know I do.

I went to Baltimore and the bakery last September or October to meet everyone, and Malice was waiting for her at the airport with that sign. I have it proudly pinned to the bulletin board above my desk at Authentic Entertainment back in Los Angeles.

WRITING *ACE OF CAKES* (Part Two)

Miriam Leffert, writer

ACE OF CAKES
EPISODE 208
10/29/07

ACT ONE	ACT ONE
	MONTAGE OF BALTIMORE EXT. BAKERY - MORNING INT. BAKERY
DUF2-B-1019-1 13:06:16:06 DUFF is walking around the bakery with a toilet seat cover around his neck. The lid rests against his head.	
	DUF2-B-1019-1 13:06:20:15 DUFF I want everyone to be very serious
DUF2-B-1019-1 13:06:57:29 GEOFF yawns and gives DUFF a nonplussed look.	
DUF2-B-1019-1 13:07:44:02 KATHERINE looks sleepily at DUFF. She doesn't seem surprised by the sight of her boss wearing a toilet seat.	
	DUF2-B-1019-1 13:10:25:14 DUFF walks up to MARY ALICE, who is writing the shopping list.

ACE OF CAKES CONTINUED
EPISODE 208
10/29/07

ACT ONE	ACT ONE
	MARY ALICE: So are you going to Home Depot like that?
	DUFF: Yeah. I will walk into Home Depot just like this.
	MARY ALICE: Is toilet seat on your list?
	DUFF looks down at the toilet seat under his chin.
	DUFF: (Laughs) Evidently.
	MARY ALICE: Do you need to be reminded to buy a toilet seat?
	DUFF: (Laughing) I don't think I need to be reminded to buy a toilet seat.
	MARY ALICE: I'll hold it and you spin.
	DUFF makes a flushing sound and spins, pretending to be flushed down the toilet. He cracks up and pops his head back up the toilet seat.
	MARY ALICE: Nice.

A writer's job on a reality show is to view hours and hours of footage in search of the "good stuff." We pick out the storylines and carefully craft and juxtapose reality scenes and interviews to create a script for the editor. This is not an easy job on *Ace of Cakes*; my first script could have been a miniseries. Duff and his staff just hanging out in the bakery were so hilarious that figuring out what to cut was almost impossible. And it hasn't gotten any easier!

Unfortunately the scene above was cut for time. I keep a whole treasure trove of orphan scenes, hoping to find them a home in future episodes. Luckily, one of the other writers was looking for a funny bit to open her script, and that's how the great Toilet Bowl Scene was saved from the cutting room floor.

That is the magic of this show. You never know what crazy cake someone is going to order, what outlandish thing Duff is going to do this time, how Mary Alice will talk Duff out of his harebrained idea, or what's going to come out of Geof's mouth next. Not a day that goes by that I don't say to one of my coworkers, "You have to come see this."

Knowing that a place like Charm City Cakes actually exists is kind of like discovering that there really is a Santa at the North Pole—if Santa had a serious potty mouth, a penchant for blowing things up, some really naughty elves . . . and was Jewish. There is truly something for everyone in this show. I love that it's a huge hit with hipster college kids and five-year-olds alike. As corny as this sounds, there's a "magic" at Charm City Cakes, and I feel pretty darn lucky to be a part of it.

230

BEHIND THE CAKE

See his story in
ACE OF CAKES episode 605,
"Macy's and the Big Apple"

WITT GIANNINI

Back in 2002, Blair and Gene Giannini ordered a cake for their son Witt's first birthday. Now, for Charm City Cakes, the phrase "back in the day" refers to when I was working out of my house with only Geof at my side. Witt's cake was a cute, brightly colored creation with blocks on top spelling out Witt's name. Luckily they loved it—so much so, in fact, that they've come back every year for Witt's birthday cake.

Their annual cakes always tie into the theme of the party they throw. Over the years Witt has had a replica of his pug, Truman; a pin-the-tail-on-the-donkey cake; a Hawaiian surfer dude cake; a '57 Chevy convertible; and a cowboy-themed cake. Being able to watch Witt grow up over the last six years has been a treat for all of us at the bakery. And having six-time repeat customers is the highest compliment there is!

Every year when Mary Alice purchases a new yearly calendar for the bakery, one of the first things she does is mark off the third weekend of October for Witt's cake. Even though he's literally growing older in front of our eyes, we hope he never gets too old for a birthday cake from Charm City Cakes.

When I first met Duff, I was literally surprised. As a birthday gift to me, my boyfriend secretly planned a trip to Baltimore. When we arrived at Charm City Cakes, seeing everyone sitting at the table was a bit surreal for me. It's my job to watch them working, and until that moment I had only ever seen them on television. It was very strange to step into the reality. I was even more surprised when Anna brought out an orange octopus birthday cake they'd made for me. Duff gave me a big hug, thanked me for my work on the show, and welcomed me to his home. He's such a nice person, and he talked to me as if we'd known each other for years. We toured the bakery and the basement where the interviews are taped and his band rehearses, and then Duff showed me a few bakers' secrets for making amazing cakes. Everyone at Charm City Cakes was exactly as I thought they would be—incredible people and artists.

I started working at Authentic in January 2006. It was here that I first met Kelly McPherson, supervising producer. He and I hit it off straight away, and he liked my style of editing so much that he asked me four months before *Ace of Cakes* began if I would edit it. It's such a thrill to be involved in a project that became an instant success!

At Authentic Entertainment, I edit *Ace of Cakes* using editing software called Final Cut Pro. When I start a new episode of *Ace of Cakes*, I receive around three hundred hours of footage that the assistant editors have digitized onto media storage drives. Using Final Cut Pro, I can easily scan through all the digitized media and locate the most humorous sound bites and the best shots of cakes to use in each episode. In addition to all the footage, I also receive a transcript binder with all the interviews from Duff, Mary Alice, and Geof. It usually takes me two or three days to organize the footage and read all the transcripts before I begin editing. A writer gives me a script for the show, and I have three weeks to turn that into what the viewer will see when the show airs. One of the hardest parts of my job is having to cut out funny scenes in an episode if a show is too long. To date, my favorites are the Jay Leno, Super Bowl, King Tut, and Harry Potter episodes.

PRODUCING *ACE OF CAKES* (Part Six)

Rachel Whitty Hajj, producer

"*Oh, my God, I love that show!*"

"Do you get to eat a lot of cake?"

"I love Duff!"

"Do you get to eat a lot of cake?"

"My wife is a huge fan."

"Do you get to eat a lot of cake?"

"What do they taste like?"

"Do you get to eat a lot of cake?"

And then they ask, "So what exactly do you do on the show?" I tell them I'm one of the producers, to which they say, "Cool . . . so what exactly do you do on the show?" Uggghhhhh. Here we go . . .

There's a running joke in L.A. that if you ask anyone—your waiter, your barista, the guy tearing your ticket stub at the multiplex—"What project are you working on?," they've all got an answer.

After graduating from the University of Georgia, I decided to make the big move to Los Angeles. Though my life has changed a lot over the years, the one constant—the one question that comes up in every single conversation—is, well, you guessed it, "What project are you working on?" For the past two years I've had the pleasure of answering, "*Ace of Cakes.*" And the reaction is always the same: eyes widen, smiles blossom, and faces light with excitement:

I'm sure you've noticed in the opening credits of your favorite show or movie a whole list of people who've worked on the project, including multiple variations of the title "producer." Here in Hollywood we've got executive producers, co–executive producers, field producers, associate producers, and of course, just producers. On *Ace of Cakes* I'm a bit of a hybrid. If you took Nancy Drew, a traffic cop, a den mother, a bill collector, a professional liaison, and a Girl Friday and threw them into Duff's industrial thirty-quart mixer, you'd start to get an idea of my job on the show.

Though the show is shot on location with our

field crew in Baltimore, all the tapes and notes are sent back to us at the offices of Authentic Entertainment. Surprisingly, I've never been to the bakery, and believe it or not, I've yet to actually meet anyone of my "coworkers" on the Charm City Cakes staff in person—but I feel as if I know them as well as I know everyone here. As if she were not already busy enough, I'm on the phone with the gatekeeper herself, Mary Alice, two or three times a day, and there's a constant daily flow of emails between us. I simply couldn't do my job without Malice.

My job as producer runs the entire gamut of planning what we're going to be filming months from now all the way through making sure the final episode of the season gets delivered to the network. I do everything I can to help things run smoothly from prepreproduction to postproduction. I work very closely with our executive producers and do what I can to assist them with all the minutiae of running a show. I create calendars and end credits, gather photos and sketches, and organize a lot of paperwork. I make sure the tapes from the field go through our postproduction department as quickly as possible. Once the writer has finished a script, I have to make sure the editors have everything they need to start "cutting" their assigned episode.

Once a decision has been made about which particular cakes we're following for an episode, I get cracking. I call clients to see if they'd like their cake featured on the show. Then I call the locations for the parties in order to get their approval and to get location releases signed. Because of the wide variety of venues and events that order cakes, I'm on the phone with hotels, stadiums, country clubs, private homes, public parks, boats, bars, and restaurants. You name it; we've shot there.

Now comes the fun part: rights and clearances. If Charm City Cakes is doing a cake in the shape of the board game Operation, a Cessna airplane, a Royal typewriter, or whatever, we have to get permission from those companies before we can film or broadcast footage of their copyrighted material or intellectual property. I'm the one who tracks down the right person in the right department at the company headquarters. I end up leaving a lot of peculiar messages: "Hi, my name is Rachel and I'm calling from *Ace of Cakes* on Food Network, perhaps you've heard of us. Do you know who I should talk to about getting approval to broadcast a cake version of a Scrabble board?"

As we're constantly under deadline to get the show shot, edited, and delivered for an airdate, I'm always under pressure to make sure we have all the proper releases. Since I've started working on *Ace of Cakes*, there's rarely been a day where I'm not anxiously stalking the fax machine!

I personally don't have much to do with the creative process of the show, which is in the hands of our executive producers, director, writers, and editors. My responsibility is to support them and make sure nothing gets in the way of "the funny." Maybe next time when someone asks me what I do, I'll just say that I'm kind of a mixed-up version of Nancy Drew, a traffic cop, a den mother, a bill collector, a professional liaison, and a Girl Friday.

And by the way . . . I never get to eat the cake.

EDITING *ACE OF CAKES* (Part Two)
M. J. Loheed, editor

On November 30, 2006, this email arrived in my inbox:

To: MJ Loheed <mjloheed@email.com>
From: Kelly McPherson<kmcpherson@email.com>
Subject: Ace of Cakes

MJ,

My name is Kelly McPherson—I'm currently producing a reality series for Food Network called *Ace of Cakes*. We're looking for someone to edit an upcoming episode and Rebecca Short passed your resume our way.

The show centers around Duff Goldman and his staff of cake decorators in Baltimore. It's very funny and definitely a departure for Food Network. If you're interested let me know.

Kelly McPherson

My first thought was, Cake decorators? Are you $&)%ing kidding me? It seemed another sign that my career was spiraling down the giant hole of stupidity that's engulfing television. However, ever the freelancer, I replied that I was interested even though I definitely was not. I doubt anyone came to this project with more doubts than I, and no one was more surprised that *Ace of Cakes* is a good show—scratch that, it's a great show. In my opinion, it deserves an Emmy!

Ace of Cakes does things that very few reality shows do. It's cool without being exclusive. It doesn't attract its audience by slamming anyone. It's not celebrity-driven (although I suppose everyone in the bakery is kind of famous now). It's not even a proper cooking show because no one is going to learn more than a tidbit here and there about making cakes. It works because every cake is not a recipe but a story: Who's it for? What are they celebrating? Will it be difficult to make? Did someone drop it? How did

they get cake to do that? I wonder what fondant tastes like? (To me it tastes like Cap'n Crunch.)

It also reminds us that life has milestones that should be celebrated and cakes make delicious edible mile markers.

Video editing can be pretty freakin' boring, but working on *Ace of Cakes* has been really fun for me precisely because it's so unlike any other show. As editors we're really given free rein to use music we like and hammer away at it until we can achieve some kind of sublime artistic expression. Yeah, that's right, I said it: sublime artistic expression. Go back. Look at the show. See what we've done. Feel free to disagree. You're wrong if you do. We don't always hit that level, but sometimes we do. I'm pretty jaded, but a few times this little show about a cake shop gives me goose bumps, so I think we must be doing something right.

So most of the time I like to sum up Ace of Cakes up like this:

Best. Job. Ever.

On location in Alaska

It didn't take long for me to realize what a great shooting atmosphere I had landed in Baltimore. After a couple of days of getting feedback from Matt, our director and a Season One veteran, I embraced the shooting style and have loved it ever since. The show was refined from the first rough cut I had seen, and I started to realize how well the shooting angles worked for the bakery and the artistic cake-making process. As I'm not the most artistic person, learning to vary my shooting style was a pretty fun and rewarding challenge.

Shooting at the bakery is one of the best work experiences I've ever had. Duff is one of my favorite storytellers, and he's always willing to go out of the box—which makes him great to work with. This overall positive vibe makes it different from some of the less favorable TV experiences I've had. In production you tend to rotate into and out of crews a lot, and people who come in even for just a few days or weeks all comment on how special the work environment is.

After working camera, I'm now in the field working as the supervising producer. My job now entails keeping track of the developing stories in the bakery each week and serving as an intermediary between everyone out in the field (Baltimore) and everyone back in the office (Los Angeles). I also have to keep track of Duff, which isn't always so easy. We like to say he's a human pinball, bouncing all around the bakery

Believe it or not, I actually couldn't handle *Ace of Cakes* the first time I saw it . . . just didn't like it. Perhaps it was the rough demo reel combined with too much turbulence on the airplane, but as I came from a traditional news background, the whole style of crazy shooting and editing was hard for me to stomach. A few months later my attitude toward the show began to soften. The show I had been working on was done shooting for the season, and I learned that *Ace of Cakes* was going into a second season. In production you're always looking for your next job, and when there was an opportunity to fill in on camera for three weeks on *Ace* I took it. Little did I know it would turn out to be one of the best opportunities of my life.

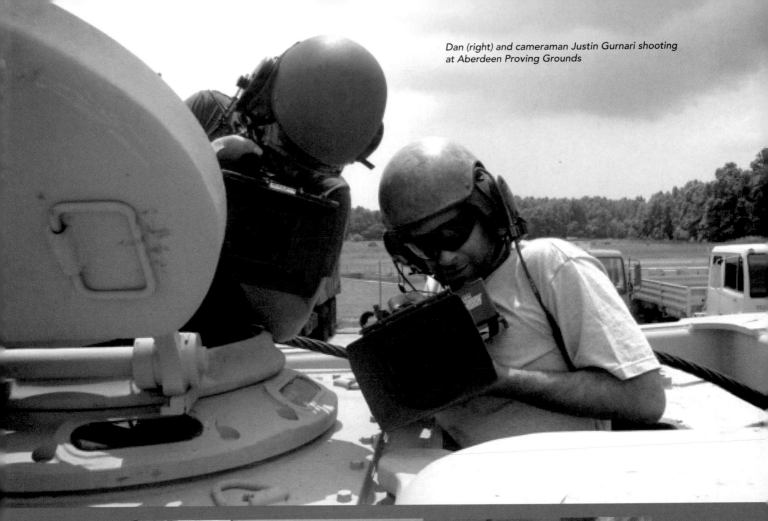

Dan (right) and cameraman Justin Gurnari shooting at Aberdeen Proving Grounds

No one had the heart to tell Dan it was a cake.

Our crew takes a quick break from filming at Oriole Park at Camden Yards.

At the frolf course near the bakery

from person to person, camera to camera, and cake to cake. His personal style keeps him very focused on and engaged with whatever he's doing or whoever he's talking to . . . and these days he's got a lot on his plate!

I have to admit, being out in the field does give us one huge advantage over our team back in L.A.: we get to eat a lot of cake. Though brownie is probably my favorite flavor, Adam once baked an incredible-tasting espresso flavor, as well as a special one-time-only Kahlua-flavored cake for Lebowski Fest. The chocolate peanut butter and the famous pumpkin chocolate chip are also pretty high on my list of favorites. Though I can't eat as much as Geof or Joe the intern, there are definitely some days—such as Fridays, when we're there all night—that I can throw back a pretty decent amount of cake.

BEHIND THE CAKE

See their story in
ACE OF CAKES episode 506,
"Lord Stanley"

DAVID AND MICHELLE REXRODE

I've made a lot of wedding cakes in my day, but none has held a special place in my heart quite like the replica of the Stanley Cup we made for Dave and Michelle Rexrode. This one just blew us all away.

Like me, Dave and Michelle love hockey. In fact, they met because of their shared love for the Washington Capitals. Both are season ticket holders who met on the Capitals message board, so naturally when they decided to get married, they knew that their wedding reception would incorporate hockey. After seeing the cake we created for the NFL for Super Bowl XLI, they knew we would be up for the challenge of creating pro hockey's ultimate prize—in cake.

How do you best replicate such a one-of-a-kind object? We were lucky enough to get a visit from Lord Stanley's Cup itself! I couldn't believe I actually got to touch the most recognizable symbol in the NHL. Nothing could top that. . . . Well, unless you could eat it!

Obviously I've seen my fair share of wedding receptions, but when I delivered the cup to to Dave and Michelle's wedding reception, I was pretty blown away by what I saw:

✦ They used hockey sticks as centerpieces and hockey pucks as wedding favors.

✦ They wore jerseys over their tuxedo and wedding dress.

✦ They were announced by the actual Washington Capitals PA announcer.

✦ They made their entrance under an archway of hockey sticks.

✦ They even had a referee call "holding" during their first dance.

That was a reception I was proud to be a part of!

And when I got there, I found that the best man was in the hospital and the groom's father was standing in in his place, so I piped his name on the side of the trophy where the rest of the wedding party was listed. He was the ultimate replacement player.

Though I wasn't able to stay for the cutting of the cake, I later heard two wonderful facts: one, that the entire cake was eaten by all 250 ravenous wedding guests (you'd be surprised how many don't get eaten), and two, that Dave and Michelle are now expecting their first little "mite" hockey player of their own.

Duff is fond of saying "Look at me, I'm far from what people think of as your typical baker." Sometimes I think people would be hard pressed to believe I actually work in TV production. Both of us are ex-athletes who loved rough sports, especially ice hockey, lacrosse, and rugby, which I think accounts for our in-your-face, devil-may-care personas. But I was a little curious about how Duff would react to meeting a new member of the *Ace of Cakes* production team who was also named Duffy. Sure enough, when we finally did meet, our eyes locked, and he threw down the gauntlet and said, "Yeah, you're going to have to change your name to Steve." We both laughed, and I told him he'd have to get used to having another Duff around, because it's the only name I answer to. It's been a beautiful friendship ever since.

With the constant demands of a tough production schedule, doing audio for the show is no easy task. It seems as if the bakery staff is expanding every day, which makes for more mics, more action, and more multitasking. The same goes for events and deliveries—one week it's a nice birthday or a wedding at the row house around the corner, and the next thing we're all jumping on a plane to film a cake for the Super Bowl. Though a typical weekend used to entail a cake drop-off at some small Baltimore wedding, now we're driving further, filming larger events, and meeting more and more interesting people.

I remember the exact moment we realized *Ace of Cakes* had finally made it: we'd driven up to New York to film some scenes for the Super Bowl episode at the NFL's headquarters, and when we were driving through Times Square we heard all this screaming and yelling over our radios. I looked up, and Duff and Geof were staring right back down at us—*from a larger-than-life* Ace of Cakes *billboard*! Soon after that, everyone I knew started raving about the

Sutton Hoo cake

ton Monument Christmas lighting ceremony. I have to admit it was a little scary at first, but when I heard Duff laugh through his mic, I could only giggle. Only Duff could brush off a fall like that and laugh about it.

My favorite cake that has come out of Charm City Cakes has to be Geof Manthorne's Sutton Hoo Cake.

That cake was truly amazing. Geof's attention to detail and his dedication get stronger every week. And hands down my favorite cake flavor is Adam's pumpkin chocolate chip using handmade Godiva chocolate to replace his regular chocolate chips.

It's been great to witness the true side of Baltimore, which is often portrayed in a negative way. It's really an artistic, bright, and lively city. While Baltimore has become my new home, the Charm City Cakes bakery staff and *Ace of Cakes* production crew have become my family. We've all had so many life-changing experiences along the way, but the biggest change I've had. here is that I met my future wife! If it hadn't been for this show I wouldn't have found the woman of my life, so I have to thank Duff and the bakery staff for my success. I can't wait to see what my wedding cake looks like!

show and asking me how they could meet their favorite prime-time bakery staff.

The funniest memory I have is when Duff fell backward off the stage at Baltimore's Washing-

It has been said that movies are life with the boring stuff taken out. I would say that the boring stuff of a reality writer's life consists of watching other people's boring stuff in order to take *out* their boring stuff (ooh . . . meta . . .).

On shows I've worked on in the past, my job has been to go through a week's worth of footage in order to piece together the interesting bits that will support a storyline and voilà—out of the boring emerges something entertaining (or at least watchable). Imagine my delight when I started working on *Ace of Cakes* sometime during the second season and discovered what everyone and their mothers already knew—these people aren't boring *at all*.

They're funny! And smart! And crazy talented! Holy trifecta, Cake Man!

Life at Charm City Cakes is always, in all ways, interesting. From the myriad clients and their kooky orders (a turducken cake for a family of vegetarians? What the . . .) to the insanely talented decorators (A "glass" car windshield made out of sugar? No problem!) to the "Ace" himself, Duff Goldman.

Ah, Duff.

Pure. Viewing. Goodness.

Every episode, I'm again amazed that our greatest challenge as writers is what to leave out. Can you imagine? It may not seem like much to you, but trust me . . . it is a dream.

I signed up for this job because the show runner, Kelly McPherson, seemed as if he'd be a cool boss. It turned out he may be the coolest boss ever, on the coolest show ever, where Duff is the coolest boss ever (ooh . . . super-double-bonus-meta).

Pinch me!

Cut to: Two years later, and I'm still at the bakery in Baltimore having the time of my life. The events and locations *Ace of Cakes* take us to exceed anything I ever could have envisioned: we've been to the Super Bowl, a navy battleship to celebrate the author Tom Clancy's birthday, the United Nations for a special celebration with humanitarian and the James Bond actor Roger Moore, even out to L.A. for the premiere of *Kung Fu Panda*, to name just a few.

Though I started in a position called AC, or assistant camera, I've now moved into the sound or audio position and have come to refer to myself as an *Ace of Cakes* "lifer." Our cast and crew have become like a family to me, and there's no place I'd rather be.

Doing audio on the show is a funny (and sometimes technically frustrating) job. Listening to everyone's mics at once, you hear all kinds of things you thought you'd never hear. Whether it's Tuvan throat singing, humming, whistling, power tools, burping, or just some really goofy conversations, there's always something inter-

Ever since high school, all I've ever wanted to do is get paid to travel, so when I found a job at Authentic Entertainment I was ecstatic. In my first two years of working for the production company, my assignments have taken me to Hawaii, Italy, Brazil, even Japan. I was doing what I'd always wanted to do, and I was happy. So you'll have to forgive me if I wasn't expecting a lot of excitement when they asked me to go to Baltimore to work in some bakery . . .

Nick Rush with supervising producer Daniel Hops

esting coming over my headphones. As sound guys, we wear a harness around our shoulders that straps a bag onto our torso. This bag contains a six-channel mixer connected to six wireless receivers. It weighs around thirty pounds, so you can imagine why I've come to refer to my bag as "my baby." Almost all the audio on *Ace of Cakes* is done wirelessly, which means every member of the bakery staff wears a wireless microphone that sends his or her audio—via radio frequency—to one of the six wireless receivers. It's my job to scan among the frequencies and pull up the audio for whomever the camera is pointed at. I then mix whatever audio is needed down to two channels (left and right) and send what I'm mixing—via two wireless transmitters in my bag—to the camera, where the audio gets recorded onto the tape along with the video.

It can be a lot to think about sometimes, but we have fun with it too. We've set up what we call "bakery radio" by hooking up an iPod to one of our extra wireless microphones. Duff even let me throw a concert in the basement once! Whether we're on the *Ace of Cakes* crew or the Charm City Cakes staff, the one thing we all have in common is that we play as hard as we work.

Duff and Nick pose with the Stanley Cup.

The Crew of ACE OF CAKES

SHERRI CHAMBERS FISHER
Decorator

Hometown: Catonsville, Maryland

Education: Postbaccalaureate teaching certification, Towson University, Towson, Maryland; BFA, magna cum laude, Purchase College, Purchase, New York; Independent Studio Program, Slade School of Fine Arts, London

Favorite hobbies: Synchronized swimming; making costumes; playing with my puppies, Yoda (boxer) and Twiggy (Boston terrier)

Fun fact: I met my husband on a blind date.

Favorite movie: *Breaking Away*

Favorite books: *How to Pick a Peach* by Russ Parsons, *Franny and Zooey* by J. D. Salinger, *The Poetics of Space* by Gaston Bachelard

Favorite music: Pixies, B52s, Fleetwood Mac, Talking Heads

Favorite nondessert dish to create or eat: Pickles

In her own words . . .

In 2002, upstairs at a local club here in Baltimore called the Ottobar, a birthday gathering for my new friend was under way. Her name: Mary Alice. Suddenly, some guy I didn't know showed up with one of the strangest and most interesting cakes I'd ever seen: it was white and red with these sort of paisley-shaped pieces sprouting out the top and covered in shiny silver balls. I remember thinking, Wow, making *that* looks like fun. A couple of years later, when that goofy dude with the cake would be my boss, I'd learn that those tiny balls are called dragées and about a million other things about cake decorating I never thought I'd ever know . . .

In the summer of 2004, Geof was helping me with a play I was directing for Fluid Movement (a Baltimore-based performance art troupe) called *Earth, Wind and the Baltimore Fire*. It was a snappy recasting of the Great Baltimore Fire as a funktastic, flamenco-flavored fantasy. And when it came time to cast the role of Baltimore's mayor circa 1904, who better than Duff? After he agreed to be in the show, on the first day of rehearsal he came armed with a giant box of cake to share. That was the first time I had really spent any length of time with him—and my first taste of pumpkin choco-

TIP *Always make a sketch. Doing this first helps simplify and translate complex forms and ideas into the basic shapes you will need to construct. It also allows you to address structural questions before it's too late.*

late chip cake. Both were out of sight! The actor playing Duff's wife was a seven-foot-tall drag queen; the two of them together stole the show. We immediately became great friends.

Later that summer I decided to leave my job as an exhibition designer for the Smithsonian and go back to school to become an art teacher. The bakery had grown larger—it was finally out of Duff's row house and into a small

TIP *When working with modeling chocolate, if your hands get too warm, coat them with a thin layer of cornstarch. This helps slows the melting process by creating a thin barrier between the heat of your hands and the chocolate.*

kitchen space above a Korean karaoke bar. Geof mentioned that the bakery was looking for some help, and he thought it would be the perfect part-time job for me. After a brief chat with Duff (which I recall consisted of him asking little more than "You can make stuff, right?"), I suddenly found myself working on my first cake. Coincidentally, it was a flamenco-themed wedding cake.

At that time, there were just five people on staff, and Anna had just started working with us as an intern. What I initially liked about the bakery is what I think still makes it unique: everyone who worked there had another life or interest. As musicians, graphic designers, artists, and even massage therapists, everyone brought different experiences and interests to the bakery, and this diversity made it a fun and exciting place to work.

The busier we were, the more fun we would have. Since most of our cakes were scheduled for delivery on Saturdays, our friends soon realized that life at Charm City Cakes consumed our Friday nights, and they would stop by the bakery to hang out and drink beers while we worked. Occasionally, when it looked as if we had too many complex cakes going into Friday, Duff would work his magic. He'd sit down after everyone left on Thursday night and go to town finishing cakes on his own. When the staff arrived for work on Friday morning and saw their cakes magically completed, it felt like Christmas morning! One of my all-time favorite memories from the old space was this one late Friday night that was just stretching on and on and on. As we were working away quietly, completely exhausted, our ears perked up as we heard the sweet sound of an ice cream truck approaching from down the street. Duff popped up out of his seat like a piston, ran out the door, and returned with banana splits for everyone.

As a student at Purchase College, my main area of study was sculpture, so I tend to approach the materials at the bakery as if they were more traditional sculptural media. Fondant works a lot like Sculpey (polymer clay), modeling chocolate has the flexibility of clay (but not the stability), and cake itself can be carved like wood or stone (but you have to talk to it nicely). It's been the creative translation of my knowledge of these more traditional media to cake-decorating materials that has really allowed me to explore and kept me interested in the work. Easily by far my favorite cakes to create are the animal cakes, as I enjoy experimenting with how to transform real textures into cake. I love it when a cake takes on its own personality.

When I originally started at the bakery, I was studying to become an art teacher, and now I teach drawing, painting, and sculpture at a local art magnet high school, all while continuing to work part-time at Charm City Cakes. Since most of my students are fans of the show, *Ace of Cakes* has become an invaluable teaching tool. It allows for the concepts discussed in art class, such as good craftsmanship and creating a uni-

fied design, to be accessible in a unique and unexpected way. I find that when I'm teaching I tend to use food references in explaining sculpture techniques to my students, and when I'm sculpting, I find my experience as a cake decorator informing my technique.

Having worked at the bakery since 2004, I've sculpted more horses and motorcycles than I can count, but the work remains fun and new, and my techniques are always evolving. Each new person who joins our team at the bakery brings a new perspective and helps to keep things fresh and exciting.

TIP *To give an animal cake more life, determine the most expressive feature of the animal (droopy jowls, hunched-over shoulders, sad eyes, long neck, wrinkly skin, and so on), and focus your energy on creating that feature. This will give the cake a focal point and recognizable quality.*

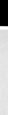

MARK MULLER Porter

Hometown: Towson, Maryland

Education: BA in literature, University of Maryland, College Park

Fun fact: When she was a child, Mary Smith was bitten in the face by a horse. As a result, she now prefers to be photographed from her left.

Favorite movie: *Andy Warhol's Heat,* directed by Paul Morrissey

Favorite book: *Peasants and Other Stories* by Anton Chekov

Favorite music: Statler Brothers, Richard Harris

Favorite nondessert dish to create or eat: Ribs

In his own words . . .

I first met Duff early one morning after agreeing to deliver a cake to Virginia with Katie Rose. He helped us load a cake sculpted to look like Darth Vader's helmet into one of the delivery vans and instructed us to call if we encountered any problems. The drive was supposed to take three hours, but sometime during the second hour, Darth Vader's head began to sweat from the extreme heat. We called Duff, who reminded us to keep the air-conditioning on high. I spent an hour watching the cake melt through the rearview mirror. As I drove, Katie attempted to fix it, using royal icing to glue patches of black fondant over the cracks in its helmet, but the face had become completely warped. After another call to Duff, we decided that the cake was too far gone and drove back to Baltimore. When we arrived at the bakery, Duff was livid, but it was a relief that his anger wasn't directed at either of us. He destroyed the cake with his hands, punching it repeatedly and ripping the fondant off of its sagging face. He ended up paying us in spite of everything and remade the cake himself (he delivered it personally the next day).

A month or so later, during my last semester of school, my friend Charlie told me he was moving and needed someone to take over his job sweeping Charm City Cakes. I accepted and started coming in twice a week to make some extra money. After a few months of sweeping, Duff asked me if I'd be interested in taking on more responsibilities at the bakery. These included all of the janitorial duties that I had done previously but extended to include the procurement of any supplies needed by the decorators and in the bakery.

I spend a couple of days each week picking up supplies and occasionally hunt for obscure things that can't be made from cake, such as the glass on a gumball machine or a spindle for a slot machine. More recently, I've started to handle inventory and ordering for the bakery.

My First Cake

I have no background in food preparation, sculpture, or design, but when asked if I would try to make a cake for this book, I was excited and agreed to do it. This is my first attempt at cake making, and though I'm sure that it shows next to the work of the bakery's decorators, I'm personally happy with the way my cake turned out.

For my cake design, I chose to replicate an image of Freddy Krueger from the *Nightmare on Elm Street* movies. I located a picture of his face carved into a pumpkin and decided to model my cake after it. My first step was to dye fondant in the colors that would make up the cake. Initially, I thought that I'd apply two layers of fondant to the cake and cut the Krueger design from a pumpkin-colored outer layer, revealing a bright yellow layer underneath. Mary Smith, who had made a cake using a similar technique a few months prior, suggested that the number of thin lines on Freddy's face would make it impossible to support an outer layer. Instead, I settled for putting a bright yellow face on the cake, in the hope that it would look like light shining through. I ended up dyeing fondant in four colors: a big chunk in the pumpkin color, some bright yellow to look like light, black for the shadow, and brown for the stem.

Next, I set out to carve and cover my cake. Ben and Anna gave me helpful suggestions,

T.R.C. - 1991

TIP *Keeping track of the products and ingredients that are needed for a project can be confusing; create a list.*

and I ended up working with a saw and some small knives to best approximate the shape of a pumpkin. Once I felt confident about the shape of the cake, I covered it in a thin layer of shortening (which acts as an adhesive between the cake and fondant). I tried three separate times to roll a solid, thin layer of fondant that could cover my cake. This stage was particularly difficult, but with Ben's help, I was able to achieve a smooth (if not completely natural-looking) effect.

After shaping and covering the cake, I was finally able to focus on Freddy Krueger's face. I used a stencil to cut out the lines of Krueger's hat, face, and blades in yellow fondant, then carefully applied them to the cake with a damp cloth. Mary Smith helped me spray a layer of vodka onto the cake to remove some of the imperfections and cracks in the fondant. It was great to have the help of my talented coworkers on this project, and I enjoyed working on my first cake, even if it was just a dummy.

I remember that before they starting filming *Ace of Cakes*, Anna showed me a demo DVD made by the producers. The idea that people I knew, at a bakery I knew, would be featured on TV was hard to believe—but I was really excited for Anna. For the first episode, they brought a digi-

tal projector into the bakery, where Duff threw a party and we all watched it together—and I remember thinking it was completely surreal to see people in my everyday life being featured as part of a reality show.

One time someone sent potato guns to the bakery, and we all broke them out and had a lot

Mark watches as Ben pours liquid sugar into a mold.

Producer Maryn Peters OTFs cameraman Mark Lefleur for Ace of Cakes. (OTF means "on the fly"—the opposite of a formal interview.)

TIP *If you're planning to save icing and are using a tip, put a pin through the tip so that it won't dry out.*

of fun with them. Everyone's always making jokes and stuff; the interactions can get pretty hilarious.

But in addition to the fun and good times, one of the things that make me proud to be associated with the team is Duff's sense of charity—he's really good at giving back. The other day I

was helping Duff and Mary Alice and everyone put together care packages for soldiers stationed overseas. When we do things like that, it just adds to the feeling that Charm City Cakes is an incredibly special place to work

On a more personal note, one of the things that makes this place so special is the way newer employees are brought into the fold. Everyone here is great about giving people a chance, helping people click, making them feel welcome. And I think that comes from the top down: Duff takes everyone on vacation, we all eat dinner together, work together, and play together. Things like that go a long way toward forging friendships and relations beyond the traditional workplace.

TIP *When dyeing fondant, add food coloring gradually or it might just end up brown.*

The staff of Charm City Cakes with their puppet doppelgangers.

THE BANDS OF CHARM CITY CAKES

I started Charm City Cakes because I'm in a band and I knew that the only way I was going to get any time off was if I was a boss. So I organized Charm City Cakes as a one-man company that would allow me to play music whenever I wanted to. Looking back on it now, it makes perfect sense that we've grown to attract similarly minded artists and musicians. We haven't deviated from my initial dream—to have a place where I could work and play music—but for as crazy big as the whole enterprise has gotten, everybody in the bakery is encouraged to pursue their art—be it music, synchronized swimming, roller derby, taking pictures of cats or dogs, or simply having cats.

We also have epic iPod battles. One day one of our *Ace of Cakes* audio techs figured out a way to tap into the old overhead speaker system, and now the place is totally wired for sound. We like music. We all listen to lots and lots of music. We fight over stereo rights. It's sad when we're filming because we don't get to listen to music.

. . . soihadto . . .

Most of us are in bands, and we play music as well. Here's the rundown:

- ✦ I play bass in the postrock band . . . soihadto . . .
- ✦ Elena plays bass and sings in the Squaaks.
- ✦ Geof is a singer/songwriter/ guitar player and plays trumpet in The Baltimore Afrobeat Society, which is probably the finest tribute to Fela Kuti in this country. I also happen to be Geof's biggest fan.
- ✦ Anna and Katie Rose are in their own imaginary band, the OW-OW-OWL-ETTES!
- ✦ Mary Smith is a rockin' DJ.
- ✦ Ben plays drums in the band Field Athletic.
- ✦ Lauren's boyfriend Ken plays guitar in the band Ponytail.

The Squaaks

The Lexie Mountain Boys

...soihadto...

I ♥ DIZZY ISSIE'S
300 W. 30th St. • Baltimore, MD
(410) 235-0171

I ♥ REMINGTON
Baltimore, MD

ORANGE
The Legendary British Guitar Amplifier

CHARM CITY ROLLER GIRLS
www.charmcityrollergirls.com

CHARM CITY CRAFT MAFIA
CHARMCITYCRAFTMAFIA.COM

HFBL TATTOO
410 235 5936
HAMPDEN

Save the Date

Jessica & Rommel • 09.29.07

G A B #   ► OK ◄   ORANGE
                                 TUNER

0   10   0   10

Tone   Volume   Power

- Katherine is a member of the Lexie Mountain Boys, and her boyfriend, Alex, is in the band Beach House.

- Although she will never admit it, Mary Alice can sing like a canary, and her older brother is the lead singer of the rock band Clutch. The very first cake I ever made was for Neil's wedding, so in a way, you could say Clutch was the band that started it all.

- After filming, our entire film crew turn into rock-and-roll gods when they're relaxing and playing Guitar Hero and Rock Band. They get to be any band they want.

I'm constantly amazed how many people here are in bands. They used to call Baltimore "The City That Reads," but I say Baltimore is "The City That Rocks."

Dear Mom,
I love you.
Do you think
I should throw
this away? Lauren

LAUREN FRIEDMAN Decorator

Hometown: Durham, North Carolina

Education: Durham School of the Arts, Maryland Institute College of Art

Favorite hobbies: Karaoke, figure skating karaoke

Fun fact: My senior thesis project was a birthday party that nobody came to and videos of me "figure skating" in socks on a hardwood floor.

Favorite movies: *A Muppet Christmas Carol, The Little Mermaid*

Favorite books: *A Heartbreaking Work of Staggering Genius* by Dave Eggers, *The World Without Us* by Alan Weisman

Favorite music: Ponytail, Animal Collective, country radio

Favorite nondessert dish to create or eat: Fries

In her own words . . .

I'm an only child and, having no one to play with, I watched a lot of TV growing up. I usually would draw or do little art projects while I sat there, so I guess that makes television my biggest first inspiration (ha!). When I was five, my mom signed me up for a community theater group, I think because she wanted to get me out of the house. I continued with the group until I graduated from high school.

For middle and high school I went to an arts magnet school, where I studied theater and sculpture. In middle school, I worked a lot with clay, and I can credit those years with preparing me for my job at Charm City Cakes. I decided to attend the Maryland Institute College of Art because it was relatively close to home, and I thought art school would be more fun than regular school. I studied performance, video, and conceptual art in the General Sculptural Studies department.

The first time I really learned about the bakery was when I saw one of the first episodes on television. It was the Preakness episode (Episode 101), in which Duff has to walk the cake across the track and through the crowds of drunken college students. I remember thinking, Oh, yeah, this is that show about Baltimore! Baltimore's really getting a lot of attention lately. I vaguely knew Anna and Katie from around town, but when Ben got hired, he became my first actual friend in the bakery.

I got an opportunity to intern through Becca, the intern before

THE UNAUTHORIZED BIOGRAPHY OF LAUREN FRIEDMAN
By her best friend, Elizabeth Zephyrine McDonough

Lauren's parents got her out of one of those machines with the claw that reaches down to grab stuffed animals. From a young age, she learned what it means to have a giant metal thing come down and claw your head. Though she's by no means a snob, Lauren enjoys the finer things in life: mascots, country music, baby versions of things, and fries. Mostly things that could be found at a fair. Lauren, along with the rest of the population, enjoys fairs. When not at a fair, Lauren spent much of her time as a young child sucking up anything and everything TV (or as she liked to call it, "Mom/Dad") had to offer. This helped her blossom into a beautiful pop-cultured young woman and probably played a part in landing her a role as a mental patient who thought she was a television!

But in all seriousness, if anyone is a TV, it's Lauren. And now, as if that weren't enough, she gets to be on one. After being introduced to Duff by Ben, Lauren began an internship with Charm City Cakes that eventually blossomed into a cake-decorating position that will, fingers crossed, eventually blossom into her taking over as the lead personality of the show, as well as winning eight gold medals in the 2012 Olympics.

When she's not being a TV or being on TV, Lauren can be a real outdoorsman. Unfortunately, a near-fatal bowling injury ended her glory days in the lanes (ages five to eleven), but, resilient as ever, she decided to take up another gentleman's sport: softball. This athletic rebirth proved to be a life change that would give way to yet another life change: a life-changing nickname that would change her life forever. That nickname was Magnet Head. It was on accounta she had a tendency to attract lots of softballs to her head—being thrown by pitchers, catchers, her own teammates even. Let's just say, when the girl stepped up to the plate, nine times outta ten, you could bet the ball was gonna hit her right in the head. And one-a those times, it musta hit somethin' right, 'cause she went on to score a 1 on her Calculus AP test, graduate college, and finally make her debut on TV as a brilliant cake decorator. She is also the world's resident expert on pizzert (dessert pizza).

She is thrilled to be working with Duff and everyone else at Charm City Cakes and gets down on her knees and thanks that giant silver claw thingy (God) every day for giving her the best job in the world.

me. When I found out she was interning at the bakery, I nearly pushed her to the ground, I was so intensely jealous. Anyway, Becca and Ben were nice enough to nag Anna until she called me to come in for an interview with her and Duff. I was *really* nervous, but Duff and Anna were really nice. Duff told me about the intern's duties, including listing "building boxes" about four times, something I never once had to do. He's so crazy! Even though I was totally nervous

and freaked out, I had a pretty strong feeling that I was in. Anna called me a few days later to tell me I had the internship, and the rest is history!

On my first day interning, I was immediately put to work dyeing fondant for a cake that was being followed, so the anxiety of starting a new job was magnified a million times because I was being filmed within two minutes of entering the bakery. Incidentally, the cake I was working on

ended up being canceled just as I was finishing dyeing the last bit of fondant, so it never made it onto the show (thank goodness)!

I was definitely nervous for my debut on the show, because I didn't really know what I would be saying or doing or if I'd look silly or weird. After the initial shock, I can say that I mostly enjoy it. It's exciting to see what things make it into the final edit of the episodes. It's especially exhilarating when something really funny that happened in the bakery gets used for the show, because we get to relive the moment and it can be preserved for posterity.

I haven't been on the show long enough to get recognized, but I'm starting to get phone calls and emails from my old teachers and high school friends, which is really fun. If I didn't hear from people whom I haven't spoken to in a while, I would probably

think *Ace of Cakes* was shown only on my own television. It's hard to imagine that we're seen by people all over the country.

I love my job, so I actually like reliving my work days in shorter, funnier doses. I also really appreciate the opportunity for my parents to see me on TV, because there's no doubt that I have a great job and am working hard.

I don't know if I can pick a favorite episode. One of my favorite moments is from the "Elephant Delivery Service" episode, which opens with Duff trying to climb into the van while wearing a huge pink elephant costume. It's the unedited shot of Duff slowly and si-

had only four characters completed. At that point, Ben and Katherine convinced me that the cake looked great and that it wouldn't matter if I'd done all six figures or not. So I ended up just sticking the figures wherever I felt like they looked good. *Big mistake.* Somehow, pictures of the cake made their way onto a *Star Trek* blog, where Trekkies immediately noticed the incorrect placement of many of their beloved characters, and boy did they make their feelings known. Within a few days, a bunch of popular tech blogs had picked up the story, one of which proclaimed, "*Star Trek* Cake Upsets Nerds." The story even made its way as far as the *Los Angeles Times*! Needless to say, I was mortified. The bride and groom loved the cake, but I re- alized that my audience is much broader than just our clients. Most important, I learned that the next time I do a cake about a hugely popular science fiction show or movie, I'm going to get every single detail right, be- cause those Trekkies are a rough crowd.

The second cake I did

lently struggling to cram himself in that's just a hilarious image.

My very first cake was a replica of the bridge of the *Starship Enterprise*. I'm pretty sure Duff gave me the assignment because it included a bunch of little chairs; I've been pigeonholed as the tiny furniture maker of the bakery. The cake also included about six figures, all the central characters of *Star Trek*. As this was the first cake I'd ever done on my own, I worked very slowly. By Thursday night (the cake was due Friday), I

on my own was an eleventh-birthday cake for a girl named Lauren. It was for her scrapbooking sleepover, so I made gum paste figures of every girl who was attending the party, plus little sleeping bags and scrapbooking supplies. Basically it was a cake representing the event it was made for, which is a funny idea in itself. I liked it because it turned out really cute, and I enjoyed the fact that it was for a little girl with the same name as mine!

Anyway, cake is one of my favorite things in the world. Where there's a cake, there's a party, and where there's a party, people are celebrating! And they're happy! Any cake is my dream cake! I love cakes!

> **TIP** *If you don't have a small circle cutter, use the end of a large piping tip.*

EPISODE GUIDE

Food Network presents in association with Authentic Entertainment, Inc.

ACE OF CAKES

Created by: Willie Goldman, Dana Leiken Richards, Lauren Lexton, and Tom Rogan
Executive Producers: Lauren Lexton, Tom Rogan, Kelly McPherson, Jeanne Begley
Co–Executive Producers: Willie Goldman and Dana Leiken Richards
Co–Executive Producer (Episodes 312, 313, 401–411): Jack Tarantino

Cycle 1: Season One (6 episodes)

Cycle 2: Season Two (13 episodes)

Cycle 3: Season Three (13 episodes) and Season Four (13 episodes)

Cycle 4: Season Five (13 episodes) and Season Six (13 episodes)

Cycle 5: Season Seven (13 episodes) and Season Eight (13 episodes)

SEASON ONE

Triple Crown Cake

Production no.: DB101
Original air date: August 17, 2006
Writer*: Miriam Leffert
Director: Jeffrey R. Daniels
Editors: Grayce Lackland, Matthew Monte

Chef Duff Goldman, proprietor, owner, and operator of Charm City Cakes, explains that the largest order of the week is a fifty-pound masterpiece for Baltimore's Preakness horse race. Later in the day, an old friend of Duff's stops by the bakery to select her wedding cake: a clean and classy beach motif, complete with edible sand and seashells. Duff gets to work building the scale-model base of the cake with real wood and rope, using an assortment of power tools. With less than twenty-four hours to complete the cake for the horse race, Duff pulls an all-nighter with sous chef

Geof, loads the cake into his delivery van, and races across town to the Pimlico racetrack, just in time to cross the racetrack and a sea of partying college kids to complete the delivery.

Featured cakes: Preakness, Jeep, Dental School Graduation, Fish-in-a-Basket, Sweet Sixteen, Cell Phone, Black Belt

Special appearance: Lieutenant Governor Michael Steele

Decorative techniques: Base construction, modeling chocolate, dowel insertion, gum paste seashells and black-eyed Susans, graham cracker crumbs for sand, piping, airbrushing

Featured organizations: Pimlico Race Course

Fun fact: Though this was the first episode to air, portions of episode 105 were first shot in Los Angeles and edited into that episode.

"Technically I am the executive sous chef of Charm City Cakes. This is a title that

Duff gave me; I don't really know what it means."

— GEOF

"Well, we kind of specialize in not small and not simple."

— MARY ALICE

"Real men prefer caulk."

— DUFF

Hell Week

Production no.: DB102
Original air date: August 31, 2006
Writer: Dustin Rubin
Director: Jeffrey R. Daniels
Editors: Jeanette Christensen, Grayce Lackland, Matthew Monte

With just five days to complete twenty-seven cakes, there's a whirlwind of activity at Charm City Cakes. Geof and Richard

---

*A note on our writers: Nothing on Ace of Cakes is scripted. Working with the show's editors, the writers watch all the footage from the field and generate a technical script in reverse that's used to create narrative "storylines."

construct a cake in the form of a tequila bottle out of crispy cereal treats to give the cake added stability. The most challenging cake is modeled after a client's German Shepherd and will require a complex multitiered base/skeleton out of wood and metal. Once Sherri has carved, stacked, and iced sheet cakes, Duff and Geof get to work quickly applying fondant to the odd-shaped dog cake. With all cakes now completed, the bakery has less than twenty-four hours to deliver them. Duff and Geof explain the complexities of delivering different types of cakes. All deliveries are completed, and another successful week at Charm City Cakes concludes.

Featured cakes: Tequila; German Shepherd; Naval Academy Graduation; Haggarty, Tisch, Wingate, Zak, Powell, Callar, Churlin, Hunt, and California Scenes Weddings

Decorative techniques: Crispy cereal treats usage, fondant application, fondant crack repair.

Caketastrophe: Duff must repair a fondant crack in the bottom tier of an already painted cake.

Fun fact: Sound mixer Josh Spector appears in a half-second cameo in this episode.

"Sherri is like the Swiss army knife—she can do anything."

—DUFF

"Ever notice there's always peas in throw-up? Even if you haven't had peas, there's peas."

—DUFF

"High five? I don't play that jive."

—GEOF

"We call a turn like this a cake killer."

—DUFF

Wedding Cakes and Headaches

Production no.: DB103
Original air date: August 19, 2006

Writer: Miriam Leffert
Director: Jeffrey R. Daniels
Editor: Grayce Lackland

To celebrate her mother's eightieth birthday, a client asks Charm City Cakes to design a cake in the form of her mother's favorite hat. Duff and the staff go the extra mile, creating an edible hatbox out of gum paste and edible tissue paper. For his dad's birthday, Duff replicates a World War II–era "flying wing" plane, which he will trick out with a series of fireworks. While Duff and decorator Richard perform a fireworks test for his dad's cake, Geof places fondant stripes around the hatbox and the entire Charm City Cakes team gets to work completing all their cakes for the looming weekend deadline.

Featured cakes: Beardsley Wedding, Hatbox, World War II Flying Wing, Grape, Lavender Anniversary

Special appearances: Rahn; Steven; Peggy, Dorothy's daughter; Dorothy; Morrie; Luke

Decorative techniques: Royal icing application, gum paste construction, piping and painting design outlines, fondant application, fireworks

Fun facts: Even though this was the third episode completed, Food Network aired it two days after the series premiere and a week prior to episode 102, Hell Week. Duff's band, . . . soihadto . . . , played "Searching for the Cure" in this episode. This is the first episode to feature appearances by Duff's family.

"It's not Charm City Cookies. It's not Charm City Meat Loaf."

—DUFF

"She's taking our baking for granite."

—MARY ALICE

"You got to be real fast with it because it will dry out, it will crack, but yet you have to be really, really gentle with it at the same time. Fondant's like a woman, but I won't get into that now."

—GEOF

"Why is it that everything is done and we're not done? Can somebody tell me why everything is done and we're not done yet?"

—DUFF

"Just checking on my investment in culinary school."

—MORRIE GOLDMAN

Life's a Zoo

Production no.: DB104
Original air date: September 7, 2006
Writer: Dustin Rubin
Director: Jeffrey R. Daniels
Editors: Grayce Lackland, Jacob Lane

The Baltimore Zoo asks Duff to create a pair of flamingos for a black-tie event. While Duff uses an arc welder to join the metal support rods to the base of the Flamingo cake, Sherri must help area baker and Food Network personality Warren Brown create a replica of the U.S. Capitol dome for a cupcake-tower wedding cake. Duff and Richard use sanders and blocks of Styrofoam to shape the flamingo heads. Duff and Geof cover the flamingo framework with fondant. Sherri works on the dome and cuts out fondant flamingo feathers. Duff airbrushes the flamingos pink. Once the flamingos are completed, Duff and Sherri must hold the oversize cake diagonally in the cargo space of the delivery van so it doesn't collapse while Mary Alice drives them to the zoo.

Featured cakes: Flamingo display, Fist of Rock Groom's, Capital Dome Wedding topper

Special appearances: Warren Brown; Lainie Contreras; Matthew Mulkey and Ruth Martin, groom and bride; Barbara Queen, bride

Decorative techniques: Chocolate sculpting, fondant application, layered airbrushing technique, gum paste figures

Featured organizations: Zoomerang, Baltimore Zoo

Fun facts: Duff first appeared with Warren on the premiere episode of his Food Network series *Sugar Rush*. Warren owns and operates one of his Cake Love specialty shops in nearby Canton. The stained-glass mosaic featuring the Charm City Cakes logo was made by Duff's mother, Jackie, an accomplished stained-glass artist.

"I hope someone there can give me the fist of rock. That sounds kind of dirty, though, doesn't it?"

—GEOF

Duff Goes Hollywood

Production no.: DB105
Original air date: September 14, 2006
Writer: Miriam Leffert
Director: Jeffrey R. Daniels
Editor: Grayce Lackland

Jay Leno has invited Duff to appear on *The Tonight Show* with a cake resembling a 426 Hemi Cuda car engine. Duff and Richard head over to the tool area, where they build a special housing for engine fireworks. Meanwhile, Mary forms miniature gum paste Chesapeake Bay blue crabs for a local seafood restaurant's anniversary cake. Richard constructs edible corn cobs out of crispy cereal treats and painted yellow fondant. After a quick cake-cutting ceremony at the seafood restaurant, Duff packs up for the big trip to L.A. Duff presents Jay Leno with the engine cake, handing the host a hand trigger and asking him to start the engine. The pyrotechnic display goes off with celebratory fanfare.

Featured cakes: Leno Engine, Philips Seafood, Crocker Family/Habitat for Humanity

Special appearances: Shirley and Brice Philips, Erica Crocker, Chuck Hughes, Jay Leno, Mike McCarey, Willie Goldman

Decorative techniques: Royal icing mixing, fondant rose construction, faux corn construction, use of wood-grain tool, buttercream application, pyrotechnic work

Featured charity and organizations: Habitat for Humanity, Philips Seafood Restaurant, *The Tonight Show*

Fun fact: Duff and Geof's arrival into Los Angeles was the very first sequence filmed

for *Ace of Cakes* but was inserted into this episode for continuity purposes.

"Well, if this was the Philippines, you could."

—DUFF, responding to an eight-year-old Brownie who asked if she could work at the bakery

"You ever hear the term 'witchadidja?' 'Like, ya ain't bring the truck witchadidja?"

—DUFF

"We need a cake suppository. Or a cake depository."

—DUFF

"I don't cut cake. I don't bake cookies. I don't cut cake. So far, you've seen me do both."

—DUFF

"You can't let the cake tell you what's going on. You gotta hump, smash it down. . . . You know, if it's not level, make it level. This isn't the shape that we want, we're going to make it the shape that we want. You can't let the cake push you around."

—DUFF

Cake Walk

Production no.: DB106
Original air date: September 21, 2006
Writer: Dustin Rubin
Director: Jeffrey R. Daniels
Editors: Grayce Lackland, Jacob Lane

The biggest order this week is a birthday cake for the Maryland Science Center built to resemble a brontosaurus wearing a birthday hat. Duff constructs the internal skeleton of out of copper pipe, while Mary pipes an incredibly intricate detailed Mehndi Henna tattoo pattern on cake for an Indian wedding. With just sixteen hours until delivery, Sherri abandons molding the dinosaur with crispy cereal treats and uses modeling chocolate instead. When the dinosaur cake is finally finished, Duff delivers it to the science center, where he playfully mixes it up with the dinosaur mascot. Much to the delight of the organizers and all the

kids in attendance, another delivery is successfully completed.

Featured cakes: Cartoon Dinosaur, Mehndi Wedding, Bumper Car

Special appearances: Gary Landsman, Charlie the Cleaning Guy

Decorative techniques: Crispy cereal treat usage, cake carving, piping, airbrushing, modeling chocolate work

Featured organizations: Glen Echo Park, Maryland Science Center

"I think a solution will present itself."

—DUFF

"One of the things about working at Charm City Cakes is that you gotta be mature."

—DUFF

"I think I almost got my ass kicked by a guy in a dinosaur suit. Oh yeah, I'll show you extinction."

—DUFF

SEASON TWO

Chi-Town and Wedding Gowns

Production no.: DB201
Original air date: January 18, 2007
Writer: Miriam Leffert
Director: Todd Strauss Schulson
Supervising editor: Grayce Lackland

The second season of *Ace of Cakes* kicks off with several new additions to the bakery, including an icer, Elena, and a decorator, Katherine. The Charm City Cakes team has been asked to create a red velvet 10-point buck groom's cake, a punk rock wedding cake, and a vintage postcard–themed wedding cake for a childhood friend of Mary Alice's. But the most challenging cake of the week is a model of Wrigley Field for a surprise eightieth-birthday party in Chicago. Duff puts the meticulous Geof in charge of the stadium cake. With the cake loaded in the van and 699 miles to go to Chicago, Duff hits the road. As he enters the home and tells birthday boy Joe Kurcz that everything on the cake is edible, he responds, "I didn't know that was a cake!"

Featured cakes: 10-Point Buck Groom's, Wrigley Field 80th Birthday, Bamboo Wedding, Punk Wedding, Postcard Wedding

Special appearances: Tim and Linda, punk cake; Jonna, postcard cake bride; Ed Kurcz; Joe Kurcz, Cubs fan birthday boy; the entire Kurcz family

Decorative techniques: Cake carving, straw usage, fondant crack repair, painting, fondant application, piping, graham cracker crumb usage

Caketastrophe: The Bamboo Wedding cake develops a crack in the fondant that Duff repairs with royal icing.

Featured organizations: The American Visionary Art Museum, Wrigley Field, The Engineering Society of Baltimore

Duff: "Don't be afraid to delegate. Seriously. Even to me."
Geof: "Oh, I plan on that."

"You can either hide it with flowers or learn how to fix it."

—DUFF

"I don't think the Cubs have won in, like, a hundred years, but I guess he's going to get a nice cake."

—GEOF

"They made a stadium that looks like my cake."

—DUFF

"I'm going backwards, and I'm built like Barney Rubble."

—DUFF

The Boss Is Gone

Production no.: DB202
Original air date: January 24, 2007
Writer: Heather Mitchell
Director: Todd Strauss-Schulson
Supervising editor: Grayce Lackland
Editor: William Jarrod Burt

With Duff away delivering the Wrigley Field cake from episode 202, Geof is in charge

and hates it. Meanwhile, Mary Alice is drowning in emails. Mary Smith works on icing a Chinese Take-Out Container cake for a birthday celebration adorned with gum paste Netflix packages on the sides. And repeat customers Jeff and Natalie McAndrew have ordered an anniversary cake in the form of their house, complete with all the homeowner disasters such as flooding basements and broken wells, while Mary Alice drives across town to Glass Block of America to pick up glass blocks for Geof's challenging art deco cake. Meanwhile, from Gary, Indiana, Duff explains his recipe for true road food, which involves cooking potatoes on the engine of the car and tying beans to the exhaust pipe.

Featured cakes: Chinese Take-Out, McAndrew First Anniversary, Art Deco Guglik Wedding, Gyro with Fries, Dogs Playing Poker, Philips Mountain Wedding, K-9 Sixty-fifth Birthday, Van Gogh "Starry Night"

Special appearances: Jeff and Natalie, McAndrew home anniversary cake clients; Jennifer and Jim, Chinese Take-Out birthday cake clients; Keith and Tasha, wedding cake clients

Decorative techniques: Icing, carving, gum paste vegetable creation, modeling chocolate work, extruder work

Caketastrophe: Broken dog cake

Fun facts: This episode originally aired out of sequence with "Great Scot" to help introduce *Dinner: Impossible.*

"We've had clients that have gotten wedding cakes from us and then called a year later, and I'm thinking that they're calling for their anniversary topper, and they're really calling for a baby shower cake. . . . It's just you get the highlights of these people's lives and their families, and it warms your heart."

—MARY ALICE

"Certain flavors are more difficult to carve than others. You got all these chocolate chips in here, it's hard to cut through a chocolate chip. I wouldn't mind living inside of here, it's got your food groups, it's got the pumpkin group, and the butter group, and the chocolate group."

—GEOF

"Bacon makes everything make better."

—DUFF

"Oh, my god—if those people don't flip out over this cake, I'm going to stab them in the neck with this key."

—DUFF

"Always thinking. About what, I have no idea . . . but always thinking."

—DUFF

Four Weddings and a Rat

Production no.: DB203
Original air date: February 8, 2007
Writer: Miriam Leffert
Director: Todd Strauss-Schulson
Editor: Grayce Lackland

Two women are getting hitched, and when it comes to their wedding cake, they've decided to mix traditional and nontraditional. A special Thai Pagoda cake is paired with a Brooklyn Bridge–themed cake to reflect the couple's unique heritage. Geof hopes his next Jeep cake doesn't suffer the same fate as his first. And finally, Charm City Cakes decorator Erica is getting married and has ordered an unusual wedding cake: a male and female owl perched on a branch. When one of the owls is in danger of collapsing, emergency cake surgery is performed by attacking the problem from the bottom up.

Featured cakes: Rat Wedding, Thai Pagoda Wedding, Brooklyn Bridge Wedding, Owl Wedding, Jeep Groom's, Tree Wedding

Special appearances: Erica and John; Josh and Caryn; Jeep cake clients; Mary Pat, Tree cake client; Shelley and Jacq, Rat cake client; Cathy and Adrian Pagoda and Bridge cake clients

Decorative techniques: Cake carving, gum paste bridge and manhole contstruction, nonedible "tree" cake element, airbrushing, luster dust and vodka mix hand painting, fondant "roof" construction

Caketastrophe: When one of the owl cakes begins to lean to one side, a hole is drilled underneath for the insertion of a straw support.

"It's a confusing map; this map is not to scale, and I'm a very 'to scale' person."
—GEOF, lost while driving

"The best way to learn is to do it wrong, and then learn from that."
—GEOF

"Charm City Cakes is a family. Delivering a cake to a family member, you want to get it right."
—DUFF

Great Scot

Production no.: DB204
Original air date: January 24, 2007
Writer: Heather Mitchell
Director: Todd Strauss-Schulson
Editors: Matthew Monte, Grayce Lackland

Not only does Duff don a kilt to deliver a cow cake to a Scottish wedding, he even enlists the aid of a bagpiper to help get the bakery into the mood. There's also a Sweet Sixteen cake, a magnolia-themed cake that poses some challenging problems for Anna and the Charm City staff, and, last but not least, a nervous customer orders a cake with which he plans to propose to his girlfriend. The engagement ring is located on a special light-up feature on the top of the cake!

Featured cakes: Highland Cow Wedding, Happily Ever After Proposal, Magnolia Painted Flower, Drunk Jack-O-Lantern Graphic Arts Show, Super Sweet 16 Birthday

Special appearances: Rommel, proposal cake recipient; Katheryn and Alexander, bride and groom; Suzie and Tina, birthday girl and mom

Decorative techniques: Cake carving, fondanting, icing, wooden base construction, modeling chocolate use, electronics in foam core base, gum paste flower painting, royal icing "beer foam," extruder-created fondant "hair."

Caketastrophe: The fondant hair and skin on the Highland Cow fall off overnight and have to be replaced with modeling chocolate.

Fun fact: This episode aired a week and a day early along with "The Boss Is Gone" as part of a special programming block to introduce Food Network's new series *Dinner: Impossible*. It then reran the following week in the regular time slot.

Duff: "It's my bakery, and if I want a bagpiper, I'll have one."
Geof: "I've never seen a bagpiper in the bakery. I've seen piping bags but not a bagpiper."

"All of the skin had fallen off. Yak-tastrophe."
—DUFF, after the fondant hair separates from the Yak cake

Duff: I'll probably go commando under my kilt.
Mary Alice: What? Do it after lunch.

"It's a cake of a Highland cow, which apparently is from Scotland and looks kind of like a yak and Snuffleupagus had a love child."
—MARY ALICE

Monkey Business

Production no.: DB205
Original air date: February 15, 2007
Writer: Heather Mitchell
Director: Brandy Menefee
Editors: Grayce Lackland, Kamali Minter, Steven Centracchio

Duff and the staff have several giant cakes in store for them this week. First up is a giant monkey cake they have to get off their backs: a giant King Kong for a client's upcoming Bar Mitzvah. Next up, Geof finds himself challenged by both the construction and delivery of a giant oil supertanker for the real ship's christening. Also, a couple is getting married and the groom-to-be is a DJ. His fiancée is looking to surprise him with a cake that looks like one of his beloved turntables.

Featured cakes: King Kong Bar Mitzvah, Overseas Houston Oil Tanker Ship Christening, Technics Turntables Groom's

Special appearances: Fazia and Damian, Turntable cake clients; Drew Kramer, Bar Mitzvah boy, and his family

Decorative techniques: Large-cake construction, gum paste figure construction, dragée usage, electronic light installation, fondant usage, airbrushing, crispy cereal treat champagne bottle, faux edible rock construction, modeling chocolate sculpting, refrigeration pipe tubing skeletal frame construction

Caketastrophe: When faced with the sagging gum paste bow of his ship replica, Geof is forced to get creative with a small piece of Styrofoam, fondant, and strategically placed waves.

Fun facts: Mary Smith pronounced exactly zero *g*s during the production of this episode.

"You can eat yourself, but that's it."
—GEOF

"My Bar Mitzvah was at a Turkish restaurant in a strip mall."
—DUFF

Tributes and Tribulations

Production no.: DB206
Original air date: March 1, 2007
Writer: Miriam Leffert
Director: Brandy Menefee
Editor: Grayce Lackland

The staff of Charm City Cakes rises to the occasion as they visit a firehouse for inspiration in creating a fire truck for a special charity event. Sherri, Richard, and Mary battle fatigue as they work on a unique Cinderella Carriage for a local historic theater. And Duff teams up with his little brother, Luke, to create a special treadmill cake for the twentieth anniversary of their dad's health club business, SportFit.

Featured cakes: Cinderella Carriage Olney Theater, SportFit Twentieth Anniversary Treadmill, Fire Truck Charity Benefit

Special appearances: Luke Goldman; Morrie Goldman, Duff's dad; Bob, COO of SportFit; Brad, producing director, Olney Theatre Center; DJ, firefighter, and the Howard County Fire Station; Wendy, college friend of Mary Alice

Decorative techniques: Wooden base construction, airbrushing, fondant shape creation, vodka usage, fondant work, modeling chocolate detail work, piping, dragée application, royal icing application

Featured organizations: Howard County Fire Department, Johns Hopkins Children's Cancer Unit, Olney Theatre Center

"My dad is an amazing entrepreneur; he helped me get to this point, and now that I'm at this point, I'm trying to sit down with my dad and figure out what do I do?"
—DUFF

"I'm the UFA, you're the COO, and he's the DUFF."
—MORRIE GOLDMAN

"I've never been in any drama club . . . except for Charm City Cakes."
—GEOF

Flying High

Production no.: DB207
Original air date: March 8, 2007
Writer: Heather Mitchell
Director: Brandy Menefee
Editor: M. J. Loheed

After receiving a fan video from a couple of young decorators, Mary Alice kicks off a stressful week as she's agreed to host Glitterama, a local variety show produced by Fluid Movement. The show will also feature an added bonus: Duff doing Salome's Dance of the Seven Veils. Geof's architectural skills are put to the test with a groom's cake in the shape of a famous Austrian ski jump. In addition, there is a surprise airplane-shaped cake for a husband who has just received his pilot's license—complete with a fondant figure of the pilot himself.

Featured cakes: Ski Jump Wedding, Cessna Airplane Celebration, Cake of the Seven Veils Variety Show

Special appearances: Gerard and Kevin McSorley; Robert and Kendall, clients; . . . soihadto . . . (Duff's band); Paul, "ninja"/intern wrangler

Decorative techniques: "Ski Jump" cake base and foam core ramp construction, modeling chocolate wall, airplane wood base construction, dowel struts, foam core wings, airbrushing, fondant work, piping, cake carving, cake icing

Milestones and Monuments

Production no.: DB208
Original air date: March 15, 2007
Writer: Jen Wise
Director: Brandy Menefee
Editor: Stephen Centracchio

Duff has been asked to be emcee of Baltimore's annual tree-lighting ceremony at the city's Washington Monument with Maryland governor Martin O'Malley. Not only is the event being televised, but Duff packs the cake with fireworks for an extra special surprise. Pam Shriver has contracted the bakery to make a tennis ball cake for Martina Navratilova, which Geof and Duff deliver to the Mercantile Tennis Challenge. The bakery has also been asked to create a cake replica in the form of a Campbell's Soup can for the show's second-season sponsor.

Featured cakes: Tennis Ball Birthday, Campbell's Soup Commercial, Washington Monument Ceremonial

Special appearances: Martin O'Malley; Pam Shriver; Martina Navratilova; Luther, pyrotechnics director

Decorative techniques: Fondant work, masking technique, painting, logo piping, cake carving, color mixing, wooden dowel and base construction, sponge marbling diffusion technique

Featured charity: Mercantile Tennis Challenge

"George Washington, the first president of the United States, said in his will that he would like no monuments erected to him. So within hours of his death, construction was begun upon the Baltimore Washington Monument."
—DUFF

"It's all fun and games until the governor gets his eye blown out."
—MARY ALICE

"We do tend to work awfully close to our deadlines here at Charm City Cakes."
—MARY ALICE

"The cake guy is down. Repeat, the cake guy is down."
—BALTIMORE PARAMEDIC

Caketastrophe

Production no.: DB209
Original air date: March 29, 2007
Writer: Miriam Leffert
Director: Brandy Menefee
Editors: Grayce Lackland, M. J. Loheed

It's a busy week for Charm City Cakes. This week they're busting out forty cakes (last year at this same time they had only seven on the books). Duff has been brought in by Starbucks to make a special holiday cake at Union Station in Washington, D.C. After days of working around the clock, Duff and his team have created a train that looks as if it's made of gingerbread. Duff delivers the train to scenic Union Station, where he adds the finishing touches before an audience of hundreds. It's a teenage girl's sixteenth birthday and her mom has ordered a Goth cake, complete with skulls and spiders, to celebrate. Mom is driving all the way from North Carolina to pick up the cake. Charm City has been invited to make three massive cakes for a guy's "Big Fat Greek Birthday." One of the cakes is an old theater with "It's a Wonderful Life" adorning the marquee; another cake is a girl sipping a soda at a soda fountain.

Featured cakes: Gingerbread Train Starbucks, Goth Birthday, Patterson Theater and '50s Soda Fountain Birthday, Castle Amos Birthday

Special appearances: Willie Goldman; Carter Bentzel; Starbucks marketing manager; Michael, Ashley, and Wendy, clients; Stuart and Suzanne Amos

Caketastrophe: The castle cake is accidentally dropped, and a replacement must be constructed within five hours.

Decorative techniques: Cake carving, cake sketching, fondant figure construction, display centerpiece construction, fondant work, airbrushing, piping, candy application, cake icing, hand painting, brick patterns mold usage, coordinated high-speed cake construction

Fun facts: The 1,200-seat Patterson Theater opened in Baltimore in 1929 but was nearly destroyed by a fire in the late 1950s. Saved from the fire, it went on to show movies until it finally closed. A local group worked to restore and reopen the theater.

"We really got to get it right—that's what Geof does. He does things right."
—DUFF

"We just had to stay on target. Follow the plan. And then the plan came to a screeching halt."
—MARY ALICE

"Richard came back to the bakery with the cake in trash bags. It was like cake body bags."
—MARY ALICE

"Yo, Rich, you're on the Charm City Cakes book of records: the worst f—up ever."
—DUFF

"This is extreme cake decorating!"
—DUFF

"Why couldn't I drop a two-tier round cake?"
—RICHARD

Shell Shocked

Production no.: DB210
Original air date: April 12, 2007
Writer: Heather Mitchell

Director: Brandy Menefee
Editor: Grayce Lackland

Charm City Cakes is cursed! No cake is safe. It's had three cakes fall apart in two weeks. This week it's making a cake for a graduation party in the shape of the University of Maryland mascot, Testudo the Terrapin. The team has to pull an all-nighter to make it right because the turtle keeps falling apart. In order to ward off the evil spirits, Mary Alice and the girls hold a seance in hopes they can stop the bad mojo. Duff also has to make a ninetieth-birthday cake for a local legend, Sid Mandell. He owned a famous Baltimore deli, and the cake is an exact replica of Sid's most popular dish, "The 4X4." But the biggest challenge this week is a wedding cake that has to be an exact replica of the Taj Mahal. Duff and Geoff work together to make this one of the most amazing cakes Charm City Cakes has ever done.

Featured cakes: Testudo Beck Smith Graduation, "4X4" Sid Mandell Birthday: hamburger basket, fondant buns, rice krispie hamburger patty (airbrushed), gum paste onion rings and French fries, Taj Mahal Kumar Wedding

Special appearances: Steve, son of birthday boy; Sid Mandell; Kiran, groom; Rashmi, bride; Willie Goldman; . . . soihadto . . .

Decorative techniques: Cake sketching, fondant work, cake carving, airbrushing, isomalt invert sugar pool, gum paste work, Testudo cake base construction

Caketastrophe: When the Testudo graduation cake falls apart, Mary Smith calls Geof in the middle of the night for repairs.

"We persevere here at Charm City Cakes."
—CHEF ADAM

"I love disasters. I love it when things are falling apart and on fire and stuff because that way it's, like, let's figure out how to make that."
—DUFF

"Learning how to fix a cake is a very good skill to have. Not that we ever drop or bump or nick a cake [laughs]."
—DUFF

Duff: "You don't usually descibe a cake as badass."
Geof: "Not usually, unless you're shooting fireworks out of it."

"Making a cake for somebody is a very intimate thing to do. You are taking their joy and making it into a tangible object. And that is what I think makes us successful in what we do."
—DUFF

Dr. Duff

Production no.: DB211
Original air date: May 17, 2007
Writer: Jen Wise
Director: Brandy Menefee
Editors: Steven Centracchio
Director of photography: Matt Carr

This week Charm City Cakes is all about birthdays, body parts, and the good ol' days. They're making a classic blue convertible cake for a granny with a lead foot on her ninetieth birthday. There's also a foot in a cast for an orthopedic surgeon and a CAT scan cake for a radiology company party. But the biggest thing this week is that Sherri's getting married! Duff hangs out with Sherri and her fiancé, Matt, to discuss their cake, but they end up talking about when she first started working for Duff. Mary Alice shows Duff the original records book he bought when he first started the bakery . . . she's finally finished the last page, and we get a peek at how it all started.

Featured cakes: Go Go Granny Birthday, Foot Cast Birthday, Sherri's Wedding, CT Scan Party

Special appearances: Helen ("Granny"); Sherri; Matt, Sherri's fiancé; Shahla, wife; Tracy, granddaughter; Eddie, Tracy's husband; Dr. Charles and Irene Weiner

Decorative techniques: Airbrushing, piping, cake carving, modeling chocolate "toes," fondant work, gum paste detail work and figures

Fun facts: Although this was the eleventh episode shot for the season, it aired after the hourlong season finale. This episode features vintage footage from the unaired pilot of *Ace of Cakes*.

"It was kinda gross but kinda cute at the same time. Kinda like me."

—DUFF

Playing Games

Production no.: DB212
Original air date: April 12, 2007
Writer: Heather Mitchell
Director: Brandy Menefee
Editor: M. J. Loheed
Director of Photography: Matt Carr

This week Charm City Cakes is nothing but fun and games! They're making a cake in the shape of a Scrabble board for a birthday party. Anna is beside herself with excitement because she loves this game. She owns several boards, belongs to a Scrabble club, and is a competitive player. This cake will be very near and dear to her heart. Duff teams up with another local decorator to help with a special Bat Mitzvah cake: a gum ball machine complete with a glass bowl filled with real gum balls. Also on the schedule is a slot machine for a birthday girl whose favorite show is *Ace of Cakes*.

Featured cakes: Slot Machine Birthday, Scrabble Birthday, Gum Ball Machine Bat Mitzvah

Special appearances: Ginny, Slot Machine cake birthday girl; Kyle and Stacey, Scrabble cake boy and girl; Mackenzie, Bat Mitzvah girl

Decorative techniques: Cake sketching, fondant work, cake carving, painting, piping

"When we do kids' cakes, you know you can really see him just thinking in terms of what would be so cool for this kid. And it's great because he's not thinking, you know, 'What's really going to impress the parents . . .' That's not how he thinks. He's, like, 'What is going to blow this kid's mind?'"

—MARY ALICE, on Duff

"We have the Darth Maul of Scrabble over here."

—DUFF, on Anna

"You got time to lean, you got time to clean."

—DUFF, quoting Ray Kroc

"It's like every day is arts-and-crafts day. How much fun is that?"

—DUFF

"I ate some gum balls. The white ones tasted like white. And the purple ones, they kinda tasted purple. So I can only assume that the other colors tasted as such."

—GEOF

The Super Cake

Production no.: DB213
Original air date: April 26, 2007
Writer: Heather Mitchell
Director: Brandy Menefee
Editor: Grayce Lackland
Director of Photography: Matt Carr

The bakery has been asked to travel to Miami to create a supersize cake for the NFL's official Super Bowl XLI party the night before the big game. But before they can go to Florida, Geof has to complete a very special replica of an old Royal typewriter for a very special reporter turning eighty years young, and the crew makes a cake for a Mexican Sombrero/Siesta–themed birthday. While in New York to meet with NFL executives, Duff and Geof drive through Times Square and see a large billbord for *Ace of Cakes*. For the Super Bowl cake, they bake thirty-four sheet cakes, but when Mary and Katherine make it to Miami with the supplies, the team discovers the cake will be too big to make it into their hotel's elevators, and they decide to make the cake in sections. Taking a break from cake construction, the team visits Miami Seaquarium to swim with dolphins. When they get back to the hotel, Florida's humidity poses a set of unique challenges, and they decide to complete construction at the actual venue. Despite heavy wind and other problems, Duff, Geof, Anna, Katherine, and Mary finish the cake just in time for its presentation at the party.

Featured cakes: Typewriter Birthday; Mexican Siesta Birthday; Super Bowl XLI

Special appearances: Stanley, eightieth-birthday boy, Sara, Stanley's wife, Alan, Stanley's son; Tracy, director of marketing, NFL; Dan, director of operations, Live Nation, Jamal Anderson; Paul, intern wrangler; Mico, birthday boy, Traci, Mico's daughter

Decorative techniques: Cake carving, fondant work, gum paste detail piece construction, icing, modeling chocolate cactus, crispy cereal treat hat, typewriter key piping, food coloring, fondant painting

Fun fact: Until the Season Six finale, this episode was the sole hourlong episode produced.

"I think Geof's Crockett, because all the ladies love Geof. And I'm like Tubbs, because you mess with Crockett, you mess with me."

—DUFF

Wedding Bells and Shotgun Shells

Production no.: DB301
Original air date: July 19, 2007
Writer: Heather Mitchell
Director: Rob Lundsgaard
Editor: Grayce Lackland

Kicking off a new season, Geof introduces a couple of new employees: Ben, master engineer, and Joe, the youngest intern in Charm City Cakes history. It's a busy week at Charm City Cakes. Up first, the bakery's first-ever chocolate beaver cake . . . with voodoo pin tags stuck in it. Elena carves the head and the body, and then the tail, which is made of fondant, while Catherine works on the voodoo pin tags. After whipping up a disaster cake (featuring a sinking *Titanic* and an airplane crash), Geof gets working on a helmet cake, which is ideally meant to resemble a museum relic. Decorator Sherri collaborates with Duff as he sketches out her dream five-tier wedding cake. The reception takes places at the zoo. Animals run amuck while Sherri sweetly admires the cake's workmanship.

Featured cakes: Beaver Birthday, Disaster Day Housewarming, Sherri's Wedding, Sutton Hoo Helmet Birthday, Clown, Prescription Bottle, Texas, Motorcycle, Dolphin

Special appearances: David Beaver; Joe the intern; Jack Bart; Matt, Sherri's groom; the McCutchan family

Decorative techniques: Sheet-cake carving, fondant application and detailing, piping, painting, model building

Fun fact: Sherri has major history with Duff. They met while Duff was playing the role of the mayor of Baltimore, circa 1904, in a play about the great Baltimore fire.

Mary Alice: "Are we going to do people floating in the water?"
Anna: "How tasteless."
Mary Alice: "Yeah, there's a line."

"I probably would have been in the icy water singing Celine Dion."
　　　　　　　　　—MARY ALICE

"It's real satisfying blowing up a cake."
　　　　　　　　　—GEOF

"When's the last time you hugged a baker?"
　　　　　　　　　—DUFF

"Duff and Geof and Mary Alice; they're all, like, my best friends, and I've known them for so long. And, you know, whatever strange twists and turns, we've all sort of ended up here."
　　　　　　　　　—SHERRI

"Every cake has a story; some cakes' stories are just very, very, very long."
　　　　　　　　　—MARY ALICE

"In the fourth grade in Hebrew school, I cheated on a test, and I blamed it on the dog."
　　　　　　　—DUFF, quoting
　　　　　　　　　The Goonies

BEAVERISMS

Duff: "A chocolate beaver . . . I'm just going to leave that one alone."
Elena: "Insult beaver is ready to go."

Duff: "Elena's amazing. I tell ya, man, she just came out of left field. I hired her to ice cakes, and she just whipped out this beaver that was incredible."
Geof: "It was a perfect beaver. It had that big beaver tail, big beaver teeth, beaver arms."
Elena: "I guess I'll be here when he comes to pick it up so I'll get to see the full-on reaction of Mr. Beaver. The real Mr. Beaver."
Mary Alice: "Mr. Beaver was quite thrilled with his beaver."
Duff: "When David Beaver showed up to pick up his beaver cake, he compared it to his past beaver cakes. That was the best beaver cake that David Beaver had ever seen."

Tattoos and Traditions

Production no.: DB302
Original air date: July 26, 2007
Writer: Jen Wise
Director: Rob Lundsgaard
Editor: Grayce Lackland

Paul prepares a surprise birthday cake for a local Baltimore legend, who's most often seen sitting on her porch in a rocking chair. First he carves the woman's row house out of stacked sheet cakes; then he adds a brick imprint onto the fondant. He wipes a brick red color over the imprint, crafting the rocking chair figurine and awning last. Next up is an armadillo cake for an EMT who's a big fan of the film *Steel Magnolias*. His wife's requested a replicate of the film cake . . . except the armadillo is to be dressed in an EMT uniform. Using a wooden dowel and a drill, Ben helps Elena with the construction of the head and ears. Elena paints the tip of the armadillo's nose light pink to make it look realistic. Finally, Duff, Mary Alice, and Elena take a field trip to the local tattoo parlor, where they each get new tattoos.

Featured cakes: Row House Birthday, Duck Hunting, EMT Armadillo, Plant

Special appearances: Eighty-year-old Baltimore icon Shirley; Brian, Shirley's son; Leslie, Bailey, Grace, and Joe, Shirley's

neighbors; Joe the intern; Baltimore Tattoo Museum artist; Armadillo clients: Matsui family, clients; Tracy and Elizabeth, clients

Decorative techniques: Use of wooden dowels for support and stability

Caketastrophe: The fondant roof of the row-house cake separates in transport, and Geof is sent out to repair it at the party.

Featured organization: The Baltimore Tattoo Museum

Fun facts: Anna and Ben went to art school together. Charm City Cakes offers a green-tea buttercream icing that's chock-full of antioxidants.

"You did such a bang-up job on the beaver last week."
　　　—MARY ALICE, to Elena on why
　　　　　she should make the Armadillo cake

Elena: "If I was in a really bad car accident and an armadillo was waddling to my rescue, I think I might be a little worried, but once I saw that he had all of his supplies I'd be cool with it."
Duff: "Is it better than the one in *Steel Magnolias*, you think?"
Elena: "He's gonna be way cooler. That one was just a plain armadillo. This one actually has a trade, being an emergency technician. If someone chokes on him, he could save them."
Duff to Joe the intern: "Hey Joe, the sink looks pretty full, man."
Joe: "I know."
Duff: "If I was an intern, I'd do something about it."
Joe: "Oh, no, I got a list."
Duff: "Wait, who owns this place? Oh, wait, that's right, it's me!"
Joe: "I'll do it."
Duff: "You whine and you're sassy and you lack moral fiber."
Joe: "Well, you're full of antioxidants."
Duff: "Is that a euphemism?"
Joe: "What?"
Duff: "Exactly."

Mary (Alice) Go Round

Production no.: DB303
Original air date: August 2, 2007

Writer: Heather Mitchell
Director: Rob Lundsgaard
Editor: Grayce Lackland

It's Tuesday, and the bakery has twenty-eight cakes to do, with a Friday-heavy delivery day to add to the stress. First up, a biplane birthday cake for a customer who loves planes and golf; the customers have requested a cake of a golfer practicing his swing on the wing of a biplane. Anna convinces everyone that the golfer needs to be on solid ground. Also in the mix: a show-piece cake with a carousel replica for the 110th-anniversary celebration of the city of Asbury Park, New Jersey. The team has the clever idea of using a record player as the spinning base of the carousel. Upon completion, the Charm City crew admires the carousel as it spins. Duff says, "I do believe this is the cake of the year." Then he laughs as he and the staff realize "And there's no cake in it!"

Featured cakes: Biplane Birthday, Asbury Park Carousel, Union Memorial Hospital's 100th Birthday

Special appearances: Corrine Bell, cochair of Champions of Care for Union Memorial Hospital

Decorative techniques: Cake carving, fondant work

"So we're making a plane with a golfer on the wing practicing his swing, maybe in the spring, that's a thing. No bling bling. I can sing. K-ching!"

—DUFF

"Biplanes are cuter than a single-winged plane, I suppose. Better to be bi than not."

—GEOF

"If you know two sides of a triangle, you can figure out the third. 'A' squared plus 'B' squared equals 'C' squared. I mean, this is things that I learned in ninth grade that I didn't use for ten years, and then I used them again, and than I didn't use them for a few years. Again they come back. Stay in school."

—GEOF

Challenge Road Trip

Production no.: DB304
Original air date: August 9, 2007
Writer: Jen Wise
Director: Rob Lundsgaard
Editors: Grayce Lackland, M. J. Loheed

The first featured cake this week is a replica of Max's Bar on Broadway, where the bride and groom met. With their first drunken encounter in mind, they've also requested that the bakery make a sugar model of the groom passed out in front of the bar while being poked with a pool cue by the bride. Next up, a very unusual groom's cake incorporating the groom's elementary school picture book. The groom's mother also wants to include her son's (Clark's) childhood haiku attempts. Duff puts Anna in charge of the bakery because he, Mary Alice, and Geof are flying to Denver to judge the Food Network's Extreme Cake Challenge. There's some stiff competition, but after deliberating, Duff announces the winner of the $10,000 award: Elisa Strauss, the creator of the Psycho Sock Monkey cake.

Featured cakes: Max's Bar Wedding, Haiku Groom's

Food Network Extreme Cake Challenge cakes featured: TNT Bone, Upside Down, Swiss Army Knife, Psycho Sock Monkey

Special appearances: Keghan Gerhard; Jess; Joe the intern; Clark, groom

Decorative techniques: Fondant work, brick pattern technigue, gum paste figures, painting, piping

"Why bake when you can deep-fry? Why airbrush when you can torch?"
—DUFF, as he uses a welder in a previous cake competition clip

"And they introduced me. And they're, like, 'Here's Mary Alice Yeskey,' I'm kind of dorked, like, walking through these lasers trying not to look like a complete moron because I don't know what the protocol is for walking through a tunnel of lasers with smoke. I did the best I could. I hope I looked pretty extreme."

—MARY ALICE

"Is it a beer o'clock at the bakery?"
—MARY ALICE, to Jess on the phone as she checks in on the bakery

Duff: "Is Katherine haikuing?"
Katherine: "Tying big white sails, the lemon curd pirate ship, Ben and Katherine work."
Duff: "It's lime curd. It's a lime curd pirate ship."
Ben: "It doesn't taste like lime, but I'm not gonna say anything."
Duff: "What do you mean, it doesn't taste like lime? I made it myself."
Ben: "Give it a taste."
Duff: "It totally tastes like lime."
Katherine: "Here's a lime curd pirate ship."

"This is what's being called the Haiku cake, and I am piping what's being called the Haiku, but it's just a poem. It's not a haiku. It's a good poem."

—KATHERINE

"I wouldn't want my grandmother knowing that I was passed out drunk when I met my future spouse, but hey, yay for honesty."
—MARY ALICE, on the backstory of the Max's Bar wedding cake

Anna: "Next time you go out of town, we'll really show you what it's like for us to not come to work."
Katherine: "Yeah."
Anna: "If that's what you want?"
Duff: " 'Hi, my name's Anna, and I'm a smart-ass.' "
Anna: "Hi, my name's Anna, and I finished all your cakes while you were gone."

"You don't wanna kill your audience, you know what I mean? You just want to entertain them. There's a difference."

—DUFF

Wishes Granted

Production no.: DB305
Original air date: August 23, 2007
Writer: Miriam Leffert
Directors: Rob Lundsgaard, Matthew R. Carr
Editor: M. J. Loheed

First up this week is a wedding cake for two parents who are getting married for the second time. They actually dropped off their kids at the bakery and gave them free rein on the wedding cake design. Together with Duff, the kids came up with a unique design—a green gorilla and a skunk sitting on a minicar with four pairs of hiking boots. Next is the cake for a Make-A-Wish Foundation recipient, Laura Cowling. Her wish is to make a four-tiered jungle/rain forest–themed birthday cake at the bakery with Duff to have at her birthday party. Laura sent the bakery a list of all the animals she wants on her cake, including "a macaw, a guerilla [sic], an orangutan, the smallest monkey in the world, a green snake, a hippo, and an elephant." Laura says with complete sincerity, "This has been one of the best experiences of my life." Finally, Southwest Airlines has ordered a replica three-foot-long jumbo jet painted with the Maryland state flag for its employees at Camden Yards.

Featured cakes: Southwest Airlines, Rainforest Make-A-Wish, Skunk/Gorilla Wedding, Soccer Ball and Shoe (aka "the 30th")

Special appearance: Make-A-Wish Foundation recipient Laura Cowling

Decorative techniques: Fondant work, X-ACTO knife detailing

Featured charity: Make-A-Wish Foundation

"I think it's tough to find a flag that's better than Maryland's. Pennsylvania's doesn't come close, I know that."
— GEOF, after Mary Alice calls the Maryland flag "The greatest state flag in the Union"

"We do Maryland flags, like, every month, and every month I say I wish we lived in a state with an easier flag, because the Maryland flag is very complicated . . . I don't even know how to describe it. It's got this sort of checkerboard pattern, and then it's got this, I don't know what it is."
— GEOF

"I love hanging out with kids. I think we share the same maturity level."
— DUFF

Cute exchange between Duff and Laura as they put the gum paste animals on the cake:
Duff: "I mean, if I was an orangutan, what would I be doing?"
Laura: "Scratching your butt."
Duff: "Well, I do that anyway."
Laura: "I do that too."

"What happens when you let Duff Goldman and two very young children design a wedding cake? You get a green gorilla in a wedding veil next to a skunk sitting on top of a car. That's what happens."
— MARY ALICE

Rock & Roll

Production no.: DB306
Original air date: August 16, 2007
Writer: Jen Wise
Director: Rob Lundsgaard
Editors: Grayce Lackland, Steven Centracchio

The first cake this week is for the Armed Forces Foundation, which provides support for soldiers and their families. It's a giant American flag with five pillars representing the Army, Navy, Air Force, Marines, and Coast Guard surrounding the Armed Forces Foundation pillar in the center. As if that weren't enough of a challenge, the cake will also have replicas of both the Washington Monument and the Capitol Dome. Next up is a thank-you cake for Clutch, Duff's "favorite band in the universe." Mary Alice's brother, Neil Fallon, just happens to be the lead singer. The bakery is going to create a replica of an orange amp. The other big cake this week is the Clipper City Pirate Ship wedding cake for a wedding full of pirate reenactors. The episode closes with Duff and Mary Alice in the front row rocking out to the Clutch concert.

Featured cakes: Armed Forces, Pirate Ship Wedding, Clutch Thank-you

Special appearances: Neal Fallon (Mary Alice's brother) and Clutch, pirate bride and groom and their pirate wedding party, Camille the intern

Decorative techniques: Fondant work, painting, airbrushing

Fun facts: Duff explains that the band Clutch is at least partly responsible for Charm City Cakes: "Clutch was my favorite band before I met Mary Alice. And not only is Mary Alice Neil's little sister, but the first wedding cake I ever made on my own was for Neil in Denver. In a way you could say that Neil was the impetus of Charm City Cakes." Though this episode was shot after episode 305, "Wishes Granted," it aired several weeks prior to that episode.

"Yarrr, it's the pirate wedding. Shiver me timbers. I think I should talk in pirate voice for the rest of the day."
— MARY ALICE

Duff: "These guys are pretty, um, what's the word?"
Mary Alice: "Into pirates."
Duff: "Yeah."
Mary Alice, "If Charm City Cakes was a pirate ship, I would probably be the beer wench."
Duff: "If this place was a pirate ship, I would be the cook."
Anna: "I would be laying on the deck getting tan reading *Us Weekly*."

"Clutch is, like, hard, but they're funky, but they're smart, but they're loud. Simply put, Clutch is the greatest band ever."
— DUFF

"Nothing says rock 'n' roll like chocolate cake."
— NEIL FALLON

Stadium Games and Eating Brains

Production no.: DB307
Original air date: August 30, 2007
Writer: Heather Mitchell
Directors: Rob Lundsgaard, Matthew R. Carr
Editors: Grayce Lackland, Chaney Moon

The first cake this week is for Crissy, who wants a very special surprise thirtieth-birthday cake for her filmmaker boyfriend, Jason, who makes horror movies. The cake is to be of Jason's head, sandwiched between two zombies who will be picking at/eating his brain. Elena draws in a crowd at the bakery as she squeezes red icing onto the cake head of Jason, so that it appears to be dripping in blood. Next up is a four-tier wedding cake covered with horizontal pleating of fondant strips, a tedious and difficult project that Anna is going to take on. And then are two stadium cakes—Camden Yards and Ravens Stadium—so Duff and Geof go to check out Camden Yards. Geof says, "It's, like, I'm making a little downtown of Baltimore in one week." When he sees the finished Zombie Head cake, Jason, the birthday boy, sums it up well: "It'll definitely be a little gory later, when we all start feasting on my brains. It's perfect."

Featured cakes: Zombie Head Birthday, Horizontal Pleated Wedding, Camden Yards Groom's, Ravens Stadium

Special appearances: Monica of the Orioles PR department; Nicole, the Orioles' head groundskeeper (the second female head groundskeeper in the history of Major League Baseball); Abby and Matt, Horizontal Pleated cake bride and groom; Audra, bride for the Camden Yards groom's cake; Jason and Crissy (Zombie Head cake)

Decorative techniques: Geof says it's best to color the modeling chocolate with a powder color to prevent it from melting, because it doesn't add any moisture. And he says the dark chocolate modeling chocolate tends to also hold up better.

Caketastrophe: Duff: "The whole thing about cake decorating is people are, like, 'How do I make horizontal stripes?' Keep making them until you do it right, you know, and then you'll get it right."

Fun fact: Elena is a cat person, and she has a Mount Rushmore photo collage of her cat up in the bakery.

Adam the baker: "I guess I could see Duff being a zombie. Sometimes early in the morning when he comes down here he kind of looks like a zombie and he kinda acts like a zombie. All

he's gotta do now is learn how to suck brains, I guess."
Duff makes many zombie noises, then says: "I've had calf brain before. Not bad."
Mary Alice: "You put any man on a baseball diamond, he's going to regress to being five years old?"
Geof: "Can we run into the wall?"
Monica, Orioles PR: "Go for it!"
Geof runs and jumps into the wall. Upon landing he says, "Oh, yeah, that's nice."
Ben, working on the skin of the Jason head for the Zombie Head birthday cake: "I'm guessing the flesh of a man who's getting eaten by zombies doesn't have to be perfect, right?"
Geof on the completed Zombie Head cake: "The Zombie Head cake was Elena's best work. It was disgusting in a tasteful way."
Duff: "You know, it was pretty funny, we can make, like, pretty much anything. But then when it comes to, like, a standard wedding cake, we're all, like, huh. Nobody here ever worked in a cake shop . . . there's a lot of traditional things that we just don't know how to do."
Sherri on the Zombie Head cake: "That is, hands down, the grossest thing I've ever seen."

"Zombies. Everybody just goes in their house and they lock the doors and block the windows and everything. Eventually they get in. But imagine if the zombies were, like, this big [he holds his two fingers a few inches apart], they'd get you a lot faster."
—GEOF

Battleships and Birthdays

Production no.: DB308
Original air date: September 6, 2007
Writer: J. C. Begley
Director: Matthew R. Carr
Editor: Grayce Lackland

First up, Charm City has to make a four-foot-tall Tower of London cake for the best-

selling author Tom Clancy's sixtieth birthday. Clancy is the only civilian American yeoman guard, or Beefeater, of the Tower of London, and the cake is to be displayed on the USS *New Jersey*. Next, Duff has agreed to make a cake for his roommate from freshman year. "Imagine me as a freshman in college." There is a pregnant pause. "Exactly." It's a Chesapeake Bay/Maryland–themed cake with black-eyed Susan flowers, crabs, beach grass, and so on, and Anna has been put in charge. Meanwhile, Elena starts on a King Tut cake, attempting to create a spitting image of the famous sarcophagus. It's for a giant surprise birthday party at the Franklin Institute in Philadelphia, which is hosting the traveling King Tut exhibit. Putting liquid black frosting on the cake, Elena says, "It's a little bit like doing my own makeup, but I'd like to think I'm a little less heavy on the eyeliner."

Featured cakes: Tower of London Birthday, Maryland Wedding, King Tut Birthday

Special appearances: Duff's college roommate, Kristopher; Tom and Alex Clancy; King Tut birthday boy Ron and his wife, Helena

Decorative techniques featured: Cake carving, icing, fondant work, painting

Featured organization: USS Battleship *New Jersey*

Duff: "He's a Beefeater."
Mary Alice: "A what?"
Duff: "The guys on the gin bottle."
Mary Alice: "You got to put it in terms we'll understand, the guys on the gin bottle."

"I think [the Beefeaters] are trained to kill . . . I'm not trained to kill."
—GEOF

"I think it is definitely going to be an Elena cake because it involves creatures that are somewhat dead."
—MARY ALICE

"I think that if I were a pharaoh and I died, my sarcophagus would just be covered with little cats."
—ELENA

"[King Tut] was a lesser pharaoh. He was, like, the Martin Van Buren of pharaohs."
—MARY SMITH

"Can you imagine Duff pulling off something like that, a major heist? He can't even figure out the delivery schedule."
—GEOF

"Don't laugh, people are going to think I'm Gothic, and then the real Goths are going to come after me and be, like, 'She's such a poser, that girl, I hear she likes the Beatles.' "
—ELENA, after Duff calls her "Princess Goth"

"That King Tut thing was just—pharaohlicious."
—MARY ALICE

Someone at the bakery: "What are the blackbirds on the Tower of London for?"

Geof: "It's an old English legend. If there are any fewer than six ravens at the Tower of London, the kingdom will fall. So what they do is, they take the ravens and they clip their wings so they can't fly away . . . that's not fair, just because of some stupid legend."

"We have to live with him [Duff] all the time, 24/7. He's here constantly, always. I'm just saying, if you get an apology cake for having lived with Duff, then there are about eleven people who need apology cakes."
—MARY ALICE

"I think I shot a missile at the Ben Franklin Bridge. Sorry, Philly."
—DUFF

Charm and Charities

Production no.: DB309
Original air date: September 13, 2007
Writer: Heather Mitchell
Director: Matthew R. Carr
Editor: M. J. Loheed

Duff's father, Morrie Goldman, has a problem. Duff is considering making a cake for the Playboy Mansion, and Duff's stepmom,

Mrs. Goldman, won't give him permission to go! Duff's turns to his brother Willie to try and make it happen. Charm City Cakes has also been asked to do another cake for Zoomerang, a charity event for the Maryland Zoo. This year the theme is elephants, and Duff quickly says, "Somebody go measure the back of the van!" Next, Charm City has been asked to make a Lighthouse cake for the Harbour School, a school for kids with special needs. Duff plans to put a motor in the lighthouse so the light within the cake will rotate, as well as a second light reflector so it will both rotate and flash. Finally, Charm City is making a cake for A Night at The Wire, a benefit held by the HBO TV show *The Wire*. This year they're honoring Ella Thompson, a legendary advocate for children in Baltimore who planted gardens in abandoned lots.

Featured cakes: Lighthouse, Elephant, Baltimore Block

Special appearances: Willie Goldman; Diedre Lovejoy, *The Wire*

Decorative techniques featured: Cake carving, icing, painting, fondant work

Featured charity: The Ella Thompson Fund

"What really makes these elephants, what makes them tick, how are these elephants—so elephantine?"
—GEOF

"In order to understand the basic shape of an elephant, I don't think you really need to go look at an elephant. But we'll just let Duff go on his little field trip while the rest of us stay here and work."
—MARY ALICE

"Elephants are supposed to have good memories, so, no, I would not call Duff the elephant of the bakery."
—MARY

"This is the first elephant butt I've ever smoothed in my life."
—BEN

"I've never had elephant cake. I can't imagine what elephant cake tastes like, but I can imagine it's endangeredly delicious."
—MARY ALICE

"Ace of Cakes rocks!"
—DEIRDRE LOVEJOY

Uncle Sam Wants Duff

Production no.: DB310
Original air date: September 20, 2007
Writer: Miriam Leffert
Director: Matthew R. Carr
Supervising Editor: Grayce Lackland

It's Roller Skate Friday at the bakery, and Mary Alice rolls everywhere on her skates. It's all part of trying to be more efficient so she can "get to and fro faster" and "put a little zazz" in the day-to-day. This is the week of cigars, wine, and tanks. Ben starts on a Humidor cake for a surprise thirtieth-birthday party at the Havana Club in downtown Baltimore. And the U.S. Army has ordered a special cake for its birthday, a cake of a M1 tank that is to be presented at Camden Yards. The Army invites Charm City up to Aberdeen Proving Ground to test-drive a tank, which Duff calls "good cake inspiration." Ben takes a lesson from the Duff school of "method cake making" and starts to wear a smoking jacket while making the Humidor cake. Meanwhile, Anna works on a wedding cake of a country wine picnic, painstakingly creating the picnic blanket with its checkered squares. Duff delivers the Tank cake (chock full of sparklers) to Camden Yards and is rewarded with the Army Medal of Excellence.

Featured cakes: Humidor Birthday, U.S. Army Tank, Edgeinton Wine Wedding

Special appearances: CWS Roger Cupolo, director, Advanced Automotive and Recovery Department; SSG Robert Morehouse, instructor, Recovery Department; David Muegge, Havana Club general manager; Michael, birthday boy; Dani and Hannah, uncredited cake decorators; Kelly and Matt; Sean Marshall, Army Recruiting, Public Affairs Office

Decorative techniques: Cake carving, icing, painting, fondant work

Fun fact: Aberdeen Proving Ground is the Army's oldest active proving ground; it was established on October 20, 1917, six months after the United States entered World War I.

"For some reason I have to take a ride in it. That way, I will really understand the tank better."

—GEOF

"The thought of Duff driving a tank fills me with a little bit of foreboding and dread, but he does have a certain tanklike quality to him. I think he'd fit well in a tank. I just don't want to be anywhere near him when he's doing it."

—MARY ALICE

"Duff always wants to put fireworks in cakes. What better than a tank to shoot something out of."

—GEOF

"We're doing a tank, cigars stank, wine I will drank."

—MARY ALICE

"This week has a motif that ties everything together. We've got cigars, booze, the U.S. Army. I know that when I'm driving a tank I definitely need a stogie and a glass of merlot. It helps with the steering."

—MARY ALICE

"My favorite part of the tank is the boom-stick."

—DUFF

"There's a fine line between being a suave dapper gentleman and sort of creepy Uncle Duff In the smoking jacket."

—MARY ALICE

"We're, like, real tank mechanics."

—DUFF

"If we were tank mechanics, everyone would be dead."

—GEOF

Coach Duff

Production no.: DB311
Original air date: September 27, 2007
Writer: Heather Mitchell
Director: Matthew Carr
Editor: M. J. Loheed

Charm City Cakes has been asked to create a special trophy cake for a basketball charity event founded by NBA superstar Carmelo Anthony, who doesn't know he's going to assist in making his own cake. Elena ices and carves several stacks of sheet cakes into the shape of a big box that will serve as the base of the trophy. Duff carves a trophy out of Styrofoam, then fills it with chocolate-covered espresso beans. He instructs Carmelo on painting the trophy base a golden brown color. Only when Duff arrives at the charity event just in time to deliver the cake does Carmelo realize he's helped decorate his own award. The bakery is also working on a special wedding cake for a jazz musician and his dancer wife. Geof molds the piano cake out a single piece of gum paste and painstakingly cuts out eighty-eight individual miniature keys. He then crisscrosses the top of the fondant with piano strings, colored wood paneling, and wires.

Featured cakes: Trophy, Piano, Navy Destroyer

Special appearances: Carmelo Anthony and his mom; U.S. Navy Senior Chief David Knight; Tracie and Laurence, bride and groom

Decorative technique: Piping

"We're going to leave off his name and all the logos, we're just going to pretend it's for someone else. I'm going to tell him [Carmelo] that he's decorating a cake for a Bar Mitzvah."

—DUFF

"I've never made a cake a day my life. You-all teach me how to make a cake, I'll teach you how to shoot hoops."

—CARMELO

"Twenty years of service, that's a long time to be stuck on a ship, I think. I'd think he would not want to see the ship anymore, but I guess it was some sort of closure, like eating your ship."

—GEOF

Duff: "I asked Carmelo if he wanted to play a little one-on-one."
Geof: "What if he screws up his ankle, goofing around with the cake guy? You going to give him a job?"
Duff: "Well, he said needed a summer job."
Geof: "He could get stuff off the top shelves."

Charm City Christmas

Production no.: DB312
Original air date: Thursday, December 13, 2007
Writer: Heather Mitchell
Director: Matthew R. Carr
Supervising editor: Grayce Lackland

Charm City Cakes is donating a cake to Baltimore's Ronald McDonald House. To give the cake an authentic frozen look, Duff airbrushes it with pearl and shine and then completes the North Pole motif with miniature snowmen. Duff and Mary Alice then head downtown to deliver donated toys and serve their cake to a group of happy kids. The bakery has also been asked to make an anniversary cake for Radio City Music Hall's Christmas Spectacular, which will feature twelve miniature Rockettes, lights, organs, a Christmas tree, and lots of glitter. Katie Rose rolls out a thin layer of gum paste to make figures of the Rockettes. Duff installs functional lights on the Radio City Music Hall cake. Finally, the team assembles the finishing touches in the lobby of Radio City Music Hall and presents the cake to the Rockettes and Santa in person.

Featured cakes: Ronald McDonald House, Radio City Music Hall Seventy-fifth Christmas Spectacular

Special appearances: Jared, Radio City tour guide; John Bonanni, Christmas Spectacular executive producer; Marianne Rowan Braun, Christmas Spectacular executive director; the Rockettes; Rapping Santa

Decorative techniques: Cake carving, airbrushing, fondant work, painting, piping gel application

Caketastrophe: The leg of an intricately painted gum paste Rockette is broken. It's up to Katie Rose to find a creative way to repair the damage.

Featured charity and organization: Ronald McDonald House, Radio City Music Hall

Fun fact: Though this episode was shot and numbered before episode 313, it didn't premiere until December, for obvious reasons.

"I have this fantasy about Geof and his whole family, like, going caroling because, like, they're all musicians. It'd be, like, the best caroling ever. But evidently it doesn't happen. But I don't accept that. In my reality, Geof's family goes caroling every Christmas."
—DUFF

"I've really never gone caroling, and I've stopped trying to convince Duff of this fact."
—GEOF

"It's eggy, it's nutmeggy, it's like being passed out under the Christmas tree. "
—GEOF, on Adam's new eggnog-flavored cake

"Don't tell the Jewish Times, *but Duff is a really big fan of Christmas."*
—GEOF

"I love Christmas, it's just joyous. I think it's the Chinese food."
—DUFF

Duff: "Get to play some Santa Claus or Hanukah Harry?"
Mary Alice: "Hanukah Harry or [giving Duff a once-over] hairy Hanukah."

"For being as short as I am and pretty much being all torso, I got dancer's legs."
—DUFF

Hairspray Premiere

Production no.: DB313
Original air date: Thursday, October 16, 2007

Writer: Heather Mitchell
Director: Matthew R. Carr
Supervising Editor: M. J. Loheed

This week the staff has been asked to do the cake for the premiere of the film *Hairspray*. Katie will create a big bottle of hair spray, complete with a hairbrush, some rollers, and cockroaches, for a finishing touch. The staff covers a four-foot tower of cake in modeling chocolate and decorates the tower to resemble a giant hair spray can. Katherine crafts edible gum paste cockroaches, complete with little antennae and red beady eyes. Once the cake's completed, the team heads down to the theater, where they encounter *Hairspray* director Adam Shankman and creator John Waters. Meanwhile, Sherri takes the lead in designing and constructing an *Alice in Wonderland* cake, building tiny chairs out of wood, while Anna works on the intricate gum paste tea set.

Featured cakes: *Hairspray* Premiere, Alice in Wonderland, Jeopardy

Special appearances: Robert and Margaret Halliday, clients; Brett Schneider, *Jeopardy* producer; John Waters; Adam Shankman; Amanda Bynes; Elijay Kelley; Nikki Blonsky

Decorative techniques: Cake carving, airbrushing, fondant work, gum paste figures, modeling chocolate work

Caketastrophe: The gum paste roaches fall onto the floor and must be remade.

Featured organizations: *Hairspray*, Jeopardy, The Charles Theatre

Fun fact: Though this episode was actually shot after episode 312, it premiered as the twelfth episode of the season.

"Being on Jeopardy *is a commitment. It isn't just trivia, it's a lifestyle."*
—GEOF

"I'll take Duff Goldman for 500, Alex."
—MARY ALICE

"The roaches, that's where they go."
—DUFF, after he has knocked all the gum paste roaches on the floor

The Harry Potter Cake

Production no.: DB401
Original air date: January 24, 2008
Writer: Miriam Leffert
Director: Matthew R. Carr
Editor: Grayce Lackland

Season Four kicks off with the bakery's biggest challenge to date: a replica of Hogwarts Castle for the fifth Harry Potter film premiere. Ben carves Styrofoam pieces that will make up the castle's many buildings, while Anna covers them in fondant. Once the interns cut out small pieces of black fondant that will make hundreds of tiny windows, the design starts to come together. Anna begins coloring and spackling the towers for an aged stone appearance. By Monday morning, the Hogwarts display piece has come together and is ready for its journey out west, where the team will construct the edible portions. Once there, Ben lays out various sheet cakes that will make up the castle's grounds and landscape. Anna creates gum paste trees while Duff melts a vast quantity of sugar to give the edible lake a waterlike appearance. After a few finishing details, the cake is finally done—and decidedly a success: at the premiere, Harry Potter actor Daniel Radcliffe admires the cake, and Duff claims, "This [is] the best cake that Charm City Cakes has ever produced."

Featured cake: Harry Potter Hogwarts

Special appearances: Daniel Radcliffe, Rupert Grint

Decorative techniques: Styrofoam shaping and carving, fondant application, liquid sugar usage

Fun fact: Valerie Bertinelli and Greg Grunberg both have split-second appearances in this episode at the Harry Potter afterparty.

Duff: "What's your magic power?"
Sofia: "Making you shut up?"

"Hey, Dumbledork, turn the lights back on."
—MARY ALICE

"If you drive through Kansas City and don't stop for BBQ, check your pulse."

—DUFF

"I am the Jew with a positive attitude towards bacon."

—DUFF

"The Fun Mover was not very fun."

—MARY ALICE

"This is very impressive!"

—DANIEL RADCLIFFE

Volcano Cakes and Mix Tapes

Production no.: DB402
Original air date: Thursday, January 31, 2008
Writer: Heather Mitchell
Director: Matthew R. Carr
Editor: M. J. Loheed

For a Hawaii-themed cake, complete with a dry-ice volcano, Ben creates the erupting volcano, and with Katherine's help—using more cake, royal icing, and a pipe for the volcano's center—completes the island's formation. Katherine paints a layer on the Maui cake, then begins adding gum paste signage and royal icing lava. Upon delivery, she demonstrates the working volcano to two very happy parents. For a Moon Bounce cake, Ben carves several stacked sheet cakes to replicate the rounded, soft, bull-nose corners of a Moon Bounce. With Duff's help, he works on structural supports, constructing the cake's outer frame using wooden dowels. Anna paints the cake's gum paste walls, which she and Ben then affix to the cake base. When the client, seven-year-old Jaylan, arrives with his mom and dad to pick up his birthday cake, Duff loads the cake into their car, while Geof tells Jaylan he's about to be "the coolest kid in school." The episode also features a charity softball game against The Sound Garden, a local independent record store, and a cake in the form of a shopping bag that's tipped over, spilling out cassette tapes.

Featured cakes: Maui Volcano and Moon Bounce birthday, Toilet Bowl Wedding (yeah, we said wedding), Sound Garden, Tractor Trailer Semi

Special appearances: Kai and his parents, Jaylan and his parents, Carrie Colliton

Decorative techniques: Dry-ice volcano, cake carving, fondant cutting, painting technique, frame construction, airbrushing, logo piping

"People appreciate that they're getting a show and that they have a story to tell."

—GEOF

Mascots and Mice

Production no.: DB403
Original air date: February 14, 2008
Writer: Miriam Leffert
Director: Matthew Carr
Editor: Grayce Lackland

Charm City Cakes must make a wedding cake for two proud Georgetown alumni in the shape of the Georgetown Hoya, a bulldog that will be taking a sizable bite out of an even larger cake. Elena carves several stacked sheet cakes into the dog's head and body, while Anna struggles with the tiered cake portion of the cake, finally settling on a design she—and the couple—are happy with. For Duff's stepmom, the team is creating a cake in the shape of her favorite Fabergé egg, a display cake she can hold on to. Duff sands off the edges of an egg-shaped cake pan and brings the two halves together to create a base. His brother Luke shows up to help paint the gold piping, but Sofia and Andrea help finish off the cake. Next, the team must create a unique French Toast Stack wedding cake with a tiny, smoking mouse popping out (an in-joke those at the bakery can't quite wrap their heads around). Katherine adorns a mouse with a beret, a mime shirt, a snazzy cigarette holder, and a little mustache and uses royal icing to mimic the authentic look of melted butter. Duff praises Katherine for a cake well done.

Featured cakes: Flower Box, Silver Subway Car Wedding, Light-up Proposal, Matzo Ball Bar Mitzvah, Fabergé Egg Birthday, French Toast Stack with Mouse Wedding, Sushi, French Fries, Beaver Birthday, Armadillo, Hound Dog, Boat

Special appearances: Luke Goldman; Ann Goldman; Morrie Goldman; Rommel, proposal cake client; Jessica, Rommel's fiancée; Caitlin and David, Hoya bride and groom

Decorative techniques: Sheet-cake carving, fondant application, piping, metal sanding, painting, royal icing application, piping gel clear coat.

"You get two Jewish kids together and they start arguing about brisket or matzo balls, it can get pretty ugly, pretty fast."

—DUFF

Airplanes and Arks

Production no.: DB404
Original air date: February 7, 2008
Writer: Heather Mitchell
Director: Matthew R. Carr
Editor: Grayce Lackland

"Transportation week" is declared at Charm City Cakes as orders for planes, trains, and . . . arks come in. Anna creates gum paste animals for a Noah's Ark cake, including fictional animals, such as unicorns, that have been left behind, while Ben carves stacked and iced cake into the ark and covers it with modeling chocolate. After resolving some major architectural snags, Duff delivers the Ark cake to the client, who squeals with delight. For a cake replica of a Boeing 767 airliner celebrating the grand opening of Delta's Sky 360 lounge, Geof re-creates the airline's logo from small pieces of colored fondant and a tiled runway base from chocolate squares and royal icing. For a Subway Car wedding cake (to be covered with graffiti), Elena stacks, ices, and carves the chocolate layers that will make up the cake. She then sprays the cake metallic silver and cuts the car's windows into the fondant. As Elena finishes her part, Duff steps in to hit the car with some of his signature graffiti, finishing up with a "Just Hitched" tag on the back of the car.

Featured cakes: Noah's Ark Bat Mitzvah, Silver Subway Car Wedding, Delta 767, Baltimore City Block, Chinese Take-out Container, Hot Dog, Open-Heart Surgery

Special appearances: Rachel, Bat Mitzvah girl; Doe and David, subway couple; Duff's former boss, the chef Todd English; cast members from MTV's reality series *The Hills*

Decorative techniques: Sheet-cake carving, painting, airbrushing, chocolate modeling, fondant carving

Fun fact: This is one of the only episodes to feature some work from Duff's previous life as a graffiti artist.

"Usually when you're doing graffiti you're not supposed to be doing graffiti—there's a sense of 'I'm doing something bad.' "
—DUFF

"This is the best-smelling cake we've ever done. It's nice to have another smell around here other than, you know, cake and fondant. It's good to have chocolate."
—GEOF

"Now we are here, we were there, but now we are here, going happily forward with cake in our bellies."
—MARY ALICE

The Spy Who Caked Me

Production no.: DB405
Original air date: February 21, 2008
Writer: Miriam Leffert
Director: Matthew R. Carr
Editor: Reverend Chaney Moon
Additional editing: M. J. Loheed

In addition to a cake decorated with hundreds of Girl Scout cookies, the bakery receives an order for an *Exorcist*-themed cake, complete with an edible possessed Regan—on her bed, puking, with her head spinning around. Elena constructs an edible replica of the bed by painting

a large piece of gum paste with a wood-grain pattern, as well as an edible replica of Regan's head. Duff and Elena build a motorized rig that will allow the head to spin, and once Elena adds green royal icing dripping from the head's mouth, she declares the cake done. Next up, Charm City Cakes prepares to make the eightieth-birthday cake for the James Bond actor Sir Roger Moore. Since Moore is a huge fan of art, as well as kids, the bakery decorates his cake with his many achievements, gum paste kids from around the world, and an edible replica of his family crest. To everyone's shock, however, hotel cleaning staff pilfer the Bond cake, and Geof and Jess are forced to come up with a last-minute replacement from a Manhattan bakery.

Featured cakes: Sir Roger Moore's Eightieth Birthday, The Exorcist, Girl Scout Cookie

Special appearances: Mary Krauser, Dag Hammarskjöld Scholarship Fund; Tony Garro, party host; Sir Roger Moore

Decorative techniques: Cookie decorating, airbrushing, wire work, fondant work, icing, painting

"I'm kind of a big deal around here."
—MARY ALICE

"Give me a nice, wet, slickery kiss."
—DUFF, quoting *The Goonies*

"This is a television program, and I can't tell you they're not going to talk about the fact that our cake was eaten by the housekeeping staff on television."
—MARY ALICE

"The housekeeper got away, but the hotel got stuck with the bill. So I guess: mission accomplished."
—JESS

Wedding Week

Production no.: DB406
Original air date: February 28, 2008

Writer: Heather Mitchell
Director: Matthew R. Carr
Editor: M. J. Loheed

A couple who met at a hockey rink has ordered a miniature wedding cake to be "towed" behind a replica Zamboni machine. Fondanting such a tiny cake proves to be more of a challenge than covering a full-size cake. Erica does the detail work on the edible Zamboni machine. After piping the rink's playfield lines and inserting goals made of gum paste, Duff rolls out fondant while Geof cuts up plastic for the rink's walls—all in time for the clients' early pickup. Meanwhile, Anna works on a cake showcasing the Baltimore skyline. She cuts 115 buildings out of gum paste, dries them using a curved Styrofoam form, and then paints them. She attaches pieces of fondant with piping gel and then places a large client-provided Rhinestone "D" on top of the cake. Geof carves and ices several stacked sheet cakes for an Off-Road Jeep cake, The clients have provided a plastic Jeep topper, so the ground itself will be the cake. The couple has also asked them to rough up the toy Jeep, so Duff, Geof, and Ben use a blowtorch and sandpaper for an authentic off-road appearance and insert the sad Jeep into a puddle of chocolate mud.

Featured cakes: Ice Hockey Rink, Baltimore Skyline, Off-Road Jeep, Monster Wedding

Special appearances: Brian and Ashley, Hockey Rink couple; Baltimore Skyline cake couple

Decorative techniques: Fondant work and techniques, cake carving and shaping, baroque piping method

Fun facts: The very first cake Duff ever made appears in a still photograph in this episode. The Baltimore World Trade Center, seen in this episode, is the world's tallest five-sided building.

"The wedding day is the peak of your beauty, and then after that it's all downhill, and then you're going to be crumply and wrinkly and dead."
—MARY ALICE

"Love is in the air, and we're providing the food."

—GEOF

"Our motto: Charm City Cakes—Always Fresh. Never Frozen. Sometimes very, very fresh. As in four seconds before you walked in the door fresh."

—MARY ALICE

Skaters and Speedsters

Production no.: DB407
Original air date: March 6, 2008
Writer: Jen Wise
Director: Matthew R. Carr
Supervising editor: Grayce Lackland

The bakery plans a wedding cake for a friend of everyone at the bakery, "Dicky," who has requested a "simple fall-themed cake. No pumpkins or other bullshit." Anna creates a neutral brownish and tannish background, a standard four-tier cake modeled off the couple's wedding invitations. Another big cake this week is a surprise birthday cake for the pro skater and skateboard designer Kris Markovich that is modeled after Kris's favorite skateboard wheel and incorporates Kris's skateboard art. Anna crafts a gum paste skateboard figure topper while Katherine replicates the skateboard wheel, covered in white fondant, and Katie Rose paints his imagery onto edible fondant. The team even realistically re-creates the tattoos on Kris Markovich's figurine. Meanwhile, Elena creates a Baby Shower cake and Geof explains he's making an edible late-fifties "German Speedster" cake.

Featured cakes: Skater Thirty-fifth Birthday, Speedster Sixtieth Birthday, Baby Shower, Fall-themed Wedding, Castle, Military

Special appearances: Kris and Amy Markovich, Katherine, Speedster cake birthday boy's daughter; Caitlin, Baby Shower cake recipient's sister, Matthew "Dicky" Dickenson and his wife, Elizabeth

Decorative techniques: Cake carving, airbrushing, fondant work, painting, piping gel application.

"We've done a few baby shower cakes. It's uncommon. Especially now, because we book up so far in advance. You'd have to know before you're pregnant if you're gonna be pregnant. I hope that no one is scheduling their pregnancy around our availability, but . . . I've seen some stranger things around here."

—GEOF

"This car was like Geof. It was so slick. Understated. Chill. Nice curves. Real suave. Nice curves. Just like Geof: nice curves."

—DUFF

"He went on this band trip to Jamaica and came back changed."

—KATHERINE, Geof's childhood neighbor

Celebration Week

Production no.: DB408
Original air date: March 13, 2008
Writer: Heather Mitchell
Director: Matthew R. Carr
Editor: M. J. Loheed

Following some playful banter about just how far one would have to screw up to get fired from Charm City Cakes, Duff, Geof, and Mary Alice discuss this week's cakes. First up: a large-scale replica of a human ear for a client, David, who is presenting it to Dr. Lloyd Minor, a doctor at nearby Johns Hopkins University who helped restore David's hearing. Because of the ear's wonky shape, Duff decides to assign the cake to Mary because of her incredible piping and carving skills. After a thorough investigation of everyone's ears, Sofia is chosen as the model. Next is a twenty-first birthday cake—an asymmetrical cake decorated with a variety of alcoholic beverages including mai tais, hurricanes, martinis—by Katherine. As Geof puts it, "It's a twenty-first birthday. Why not celebrate alcohol?" And Geof is charged with creating an intricate replica of an octagonal-domed cupola and clock tower for Mount St. Mary's University's bicentennial. Geof's cake is greeted with a standing ovation, and Katherine's

birthday cake is delivered along with some hangover advice from Mary Alice.

Featured cakes: Fork, Legal to Drink Birthday, Mount St. Mary's University Bicentennial Anniversary Clock, Human Ear Thank-you

Special appearances: Dr. Lloyd Miner, David Coriat and family

Decorative techniques: Cake carving, gum paste construction, airbrushing, fondant work, painting, Gatorfoam base construction

Caketastrophe: As he's cleaning a gum paste tuning fork, Duff accidentally breaks one and has to remake it in time for delivery.

Featured organizations: Johns Hopkins, Mount St. Mary's University

"Some things you don't really want to search on the Internet. Like human body parts."

—GEOF

"This is really ear-ie."

—BEN

"Yup, it's a lot to bear."
—GEOF, after he's told his cake looks like a huge cross

Police Cars and Wine Bars

Production no.: DB409
Original air date: March 20, 2008
Writer: Miriam Leffert
Director: Matthew R. Carr
Supervising editor: Grayce Lackland

First up is a Wine Bottle cake for a charity event, featuring Châteauneuf-du-Pape, one of the rarest bottles of wine in existence. The plan calls for a magnum bottle of wine to be made from fifteen cakes stacked on top of one another. Meanwhile, Mary works on carving a Yarn cake for a client's ninetieth birthday. The cake will be decorated with yarn, needles, partially finished sweaters, scarves, and mittens. Next up, a client has ordered a 1984 Electra Glide Harley-Davidson for her father's sixtieth birthday—and motorcycle cakes are notoriously difficult. And a police captain's wife has ordered a cake replica of her husband's police cruiser for his retirement party. Upon delivering the cake, Duff says, "Man, this is, like: great cake; great response; and I am walking away from a house full of cops, a free man."

Featured cakes: Wine Bottle Charity, Yarn Basket Ninetieth Birthday, Police Cruiser Retirement Party, Motorcycle Sixtieth Birthday

Special appearances: Sandy Malone; Captain Malone; Sergeant Hanna; Cindy Wolf; Paul (Baynesville Electronics); Georgia, ninetieth-birthday girl; Kennedy

Decorative techniques: Wooden base construction, cake carving, piping, gum paste construction, airbrushing, fondant work, painting, modeling chocolate work, electronic inserts

Caketastrophe: The weight of all the fondant on the Wine Bottle cake causes it to pull free and settle overnight. Ben repairs the cake by smoothing out the damaged areas with royal icing and then applying a new layer of fondant.

Fun facts: Duff frequently credits Cindy Wolf (who appears in this episode) as being one of his mentors. Duff, Anna, Mary Smith, and Ben playfully mock the interview-style questions they are often asked by the off-camera *Ace of Cakes* production team.

"I have a perfectly normal way of talking. I don't know what anyone's talking about."
—MARY SMITH

"That is not a motorcycle. I promised my dad I wouldn't get a motorcycle. That's a scooter."
—DUFF

"I, on the other hand, am not familiar with that because it doesn't come in a box."
—MARY ALICE, re the wine bottle

"It's great to see Duff, I'm very excited for him, I think his business is incredible, the artistic aspect of what he's doing is sort of mind-blowing. I'm very happy for him."
—CINDY WOLF

Avenue Q Cake

Production no.: DB410
Original air date: March 27, 2008
Writer: Heather Mitchell
Director: Matthew R. Carr
Editor: M. J. Loheed
Producer: Rachel Whitty Hajj

One of the week's orders includes a cake for the musical *Avenue Q*, which Duff calls "Sesame Street for adults. It's kinda raunchy but really a great story." The bakery will also be making a model of a trucking terminal for North American Terminals, which is celebrating the opening of its 100th facility. Another major cake for the week is a replica of a Les Paul electric guitar for a combination thirteenth birthday and Bar Mitzvah for client Aaron. Geof brings in his own guitar as a reference model and sets the cake up with real guitar strings. Meanwhile, the cast and puppets from *Avenue Q* arrive at the bakery for a little bit of fun and high jinks. Chucky Monster, Princeton, Kate Monster, Nikki, and Rod all get the full tour. After a brief spat, one of the puppets turns in to the camera and asks, "Can you edit that out later? We're really loving."

Featured cakes: *Avenue Q*, Trucking Terminal, Guitar

Special appearances: Aaron, Bar Mitzvah/birthday boy; the cast and crew of *Avenue Q*; Trucking Terminal clients

Decorative techniques: Base construction and painting, cake carving, gum paste construction, airbrushing, fondant work, painting, stencil usage

Caketastrophe: The staff finds an artistic solution to a problem after spilling silver paint on a nearly completed cake

Featured organization: *Avenue Q*

Fun fact: Baltimore's Hippodrome first opened in 1914, as a venue for movies and vaudeville performances.

"He is the MacGyver of the culinary world."
—MARY ALICE ON DUFF

"I haven't talked to a puppet for that long since I was a little kid . . . it's strange."
—GEOF

"If you don't love guitars, you don't love freedom!"
—DUFF

Duff's Birthday

Production no.: DB411
Original air date: April 3, 2008
Writer: Miriam Leffert
Director: Matthew R. Carr
Editor: Grayce Lackland
Producer: Rachel Whitty Hajj

The week is full of birthday cakes, including an Autograph Book cake for the fifty-sixth birthday of a client, Marion. Elena explains that as an *Ace of Cakes* fan, Marion has asked for the entire staff to autograph the cake in piping. A fishing boat cake has also been ordered, and, given Duff's stormy history with a fishing boat cake in a 2005 Food Network Challenge, he assigns it to Ben, who gets to work carving the hull from stacked sheet cakes. And the staff is excited to make a surprise birthday cake for Duff himself—a Meatball cake. Katherine forces brown and red fondant through the extruder to create an authentic meatball-like texture on the giant fondant-covered ball, Elena creates bacon roses from fondant, and Ben makes a miniature version of Duff's snowboard out of gum paste. When Duff proclaims his love of scrapple, Geof decides to make him a Scrapple cake as well.

Featured cakes: Autograph Book Birthday, Fishing Boat Birthday, Meatball 33rd Birthday, Scrapple cake for Duff

Special appearances: Hava, Autograph Book cake client

Decorative techniques: Cake carving, extruder work, fondant bacon roses (yeah, you read that right), royal icing work, cake board integration

Caketastrophe: Paint from Elena's airbrush drips over the top of the cake. She decides to turn the mistake to her advantage and uses the spill to create a colored depth to the cake book's "pages."

Fun facts: The Lead Chef Challenge segment is a play off of the cult classic series *Iron Chef* and its spin-off *Iron Chef America*. Duff takes on the role of Chairman Takeshi Kaga, the host of the original show, while Mary Alice assumes the role of the commentators. This episode features scenes from Duff's and Geof's appearance on the Food Network Challenge episode "Challenge: Mystery Cake."

"It looks like you're preparing something for Fear Factor."
　　　　—ADAM, on Geof's Scrapple cake

"The only time I ever tried to hide anything from Duff was just, like, on my . . . résumé."
　　　　　　　　　　—GEOF

Ace of Cakes director: "Potato guns don't kill people."
Geof: "Potatoes kill people."

"Drop it, or Frenchie goes."
　　　　—ELENA, holding a potato gun to Sofia's head

"I think the key to making Duff a birthday cake is to have a healthy sense of irony while you're doing it, because you're making a cake for the guy that makes cakes all day long."
　　　　　　　　—MARY ALICE

"Scrapple. There's no mistake that the word 'crap' is in the middle of it."
　　　　　　　　—MARY ALICE

"I'd rather have a beer."
　　　　—MARY ALICE, after Duff asks, "So who wants cake?"

Skate, Rattle and Roll

Production no.: DB412
Original air date: April 24, 2008

Writer: Miriam Leffert
Director: Kelly McPherson
Director of Photography: Clint Lealos No
Editor: M. J. Loheed
Producer: Rachel Whitty Hajj

This week the team will be making a cake for a Roller Derby exhibition game between the Mobtown Maulers and the Dallas Derby Devils. Mary Alice says that Duff "really wanted to do something really over the top. And kind of more, like, menacing and badass and awesome, like *Mad Max Beyond Thunderdome* scary, punk rock–like skull and crossbone evil monstrous thing." Next Duff says they've also got a Corvette groom's cake for a client, Brandon, "Who loves his '98 'Vette." Entering a dream sequence, Geof steps outside where a pink-winged, hockey stick–wielding Duff hands him a set of keys to . . . a waiting red Corvette! Sporting a vintage Members Only jacket, Geof slides behind the wheel, slips on a pair of driving gloves, dons a pair of aviators, fires her up, and tears off into the Baltimore streets. Meanwhile, Mary Smith is working on a Mom and Baby Manatee cake that a client has ordered for his wife's thirtieth birthday.

Featured cakes: Mom and Baby Manatee Birthday, Red Corvette Groom's, Roller Skate Roller Derby Bout, Soccer Ball, Book Stack, Pink-and-White Roller Skate

Special appearances: Stephanie, maid of honor Corvette cake client; Charm City Roller Girls

Decorative techniques: Cake carving; car construction, including carving, icing, gum paste, modeling chocolate, and fondant work

Caketastrophe: While delivering the Roller Skate cake, two wheels fall off and a section of fondant separates from the cake. Duff rushes to the roller rink, where he's joined by Geof and the two perform "cake surgery" and repair the damage in time for presentation.

Featured organization: The Charm City Roller Girls

Fun fact: This episode was directed by *Ace of Cakes* Executive Producer Kelly McPherson.

"You just have to kinda carve out the parts that don't look like a manatee, and then—it will look like a manatee."
　　　　　　　　—MARY SMITH

"I think I do some of my best thinking when I'm carving a cake. Carving cakes usually is my topic of thought . . . that or . . . the duality of man [laughs]."
　　　　　　　　　　—DUFF

"Yeah, it helps to have some inspiration when I'm working on the cake. I mean, I really get into it. I need to see it. Yeah, yeah, sure, you could call me a 'method decorator,' I guess."
　　　　　　　　　　—GEOF

Ace of Cakes: The Book

Production no: DB413
Original air date: Thursday, October 22, 2009
Writer: Heather Mitchell
Director: Matthew R. Carr
Editor: Grayce Lackland
Producer: Rachel Whitty Hajj

Duff declares that there are no client cakes this week, as the staff will be creating dummy cakes for the *Ace of Cakes* book. As a trio of photographers invades the bakery, Duff says, "I'm really excited to see what my guys come up with, because never are we given absolute, complete, one hundred percent no-holds-barred free rein." Anna is excited to make a three-tiered petal-shaped cake in black and white. Katherine says she's going to make a fast-food-themed cake because "it's just funny to make a cake look like other edible things." Elena is creating the postdecapitation bust of Marie Antoinette in cake. She explains, "I think she's kind of a cool horror icon . . . I really do like doing the scary cakes. I think it's really fun." Across the bakery, Duff works on an asymmetrical cake, which he calls "pretty much the design that this place was founded on." Geof adds, "The asymmetric cake really showcases, like, Duff's style, so it I think it's really appropriate that Duff did this kind of asymmetric cake for the book." Meanwhile, Ben is making a Grill cake, which he says is "like a necklace for your teeth." Duff says, "If you're going to make a grill, you gotta pull that thing off. Can't be, like, a half-done grill, because the whole point of grill is 'Yo! check out my grill!'" And Geof is replicating the Cathedral of Notre Dame, saying "I wanted to do something that challenged myself and that I would be able to use maybe some new techniques." Mary Alice says, "The Notre Dame Cathedral was probably the biggest project Geof's ever undertaken and the most amount of detail I've ever seen in a cake. It was just spectacular."

As the episode comes to a close, Geof says, "Every day something wonderful happens. I guess we make people happy, and that's wonderful," and Mary Alice adds, "Charm City Cakes is the best place in the universe to work, it just takes a very, very bizarre type of person to work here." After Anna says, "I totally feel like I found my dream job," Elena says, "I never in my wildest dreams thought I would be a cake decorator. I'm glad I am. It's totally a perfect job for me." Duff finishes with "I'm really, really happy with the way they represented who we are as a group. I'm proud to put my name on that book."

Featured cakes: Black three-tiered petal-shaped (Anna), Fast Food (Katherine), Notre Dame Cathedral (Geof), Marie Antoinette (Elena), Asymmetrical (Duff), Grill (Ben), Graffiti Signature Tag (Duff), Multicolored Henna (Mary Smith), Silver and Pink Striped (Erica), Owl (Sherri), Pink Tower (Anna)

Special appearances: Vince Lupo, Justin Gurnari, Adrienne Helitzer, Joe the intern

Decorative techniques: Styrofoam work, cake photography, airbrushing, piping, sugar jewel creation and application

Featured organization: Charm City Cakes

Fun facts: Marie Antoinette never actually said, "Let them eat cake!"

"So before you send us an email or phone call, why don't you take a look at our website? I bet 53 percent of you might find the answer there. This has been: One to Grow On."

—MARY ALICE, in a brief segment titled "A Message from Charm City Cakes" in which she explains the breakdown of the incoming calls and emails Charm City Cakes receives every day

"Everything I do tends to be a little cartoony, I guess less refined, and more kind of in your face. I have Geof for refined [laughs]."

—DUFF

"Elena's cake is the postdecapitation bust of Marie Antoinette. I'm not sure if she's going for the double entendre. But she definitely is."

—DUFF

"I'm trying to give her a breast reduction. I don't want them to be too distracting."

—ELENA

"I don't really have a need for a grill. I would get laughed at."

—GEOF

"Elena's Marie Antoinette cake was breathtaking. It was everything that Elena is good at. I think it's hilarious that we hired Elena to ice cakes, because you look at that Marie Antoinette cake and that girl should not be icing cakes. She's amazing."

—MARY ALICE

"Every day something wonderful happens. I guess we make people happy, and that's wonderful."

—GEOF

SEASON FIVE

World's Largest Cupcake

Production no.: DB501
Original air date: Thursday, July 17, 2008
Writer: Heather Mitchell
Director: Matt Carr
Supervising producer: Daniel Hopps

Producer: Rachel Whitty Hajj
Editor: Grayce Lackland

Duff and Geof create the World's Largest Cupcake for Share Our Strength's Great American Bake Sale at the Mall of America in Minnesota. Mary Smith creates a Roulette Wheel cake for a local Baltimore charity's "Casino Night." Last but not least, the decorators create a cake that's a replica of the bakery for a couple who got engaged outside of Charm City Cakes. Mary Alice also gives a tour of the Charm City Cakes and the girls discuss their fantasy marriage proposals.

Featured cakes: Charm City Cakes Bakery Wedding, Roulette Wheel, World's Largest Cupcake

Special appearances: Doug Gaddis, director of development, ARC of Montgomery County; Danny Girton Jr., adjudication executive

Decorative techniques: Cake baking, piping, airbrushing, gum paste walls, figures, and decorative items, fondant work, painting, buttercream making, cake repair

Caketastrophe: While carving a lake of suger, Duff slips and cuts himself with a knife

Featured organization: Share Our Strength, ARC of Montgomery County

Duff: I guess baking the world's largest cupcake ain't that easy, huh?
Geof: Yeah, right. That's why nobody's done it. And, besides the other obvious reason.
Duff: Which is?
Geof: It's stupid.

"Never cut toward yourself. You know, it's funny—I learn that lesson about once a year."

—DUFF

Elephant Delivery Service

Production no.: DB502
Original air date: Thursday, July 24, 2008

Writer: Miriam Leffert
Director: Matt Carr
Editor: MJ Loheed
Supervising producer: Daniel Hopps
Producer: Rachel Whitty Hajj

The bakery makes a cake that's a replica of a book cart filled with books for the National Association of Public Libraries librarian conference—complete with th specific requested that Geof be the one to deliver it. Another cake is a replica of a law professor's new book on the Federalist Papers—complete with edible Federalist papers made out of edible ink and rice paper. Duff and his team create a cake that is a tower of toys for a set of twins' first birthday party. Duff delivers the cake dressed as a pink elephant.

Featured cakes: Liberty's Blueprint, Book Launch Party Book, Book Cart Librarian Conference Meeting, Tower of Toys Birthday

Special appearances: Professor Michael Meyerson; Cali and Addie, birthday girl twins

Decorative techniques: Edible ink printing, cake carving, icing, fondant work, airbrushing, gumpaste figure construction, painting, library cart base construction, edible paper work, piping

Fun facts: are a series of articles advocating the ratification of the United States Constitution, and serve as a primary source for interpretation of it as well.

"Don't tell us it was a piece of cake"
—LIBRARIAN

Mom: "So were you challenged?"
Duff: "This was a tough one, yeah."
Mom: "You think that's tough, you should try having twins."
Duff: "I think I'd rather have my job."

Swimming with the Sharks

Production no.: DB503
Original air date: Thursday, August 14, 2008

Writer: Miriam Leffert
Director: Matt Carr
Editor: M.J. Loheed
Supervising producer: Daniel Hopps
Producer: Rachel Whitty Hajj
Underwater photography: Mark Dvornak

After feeding the entire staff ice cream sundaes on one of the hottest days of they year, Duff declare's it's animal madness week at the bakery. Duff travels to an aquarium in Newport, Kentucky, to deliver a giant cake that's a replica of the aquarium's shark ray, Sweet Pea. Duff delivers the cake and swims with a tank full of sharks. Meanwhile back in Baltimore, the staff creates a Neapolitan Mastiff Cake for the dog show that's in town—and they receive a visit from the real thing! A 125-pound mastiff puppy. Continuing the animal theme, Elena creates a machine gun–toting rubber ducky for a special surprise birthday.

Featured cakes: Sweet Pea Shark Ray birthday, Mastiff Dog Show, Rambo Ducky Birthday

Special Appearances: Andy, Emily, and Colleen; Jen Groves

Decorative Techniques: Cake carving, icing, base construction, fondant work, graham cracker usage, airbrushing, crispy cereal treat usage, modeling chocolate work, painting, gum paste eyes and machine guns.

"Hopefully this will come out awesome, because if it's not awesome, he's going to kill us."
—ELENA

Sofia: "I'm going to call human resources."
Duff: "That would be me."

Food Network Friends

Production no.: DB504
Original air date: Thursday, June 29, 2008
Writer: Heather Mitchell
Director: Matt Carr
Editor: Grayce Lackland
Supervising Producer: Daniel Hopps
Producer: Rachel Whitty Hajj

It's Food Network Madness as Guy Fieri comes to Baltimore and spends an afternoon with Duff at a legendary barbecue joint. Duff surprises Guy with a giant cheeseburger cake. Duff travels to New York to appear on *Paula's Party* with Paula Deen, then he's off to the Broadway premiere of *Cry Baby* to deliver the cake for the opening night party. Back in Baltimore, Geof builds the tallest cake in Charm City's history—a six-foot replica of the new Comcast Building in Philadelphia.

Featured cakes: *Paula's Party* Blues Guitar, Comcast Center, Hamburger (Guy Fieri), Crybaby Broadway Premiere

Special appearances: Paula Deen; Guy Fieri; Jimmy Floyd, event planner; Danny Govberg, owner, Govberg Jewelers

Decorative techniques: Cake carving, icing, stacking, base construction, piping, gum paste work, airbrushing

Caketastrophe: While delivering the tall Comcast Building cake, the vehicle's vibration causes the fondant walls to separate from the cake. Geof and Ben repair the cake by removing the damaged area and re-covering it with a piece of fondant.

Fun facts: The Comcast Center Cake is the tallest cake in the bakery's history.

"I'm not a licensed electrician."
—DUFF

"You're not a licensed lot of things."
—MARY ALICE

"I don't think anyone's ever seen Paula Deen in a bad mood, and I don't think anyone ever wants to. She'd probably fling a lot of butter at you."
—MARY ALICE

"Duff knows how to make a fat girl happy."
—PAULA DEEN

Pinball Wizard

Production no.: DB505
Original air date: Thursday, August 21, 2008

Writer: Jen Wise
Director: Matt Carr
Editor: Grayce Lackland
Supervising producer: Daniel Hopps
Producer: Rachel Whitty Hajj

Geof undertakes yet another stadium: venerable Fenway park; the bakery does a cake for their good friend, featuring the goddess/archer Diana. The cake lights up. The biggest cake of the week is a replica of a vintage pinball machine for a big pinball convention. For inspiration, a pinball machine arrives at the bakery and offers a welcome distraction for the staff.

Featured cakes: Fenway Park Groom's, Diana the Huntress Riches Wedding, Pinball Wizard Pinball Convention Display

Special appearances: Joe, Charm City Cakes web designer and Elana; Bess and Steve, bride and groom; Dizzy Issie's, Tiffany pinball cake client, Tiffany's parents

Decorative techniques: Cake carving, icing, airbrushing, styrofoam work, fondant work, gum paste work, painting, floral decorating

Caketastrophe: The staff finds a creative and artistic solution when they discover the gum paste figure from the Diana cake is facing the opposite direction of the dragee stars shooting from her arrow.

Fun facts: Daughter of Zeus, sister to Apollo, Diana the Huntress was the classical goddess of both the moon and hunting.

Lord Stanley

Production no.: DB506
Original air date: Thursday, August 28, 2008
Writer: Miriam Leffert
Director: Matt Carr
Editor: M.J. Loheed
Supervising producer: Daniel Hopps
Producer: Rachel Whitty Hajj

The actual Stanley Cup comes to Charm City Cakes for a visit, courtesy of the NHL. Duff and his team are making a replica of the cake for a couple's wedding—the bride and groom met at a Washington Capitals game and their wedding is hockey-themed. The bakery is also making a bar mitzvah dirt bike/off-road cake that is being delivered to a swanky bowling alley in Philadelphia. Last but not least, a couple who got hitched in Hawaii is having an island-themed cake delivered to their post-wedding celebration in Baltimore.

Featured cakes: Hawaiian Volcano reception cake, Dirt Bike Bar Mitzvah cake, Stanley Cup wedding cake

Special appearances: Matt, bar mitzvah boy; Michelle and Dave, bride and groom; Mike, Hockey Hall of Fame

Decorative techniques: Dry ice volcano, cake carving, icing, stacking, fondant work, airbrushing, base construction, gum paste dirt bike and figures, silver paint usage, piping

Caketastrophe: A bride informs the bakery that the tractor cake replica she ordered for her wedding will no longer be needed as the wedding's been called off. Instead of throwing away the completed cake, Geof and Mary Alice proclaim that cake is meant to be eaten and do just that.

"With food coloring, you can only get so silver . . .

. . . before you get toxic."

—DUFF

Gone to the Dogs

Production no.: DB507
Original air date: Thursday, September 11, 2008
Writer: Miriam Leffert
Director: Matt Carr
Editor: Grayce Lackland
Supervising producer: Daniel Hopps
Producer: Rachel Whitty Hajj

After Duff and Ben decide to sample a Milk-Bone dog biscuit, Mary Alice declares it's pet week at Charm City Cakes. Geof's dog, Cotton, is thrust into the spotlight, serving as the model for a cake that CCC is making for Milk-Bone's 100th Anniversary. The cake is a replica of a box of Milk-Bone Dog Biscuits and is delivered to Times Square for the commermorative event. Charm City also makes a replica of the starship *Enterprise* bridge, and a Dachshund inside a hot dog bun for a special birthday.

Featured Cakes: Milk-Bone 100th Anniversary, Hot Dog Birthday

Special appearances: Lauren, birthday girl; Jennifer and Mark, bride and groom; Willie, Duff's brother; Ivanka Trump; Amy Hammerschmidt, Milk-Bone

Decorative techniques: Icing, fondant work and stamping, gum paste figures, painting, airbrushing

Caketastrophe: When the weight of the hot dog bun forces it to split open, Duff and Katherine use dowels and foam core to hold it in place, and then employ decorative technique to mask the small crack.

Fun fact: The red fondant used on the Milk-Bone cake was the largest piece of fondant ever used at Charm City Cakes.

"Uhura sits behind Kirk, Scotty sits in that one, and then Spock sits there . . . And I'm gonna die alone."

—WILLIE

"It's like being a magician, you don't want to show your tricks."

—GEOF

Pandamonium

Production no.: DB508
Original air date: Thursday, August 7, 2008
Writer: Jen Wise
Director: Matt Carr
Editor: Grayce Lackland
Supervising producer: Daniel Hopps
Producer: Rachel Whitty Hajj

KUNG FU PANDA!!! It's all hands on deck as Duff and the Charm City Cakes crew build a giant cake for the premiere of *Kung Fu Panda* in Los Angeles. The cake has replicas of the entire cast, as well as two smoke machines on timers. Duff finishes the cake in LA and meets Jack Black at the premiere.

There's also an amazing architectural replica of a Russian Orthodox Cathedral built by Geof, and a cake that's a dead ringer for a Chicago deep dish pizza—complete with a Maryland crab and football helmets on top. While in Los Angeles, Duff gives a speech to a group of students at the Le Cordon Blue California School of Culinary Arts.

Featured cakes: *Kung Fu Panda* premiere, Pizza/Crab Wedding

Special appearances: Jackie, Duff's mom; Ashley, Duff's Sensei, Dustin Hoffman, Lucy Liu, James Hong, Jeffrey Katzenberg

Decorative techniques: Gum paste figure construction, cake carving, fondant work and rock construction, cake sketching, oven-baked clay work, airbrushing, cake carving, stacking, icing, piping, painting, flocking, fog machine usage

"Duff's pretty good with students. He's a little bit more of a leader. He's always been good at putting other people to work."

—GEOF

Geof: "I'm not gonna D.A."
Duff: "D.A.?"
Geof: "Do. Anything."
Duff: "Everyone was Kung-Fu Fighting"
Geof: "We finished this cake as fast as lightning. It was actually a little bit frightening."

Frogs to Turkey and Everything in Between

Production no.: DB509
Original air date: Thursday, September 18, 2008
Writer: Jen Wise
Director: Matt Carr
Editor: M.J. Loheed
Supervising producer: Daniel Hopps
Producer: Rachel Whitty Hajj

Operating with less than a full staff, way too many orders, and incredible heat, things get stressful in the bakery. The first cake this week is a return to Zoomerang, the Baltimore Zoo's gala black-tie fund-

raiser. This time the bakery is going to make a cake topped with edible Panamanian Giant Golden Tree Frogs. To research the cake, Duff visits the Zoo to photograph and sketch the tiny frogs. The bakery also designs a replica of one of the craziest creations in the culinary world: a Turducken (a turkey stuffed with a duck which is stuffed with a chicken), a Spaghetti Globe cake, and a jaw-dropping replica of the Lincoln Memorial for a couple who got engaged there.

Featured cakes: Turducken, Spaghetti Globe family tradition, Lincoln Memorial Groom's, Golden Frogs Zoomerang

Special appearances: Ian, Turducken fan, and Ian's family; the Zurflueh family; Laura and Bret

Decorative techniques: Fondant and texture work, cake carving, icing, base construction, melted sugar water effect, painting, airbrushing, piping

"It's pretty flattering that everyone wanted a slice."

—DUFF

Get Cake

Production no.: DB510
Original air date: Thursday, September 25, 2008
Writer: Miriam Leffert
Director: Matt Carr
Editor: Rev. Chaney Moon
Supervising producer: Daniel Hopps
Producer: Rachel Whitty Hajj

Mary Alice receives a call from a high schooler who wants Duff to ask out a potential date for prom. The first big order this week is for a client named Len who requests a cake of his favorite foods for his own living funeral. Next up, a client orders a cake for his father who invented a special machine in the Navy that measures the force of a torpedo hitting an object. Finally, Duff, Mary Alice, and Geof are asked to travel to Boston for a charity premiere of *Get Smart* to benefit the Dana Farber Cancer Institute. There, they get to hang

out with one of their biggest fans, the film's star, Steve Carell.

Featured cakes: Len's Last Supper 70th Birthday, Dynometer 80th Birthday, Get Smart Phone Booth Charity Fundraiser

Special appearances: Nick and Jeni, Paul, Roberta, and Zachary Carson, Stephen Zilliacus, Betsy and Len Homer, Nancy Walls and Steve Carell

Decorative techniques: Fondant work, cake stacking, icing, painting, airbrushing

Caketastrophe: While transporting the *Get Smart* phone booth cake to Boston, one of the fondant walls becomes damaged. Duff and Geof reface the surface with a new piece of fondant when they arrive.

Featured organization: Dana Farber Cancer Institute

Duff: "You know my rule: do it till somebody tells you to stop."
Geof: "You're gonna get in a lot of trouble someday."

"The two greatest words in the English language: Free. Beer."

—MARY ALICE

Tanks, Trucks, and Vikings

Production no.: DB511
Original air date: Thursday, October 2, 2008
Writer: Jen Wise
Director: Matt Carr
Editors: Grayce Lackland, M.J. Loheed
Supervising producer: Daniel Hopps
Producer: Rachel Whitty Hajj

After a brief look behind the scenes at the *Ace of Cakes* production team, Duff declares it's scary vehicle week at the bakery. The team makes a groom's cake in the form of an M1 Abrams Army tank for a veteran returning from Afghanistan, complete with gum paste figures of the couple. They also make a massive Mack Truck and an edible Viking ship replica for a couple of reenactors who are getting hitched at a Renaissance fair in Ohio. The team also find themselves overwhelmed with a massive order of seventy-six mini cakes for a couple's fiftieth anniversary in what Adam the baker calls, "Operation Tiny Cake."

Featured cakes: Viking Ship Wedding, Tank Groom's, 76 mini 50th Anniversary, Police Car birthday, Sports Car Anniversary, Semi Truck Birthday, Mack Truck Company Anniversary

Special appearances: Stephen Ward, Pam, groom's mom; Jenna and Brian, Viking bride and groom; Gloria and Marv, bride and groom.

Decorative techniques: Cake carving, gum paste figures, cake carving, stacking, icing, piping, airbrushing, clear sugar "windshield," digital photo frame usage

"This cake is making me want coffee and donuts."

—ELENA, while working on the police car cake

The Big Cakeowski

Production no.: DB512
Original air date: Thursday, October 9, 2008
Writer: Miriam Leffert
Director: Matt Carr
Editor: M.J. Loheed
Supervising Producer: Daniel Hopps
Producer: Rachel Whitty Hajj

Duff creates a cake for Lebowski Fest, a festival celebrating one of Duff's favorite films, the Coen Brothers' cult hit, *The Big Lebowski*. The special White Russian flavored cake is comprised of several edible iconic elements from the film, including the Dude's rug, bowling pins, a giant severed toe complete with green nail polish, and of course, all the ingredients for making a White Russian. The other big movie-themed cake is a stunning replica of the Han Solo's starship, the *Millennium Falcon* from *Star Wars*. Finally, Geof creates a traditional tiered wedding cake for his sister, Katie.

Featured cakes: *The Big Lebowski* Lebowski Fest, *Millennium Falcon* Birthday, Traditional Tiered Wedding

Special appearances: Michael, Brian; Katie and Michael, Geof's mom

Decorative techniques: Piping, White Russian cake flavor creation, cake carving, base construction, stacking, painting, airbrushing

Caketastrophe: The alcohol inside the Lebowski cake causes it to settle and the fondant to sag. Duff repairs the damage with additional fondant and paint.

"It really ties the cake together, man."

—DUFF

"I can carve you a toe. There are ways. You don't wanna know, but there's ways. I can carve ya a toe."

—DUFF

New Frontiers

Production no.: DB513
Original air date: Thursday, October 16 2008
Writer: Miriam Leffert
Director: Matt Carr
Editor: M.J. Loheed
Supervising producer: Daniel Hopps
Producer: Rachel Whitty Hajj

There are still plenty of cakes to complete before the bakery shuts down for a much needed two-week summer vacation. The first order this week is an elegant traditional wedding cake for Justin, the guitar player in Elena's band, Squaaks. Next, Charm City Cakes repeat clients Zimmy and Chris have ordered a birthday cake in the form of a large peanut butter cup complete with a rotating a breakdancer on top. Geof works on a globe-like Moon cake for a space enthusiast and aerospace worker who was born on the same day as a lunar expedition. Finally, Duff enthusiastically explains, clients Jerry and Carrie are getting married and have requested a cake shaped like a real sandcastle. Duff and Mary Alice also take a trip to Los Angeles to explore potentially opening Charm City Cakes West.

Featured cakes: Peanut Butter Cup birthday, Moon birthday, Traditional Tiers wedding, Sand Castle wedding

Special Appearances: Squaaks, Justin; Zimmy and Chris; Trena, Space Enthusiast; Jerry and Carrie

Decorative techniques: Cake carving, sketching, globe construction, icing, fondant work, painting, gum paste figure construction, airbrushing, piping, graham cracker crumb usage, electronic motor installation

"Cakes like Chris' that are very specific, it's her on the cake—no one else in the world is ever, ever, ever, ever, going to order this cake. It's one-of-a-kind and really reflects who you are and how much this person loves you. And I think that really demonstrates what we do the best."

—MARY ALICE

"Things are very expensive here. Very expensive."

—DUFF, on LA

"I'm sure we can figure out how to do it."

—DUFF

CREDITS

PHOTOGRAPHY UNIT

ADRIENNE HELITZER
STILL Productions, Inc.
www.stillpro.com

VINCE LUPO
Direction One
www.directiononeinc.com

JUSTIN GURNARI
Justin Gurnari Photography | Cinematography
www.jgurnari.com

ILLUSTRATOR UNIT

Bakery blueprint and Star Wars collage:

CHRISTOPHER TREVAS
Trevas Illustration
www.christrevas.com

Charm City Cakes animated:

RAY LAI AND BILL GREEN
Bill Green Studios
www.billgreenstudios.com

Motorcycle and Pit Droid cutaways and Charm
City graffiti:

TIM JESTER
www.j6studios.com

Basic instructions:

SCOTT MEYER
www.basicinstructions.net

Duff and the gang for Shayna:

MATT MCKENDRICK
www.cafepress.com/mattmckendrick

3ds MAX cake:

JEFF WARWICK

Charm City Cakes:

ELIZABETH HARKNETT

Cake Blueprint and Cake Kit illustrations:

MIKE RUSH

EVENT PHOTOGRAPHY

Gabriel/Russell wedding:

CAROLINE MAXCY PRIETZ
Caroline Prietz Photography
carolineprietzphotography.blogspot.com

Harrison wedding:

BILLY HUNT PHOTOGRAPHY

Leiken/Richards wedding:

SARAH HOLDEN PHOTOGRAPHY
www.sholdenphoto.com

Ruyak/Tayman wedding:

ANNE & BILL HOLLAND
Holland Photo Arts
www.hollandphotoarts.com

Siebert/Juarez wedding:

JESSICA CLAIRE
Jessica Claire Photography
www.jessicaclaire.net

Loria/Wible wedding:

JENNIFER HUGHES PHOTOGRAPHY
www.jenniferhughes.com
and
Maureen and Jonathan May

Holland/Krell wedding:

JIM KEEFE PHOTOGRAPHY

Passano/Wiggs wedding:

AMY DEPUTY PHOTOGRAPHY
www.amydeputyphotography.com

Perry/Johnson wedding:

JENNIFER JOHNSON, STIRLING ELMENDORF,
AND DAVID HARTCORN

Okkerse/Hays wedding:

BRAD ZISS

Varhaftic bat mitzvah:

LAUREN AMBERMAN PHOTOGRAPHY
www.flickr.com/photos/lauren3838photography

9:30 Club event:

JESSE OVERTON

Milk-Bone event:

DIANE BONDAREFF (ASSOCIATED PRESS) AND
COYNE PR

Cabbage Patch Kids event:

COLLEEN GILDAY AND SHEILA CLEVENGER

Crayola event:

DIANE BONDAREFF
Photo supplied by Crayola LLC and used with
    permission. Crayola®, Serpentine Design®,
    Chevron Design®, Smile Design™, and Kids'
    Choice Colors™ are trademarks of Crayola
    LLC.

Lebowski Fest and . . . so i had to . . .

WAYNE SWIKERT AND GREG "THE MAYOR"
ANDREWS PHOTOGRAPHY
www.flickr.com/photos/gregthemayor/
www.myspace.com/themayorofbroadripple/

Willey 50th anniversary:

PAULA WILLEY
www.yourneighborhoodlibrarian.blogspot.com
www.pinkpicks.blogspot.com/

Dohogne/Bryan wedding:

WILLOW MIETUS
Willow Dawn Photography
www.willowdawnphotography.com

Fidler/Morrison wedding:

KAKKI MORRISON

Conner/Idem wedding:

LISA IDEM

Pfaff/West wedding and Buchkman/Ricks
wedding:

NICOLE WOLF
SOTA Dzine/StudioThisis
www.sotadzine.com

Rabben/Forsythe wedding:

BETH FORSYTHE

Biven birthday:

MICHAEL BIVEN
www.biven.org

Gross/Daichman wedding:

MICHELLE DAICHMAN AND BRIAN MARCUS
Fred Marcus Photography
www.fredmarcus.com

Zilliacus birthday:

STEPHEN AND C. PATRICK ZILLIACUS

Elkin birthday:

JIM AND SANDY ELKIN

Marr anniversary:

SUMMER AND MIKE MARR

Lucas birthday:

STEVEN LUCAS

Rodill/Schenning wedding:

MATTHEW SCHENNING

Sincavage/Connelly wedding:

JUAN CARLOS BRICEÑO
www.fotobriceno.com

Meredyth/Roemer wedding:

JENNIFER LEE
Sunset Pics Photography
www.sunsetpics.net

Perry/Johnson wedding:

JENNIFER JOHNSON, STIRLING ELMENDORF,
AND DAVID HARTCORN

Gram/Warwick wedding:

JERRY HUEN

Mikes/Mullens wedding:

MATT ZIEMER
www.matthewziemerphotography.com
and
TANIA LEZAK
Tania Lezak Photography
www.lezakphotography.com

ADG Creative event:

JEFF ANTKOWIAK AND THERESE COOLEY
www.adgcreative.net
and
Rachel Kendrick photo
Dickson Kendrick

Lineberry wedding:

ERIN LINEBERRY AND BENJAMIN LINEBERRY
PHOTOGRAPHY
www.lineberryphoto.com
and
PETER HOLDEN PHOTOGRAPHY

Psioda birthday:

DEB AND ED PSIODA

Law birthday:

EMILY AND ANDY LAW

Furman bat mitzvah:

ELLEN COHN
www.photographybyellen.net

White/Motley wedding:

JUSTINE UNGARO
www.justineungaro.com

Firefighter Combat Challenge:

PAUL DAVIS AND ON•TARGET
COMMUNICATIONS

Hull/Williams groom's cake:

CYNTHIA KIRSCH PHOTOGRAPHY
www.kirschphoto.com

Sweet Pea birthday:

JENNIFER PIERSON AND NEWPORT,
KENTUCKY, AQUARIUM

Tourney Central event:

ANN ABELL/TOURNEY CENTRAL

McCutuchan/Musick housewarming:

MONICA MCCUTCHAN

Ole bon voyage:

BARBARA EBERHARDT

Rilley birthday:

JUSTIN RILLEY

Ward/Sessoms wedding:

WARD FAMILY

Rexrode/Polk wedding:

AMY SCHWALB
Amy Schwalb Photography
www.amywed.com

Evitts/Dickinson wedding:

PATRICK ALLEN AND SARA BAICICH
PHOTOGRAPHY
www.sarabaicich.com

Sanford/Pelton wedding:

RACHEL AND DAVE BARNHOUSER
13TH HOUR PHOTOGRAPHY

www.13thhourphotography.com

Ford/Ellenson groom's cake:

MARK KROJANSKY

Tomesek/Gil wedding:

TYSON TRISH PHOTOGRAPHY
www.tysontrish.com

Callender/Rodriguez wedding:

DYE PHOTOGRAPHY
www.lauradye.com

Krauss/Kohl wedding:

MICHELLE D. FOLTZER AND RUTH DUFFY

Williams/Fields wedding:

POWERS STUDIOS
www.powersstudios.com
Cake: Vanilla Bake Shop, Santa Monica,
    California

Hutabaret/Hucik wedding:

GLEN LAMBINICIO

Pollard/Marr wedding:

SUMMER MARR

Fox/Pollack groom's cake:

DAVID POLLACK

Wahlberg birthday:

KATHERINE WAHLBERG

Wolfson bat mitzvah

SHAUN REILLY
Zoschi Studio

ADDITIONAL PHOTOGRAPHY

Matthew Dickinson, Matthew R. Carr, Jeff Hockett, Jeffrey
R. Daniels, Daniel Hopps, John Poortinga, Nick Rush, and
Christopher Keth

FAMOUS BALTIMOREANS
John Waters by Greg Gorman

Star Wars Courtesy of Lucasfilm Ltd. *Star Wars*™
    & © 2008 Lucasfim Ltd. All rights reserved.
    Used under authorization. Unauthorized dupli-
    cation is a violation of applicable law.
Lost © Mario Perez/ABC (American Broadcasting
    Companies, Inc.)
King of the Hill © 2009, Fox

SQUAAKS PHOTO
Jim Burger
www.burgerphoto.com

PAPERCRAFT DESIGN UNIT

Build-A-Duff:

MATTHEW HAWKINS
www.custompapertoys.com

Ashley, Flaming Hearts, City Lights, and Pretty
in Pink:

RICK LYTLE
www:paperian.com/webdude/pcft.html

Cool food:

CLAUDIO DIAS
www.paperinside.com

Pirate Jack:

TANG MU
www.tang-mu.co.uk

Tubbypaws:

TUBBYPAWS
www.tubbypaws.com

Asymmetric cake:

ANTON NERSESSOV
www.youtube.com/user/hepcecob/

CHARM CITY CAKES STAFF

Geof Manthorne, Mary Alice Fallon Yeskey, Anna Ellison,
Mary Smith, Katherine Hill, Katie Rose, Elena Fox, Sofia
Rodriguez, Ben Turner, Adam Goldstein, Erica Harrison,
Sherri Chambers, Jessica Curry, Adrienne Ruhf, Mark
Muller, Lauren Friedman

ACKNOWLEDGMENTS

DUFF WOULD LIKE TO THANK:

All my parents, whose combined efforts made me who I am and kept me out of jail.

My grandmother Nana, who started my training in the arts before I knew what art was.

Every one of my teachers, who helped me realize my potential, whether they knew it or not—in particular, Mrs. Ungerer, my third-grade teacher; Jeffrey Meizlik, my high-school art instructor; Jason, my graffiti-writing partner; Art Umlauf; Mr. Sangster of Sandwich High School; Roy Templeton, who taught me how to think; and all the chefs who taught me how to cook: Cindy Wolf, Dietmar Eilbacher, Shuna Fish, Steven Durfee, Thomas Keller, Steve Mannino, Todd English, everyone at UMBC, the Culinary Institute of America, and all my friends at Food Network on both sides of the camera who have helped me learn how to cook on TV.

Mission Media for the web site and their inspired creativity.

My band, . . . soihadto . . . , for your patience when I have to cancel practice.

My friends and coworkers at Charm City Cakes, who've taken my little one-man operation and shaped what it has become today. You guys are artists beyond description. This book is not about me—it's about us.

All the fine folks at Authentic Entertainment, who have shown patience beyond measure in making us look and sound awesome. I don't know how you do it.

Last, my big brother, Willie, who has opened more doors for me and guided me through them and has been my shield, my punching bag, my navigator, and my friend.

Anyone and everyone who I forgot to thank, and there are probably thousands of you: thank you for everything.

Duff and Willie

WILLIE WOULD LIKE TO THANK:

Jay Potashnick, Jennifer Smith, Robyn Rhodes, Justin Sperandeo, Diana Kania, Juliane Kania, Joe Guilfoyle, Jason Oremland, Brian Leiken, Michael Weber, Shannon Ratcliffe, Grant Anderson, Teresa Salamunovich, Philip Kim, Harry Harris, Michael Rush, the entire gang at *ER*, my mentors at NBC and Warner Bros., and everyone in Hollywood who has had, currently has, or will have the word "assistant" in his or her title.

Adam Kolbrenner, Robyn Meisinger, and Chris Cook at Madhouse Entertainment.

Trevor Engelson and Nick Osborne at Underground Films.

Dr. Joseph and Idell Natterson.

Coffee Bean & Tea Leaf (Los Angeles), Daily Grind (Fells Point), and Ciao Coffee & Tea (Sherman Oaks) for the propellant.

The McLean High School "Tribe": Scott, Sara, Hilary, Maria, Dave, Jen, Courtney, Tara, Janice, Cece, Travis, Brent, John, Liz, Kirsten, and Dana.

And my brother Duff, for letting me stick a video camera in his face.

TOGETHER WE'D LIKE TO THANK:

All of our photographers, illustrators, and artists listed above—we are forever in your debt.

Jacob Strauss at Food Network Addict.com and Brian Ford Sullivan at thefutoncritic.com.

Steve Sansweet, Sarah Garcia, Bonnie Burton, and everyone at Lucasfilm; Troy Williams at Warner Bros.; and Gail Silverman at Paramount.

Jorge Garcia, Noreen O'Toole, and the cast and crew of *Lost*; Tony Gama-Lobo, Marc McJimsey, and the cast and crew of *King of the Hill*; the cast and crew of *The Tonight Show with Jay Leno*; John Waters, Adam Shankman, and the cast and crew of *Hairspray*; the cast and crew of *The Wire*, and everyone at Cirque de Soleil, *Cry Baby*, and *Avenue Q*.

Will Russell and everyone at Lebowski Fest.

Kelly McPherson, Lauren Lexton, Tom Rogan, Rachel Whitty, Miriam Leffert, M. J. Loheed, Grayce Lackland, Jeanne Begley, Jack Tarantino, Deb Jackson, Heather Mitchell, Dustin Rubin, Jen Wise, Trenice Bishop, Steve Centracchio, Matt Carr, Daniel Hopps, Nick Rush, John Poortinga, Josh Spector, Chaney Moon, Jeff Daniels, James Mann, Basil Francois, Duffy Nagle, Justin Gurnari, Anne Etheridge, Brandy Menefee, Camie Holmes, Kevin MacCarthy, Emre Sahin, Helga Eike, Aliyah Silverstein, Ari Devecioglu, Clint Lealos, Matthew Monte, Will Pisnieski, Kristina Scott, Brett Baldridge, David Tomasini, Nathan Peters, Maryn Peters, Katrina Parks, Rob Lundsgaard, Alex Arquembourg, Pat McElroy, Todd Strauss-Schulson, Skip Schwink, Mark Lafleur, Kari Olson, Michael Bouson, Rebecca Root, Cassie Allebaugh, Mitch Monzon, Michelle Katz, Daniel Wirsig, Alex Mercado, Jason Quinn, Steven Schwab, Andrew Van Dorn, Jennifer Bennet, Jordan Hall, Emily Kellard, Sylvan Grimm, Jamal Rashada, Paul Halperin, Edward Alfonso, Lewis Morphew, Troy Waters, Avigail Schotz, Jacob Lane, Katie Quinlan, Kamali Minter, Stefanie Zimmers, Drew Nichols, Drew Aiello, Mark Dalbis, David Mickler, Jeff Hockett, Lou Giangrande, Christian Ortega, Chris Keth, Alex Mercado, and the countless others behind the scenes at Authentic Entertainment. Thank you all for working so hard to make it so much fun.

Charles Nordlander, Brooke Johnson, Allison Page, Bob Tuschman, Sergei Kuharsky, Susie Fogelson, Carrie Welch, Brian Lando, Susan Stockton, Lisa Krueger, Katie Ilch, Nils Lundblad, Lauren Mueller, Amanda Melnick, Michael Baru, Joanne Harmon, and everyone else at Food Network for your vision, taking a chance, and believing in us.

Cassie Jones, Mary Ellen O'Neill, Liate Stehlik, Lynn Grady, Jessica Deputato, Johnathan Wilber, Lorie Pagnozzi, Karen Lumley, Susan Walsh, Ashley Halsey, and everyone at William Morrow Cookbooks and HarperCollins.

Scott Whitehead, Jeff Frankel, Andrea Torres, Marilyn Clair, and all the Mother Flippin' Winners at McKuin, Frankel & Whitehead.

Lisa Shotland, Kevin Huvane, Roxsanna Mobley, Peter Jacobs, Amie Yavor, Alonda Thomas, Simona Pop, Heather Hummel, Megan Ubovich, Heather Kamins, Arleta Fowler, Pamella LaBella, Rachel Krautkremer, Omid Ashtari, and our entire team at Creative Artists Agency.

The clients of Charm City Cakes and the viewers of *Ace of Cakes*.

You, for buying this book.

The City of Baltimore; the Baltimore Film Commission; Richard Escalante; Richard Gore and family; Sean Marshall, USAREC; the men and woman at Aberdeen Proving Ground, Aberdeen, Maryland; the soldiers and their families at Schofield Barracks and Wheeler Army Airfield, Oahu, Hawaii; A/3–25 Aviation "Stingrays"; Rich, Staci, Ruby and Charlotte Gordon; the Dibbs family, the Savit family, the Holcomb family, the Helitzer family, the entire Goldman family, A-Frame Surf Shop (Carpinteria, California); Sarah Berl; the Baltimore Orioles; the Baltimore Ravens; and the Baltimore Police and Fire Departments.

Though success always has many parents, none of this would have been possible without Dana Leiken Richards, Elayne Sawaya, Kelly McPherson, Lauren Lexton, Tom Rogan, Lisa Shotland, and Charles Nordlander.

and

The other half of our bakery family, the *Ace of Cakes* field team: Matt Carr, Jeff Daniels, Josh Spector, Camie Holmes, Daniel Hopps, Justin Gurnari, James Mann, Nick Rush, Duffy Nagle, Basil Francois, John Poortinga, Skip Schwink, Katrina Parks, Rob Lundsgaard, Trenice Bishop, Mark Lafleur, Brandy Menefee, Drew Nichols, Chaney Moon, Todd Strauss-Schulson, Maryn Peters, Nathan Peters, Jason Quinn, David Mickler, Jeff Hockett, Christian Ortega, Chris Keth, Alex Ortega, and Drew Aiello.

Above all, thanks to the sixteen artists who challenge us and only make us better every day they're in our lives:

Geof Manthorne, Mary Alice Fallon Yeskey, Anna Ellison, Mary Smith, Katherine Hill, Katie Rose, Elena Fox, Sofia Rodriguez, Ben Turner, Adam Goldstein, Erica Harrison, Sherri Chambers, Jessica Curry, Adrienne Ruhf, Mark Muller, and Lauren Friedman. It has been an honor creating with you.

And finally, our grandparents Bernie and Elinor "Nana" Helitzer, Manuel and Minnie Goldman, Mom and Ronnie, Dad and Ann, and of course, our little brother, Luke . . .

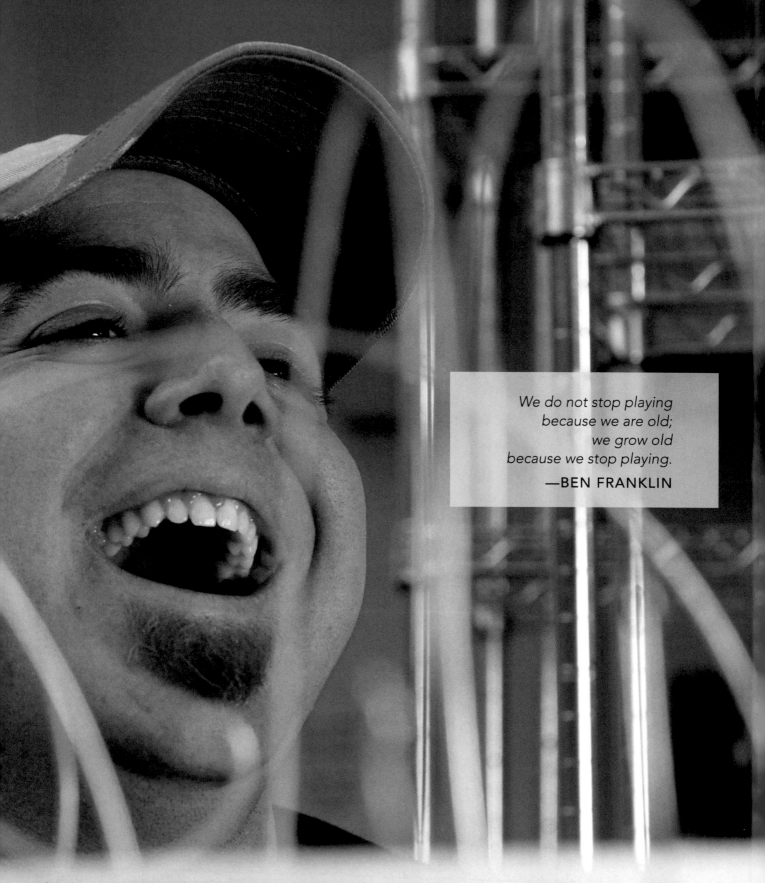

We do not stop playing
because we are old;
we grow old
because we stop playing.
—BEN FRANKLIN

In memory of Amanda Post and Jordon Abramowitz

TAKE PHOTOS OF YOUR

FINISHED CAKE! ☺

CAKE DESIGN / SPECIFICATIONS

DESIGN: CHARM CITY CAKES

DRAWN: MLR 7/8/09

REVISED: 10/20/09

APPROVED:

SUPPORTING UNDERSTRUCTURE:

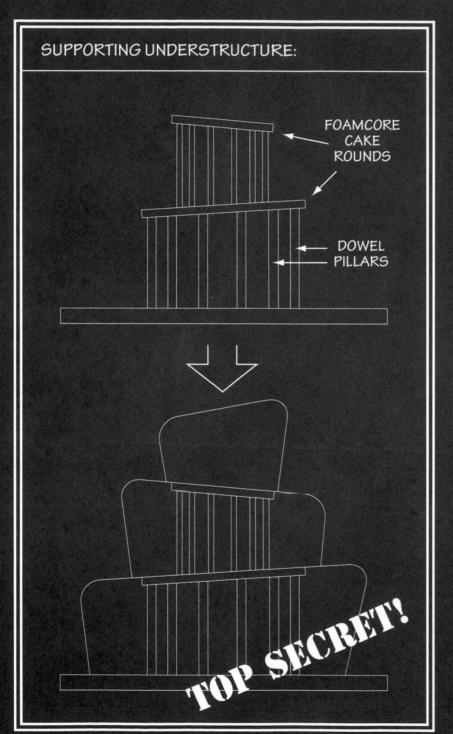

FOAMCORE
CAKE
ROUNDS

DOWEL
PILLARS

ROLLED
FONDANT
OUTER
LAYER

STACKED
CAKES

12" BASE
BOARD

TOP SECRET!